The United States and Huerta

The United States
and Huerta

by
KENNETH J. GRIEB

UNIVERSITY OF NEBRASKA PRESS · LINCOLN

Publishers on the Plains

UNP

Manufactured in the United States of America

To my parents

Contents

	List of Abbreviations	ix
	Introduction	xi
I	The Rise of Victoriano Huerta	1
II	The First Reaction	24
III	The Advent of Woodrow Wilson	39
IV	The Huerta Regime: Government and Battlefield	51
V	First Friction and Fumbling Policy	69
VI	Confrontation and Rebuff: The Lind Mission	90
VII	New Efforts and New Complications	108
VIII	The Anglo-American Confrontation	125
IX	Direct Action and Confused Intervention	142
X	The Niagara Falls Conference	159
XI	Huerta's Fall and Last Hurrah	178
	Note on Sources	193
	Acknowledgments	215
	Index	217

A section of illustrations follows page 108.
Maps follow pages 14 and 58.

List of Abbreviations

SD   United States State Department Papers, National Archives, Washington, D.C. Papers from the 812.00 file are cited by slash number only. Papers from other files are cited by complete number. See Bibliography for a full explanation of the specific files.

PR   Post Records, United States State Department, National Archives, Washington, D.C. Records of embassies and consulates are cited with the abbreviation PR and the city.

WD   United States War Department Records, National Archives, Washington, D.C. The files cited are from the War College Division and the Adjutant General's Office. See Bibliography for complete titles of the files.

JD   United States Department of Justice, National Archives, Washington, D.C. See Bibliography for the specific titles of the files employed.

Bryan-Wilson Correspondence   "Correspondence of Secretary of State Bryan with President Wilson, 1913–1915," four unpublished volumes housed in the National Archives, Washington, D.C.

AREM   Archivo Relaciones Exteriores Mexicana, Ministry of Relaciones Exteriores, Mexico City.

AHDN   Archivo Histórico Defensa Nacional, housed in the Defense Ministry, Government of Mexico, Mexico City.

Gobernación   Papers of the Ministry of Gobernación, Archivo General de México, Mexico City.

F.O.   Papers of the British Foreign Office, Public Records Office, London. See Bibliography for the specific titles of files.

Rabasa, Correspondencia   "Copia de la correspondencia telegráfica con la secretaría de hacienda," Papers of Emilio Rabasa, the Latin American Collection, University of Texas.

House Diary   Diary of Colonel Edward M. House, Papers of Colonel Edward M. House, the Sterling Memorial Library, Yale University.

The private papers of the various individuals involved are cited only by the last name. For complete details and location of the papers, consult the Bibliography. Thus, for example, the Papers of Woodrow Wilson in the Manuscript Division of the Library of Congress are cited as Wilson Papers.

Introduction

The presidency of Victoriano Huerta in 1913 and 1914 was a brief interim period separating two phases of the Mexican Revolution. Huerta was typical of the many *caudillos* who ruled Latin America in the nineteenth and early twentieth centuries. Although his opponents professed to be fighting dictatorship and depicted him as the worst in a long line of military despots, Huerta's seizure of power, method of rule, and actions while President were no worse—except for the assassination of Francisco I. Madero—than those of his predecessors. The primary historical significance of the Huerta period stems from its role as the testing ground for Woodrow Wilson's diplomacy of morality, for this was the American President's first venture into international affairs.

While the United States had recognized *de facto* governments since the days of Thomas Jefferson—and accordingly Huerta had every reason to expect American recognition—Wilson abandoned the traditional American policy and substituted his own criterion, that of opposing regimes he considered morally repugnant. He justified his actions on the ground that he opposed dictatorship and sought to promote democracy in Mexico. He considered it morally correct to intervene in a foreign country in support of democracy and sincerely believed that he was helping the Mexican people. In adopting this stance, Wilson committed a moral transgression in search of moral rectitude. It is true that he held office in an age that witnessed numerous interventions throughout the world, and at a time when the practice was considered more acceptable than at present. But Wilson did not act from the usual motives—indeed, he condemned intervention designed to protect property and eschewed the exigencies of national security. He opposed a government that could have provided stability, supporting revolutionaries who advocated reforms that would upset the economic and political structure of the country. Wilson contended that by withholding recognition from regimes that seized power through *coups d'état*, he was discouraging military uprisings and thereby insuring the continuity of constitutional government. Yet this policy would succeed only if the offending government was ousted from office, and this entailed foment- ing a revolution. Thus, Wilson encouraged coups in the name of pre- venting them.

Despite the fact that Wilson acted from what he believed to be motives of universal good, the result was American intervention in Mexican internal affairs. Even the mere withholding of American recognition exerts influence within Latin American nations, but Wilson also resorted to diplomatic pressure and overt encouragement of the forces opposed to Huerta. When these methods failed to oust the Mexican President, Wilson employed military coercion. Ultimately, the Revolution itself did not overwhelm Huerta ; rather, the American government brought about his fall. Had the United States remained neutral and refrained from supplying the revolutionaries, Huerta might well have put down the revolt and continued in power, maintaining a peace similar to that of Porfirio Díaz.

Subsequent administrations returned to a more traditional policy, and therefore, until very recent years, Wilson's action in Mexico was one of the few instances of American intervention against a dictator and American support for revolutionaries seeking a broad program of reform. The Mexican revolutionaries may well have stimulated this return to the old policy by their radical reforms and expropriation of foreign investments, for the American government would certainly hesitate to support revolutions that might injure American investors. Only in the post-World War II era, as economic and political stability returned to Mexico, did the beneficial results of the Mexican reforms become apparent. Except for occasional deviations, such as opposition to Gerardo Machado, the traditional American policy continued until the tacit opposition to Fulgencio Batista and the pressure exerted on Rafael Trujillo.

Many of Wilson's actions can be attributed to his lack of diplomatic experience, for Mexico was the first such problem to confront him. His failure to plan ahead compounded the situation. Yet the same moralism that led Wilson astray in Mexico enabled his success in domestic politics, where his struggle for justice carried the Progressive movement to new triumphs. Indeed, Wilson's difficulties in Mexico may be partially attributed to the fact that he was confronted with the Mexican problem at a time when the struggle for domestic reforms absorbed most of his energies. Wilson also failed to perceive that his accomplishments at home came in a society accustomed to democracy and hence prepared for its extension, whereas Mexico had little experience with democracy and was accustomed only to strong-man rule.

Wilson's policy failed because it was based on faulty reasoning, containing an incorrect view of Mexico. The belief that merely overthrowing the dictator in Mexico would bring democracy to that country was unfounded. But the President accepted the revolutionists' statements that they were fighting for democracy and ignored their actions. Both nations escaped a disaster from Wilson's policy only because of their relative strength—Mexico was too small to involve the United States in a major war yet large enough to render full-scale armed intervention expensive and unattractive.

From the vantage point of the present day, Wilson's policy ultimately benefited both Mexico and the United States. The initial revolutionary *caudillos* eventually gave way to more democratic regimes. Today, the Mexican Revolution is the hope of much of Latin America, representing a non-Communist way to reform. Had a Huerta dictatorship caused a delay, the Mexican Revolution would not have preceded the Bolshevik Revolution, thus raising the possibility of Communist influence. Today, the United States is thankful for the independence of the Mexican Revolution from the Soviet one; and Mexicans, on their part, while critical of the American intervention, certainly resent that action less than they might have resented American support for antirevolutionary regimes.

These considerations become apparent only with hindsight. President Wilson could not foresee this, and his policy must be judged in the perspective of his time. In this context, he departed from existing practice and embarked on a new course without achieving the desired results. For while Huerta did fall from power, the regimes that succeeded him were also authoritarian governments. Even the success of the Carrancistas did not provide stability—the immediate result was anarchy and continued struggles among rival factions. Furthermore, Wilson's support for the revolutionaries failed to improve relations between the two countries, since no Mexican government that appeared to be a pawn of the United States could survive. The United States would probably have found Huerta more amenable to its influence, at least in matters pertaining to the protection of American interests in Mexico.

Wilson's experience with Mexico reveals much about the President's character and views, and a close examination of this period shows how his bias contributed to an erroneous interpretation of the Mexican reality. Thus a careful study of the entire Huerta period, including its Mexican setting and Huerta's interaction with Taft and Wilson, provides important insights not only into American policy in Latin America but also into Wilson's more adept wartime diplomacy, for some aspects of Wilson's wartime diplomacy closely paralleled his stance in the Mexican crisis. The rigid position based on moralism was repeated—a war to end wars was strikingly similar to a revolution to end revolutions. Yet the daily conduct of American diplomacy during the war was far more skillful and reflected at least some of the lessons the President had learned in Mexico.

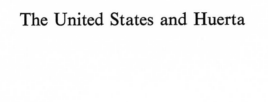

The United States and Huerta

I

The Rise of Victoriano Huerta

The forces which tore Mexico asunder during the Huerta period originated during the dictatorship of Porfirio Díaz, who ruled Mexico with an iron hand from 1876–1910. The Díaz era was a time of stability and progress, but these benefits were achieved only at the expense of individual rights. All power was concentrated in the hands of Don Porfirio and the clique around him. A small group of wealthy *hacendados* controlled nearly all of Mexico's productive land, and the bulk of the population was bound to these estates by debt peonage. Although Díaz did lay the groundwork for the future economic prosperity of Mexico, the overwhelming majority of the population perceived little difference in their meager existence.

With the approach of the presidential election of 1910, a leader arose to voice the widespread discontent: Francisco I. Madero. After unsuccessfully attempting to enter the presidential election, Madero launched a revolution in northern Mexico, and the oppressed masses rallied to his banner. Madero was hardly the typical revolutionary leader. A small man, only five feet two inches tall, he had a high-pitched, falsetto voice that did not seem likely to stir the masses. His sunken eyes, his beard, and his gentle face gave him the appearance of a shy and peaceful man, rather than a crusader. He was a "sincere, well-intentioned idealist," who was firmly convinced that he could help the masses achieve a better standard of living.[1] An aristocrat who received his schooling from private tutors in Paris and the United States, Madero had little in common with his peon supporters.

[1] Stanley R. Ross, *Francisco I. Madero: Apostle of Mexican Democracy* (New York: Columbia University Press, 1955), p. 338. Sources of general information on persons are included in the Bibliography.

1

Those who participated in the revolution that swept Madero into office in the belief that he would solve their economic and social problems were soon disillusioned, and rebel factions began to rise against him. Madero had promised everything to everybody and inevitably found it impossible to fulfill these sweeping pledges. He failed to perceive that socio-economic grievances had made him President and that economic reforms were imperative. Madero concentrated on establishing political democracy, believing this would insure the subsequent equitable solution of other problems. While he did initiate limited land redistribution, his program scarcely scratched the surface.[2] The revolutionary leader's methods of governing also disillusioned his followers. Even before his election, Madero selected José María Pino Suárez as his running mate despite vigorous opposition. Once in office, Madero placed numerous members of his family in key positions, and his brother Gustavo became the strong man of the administration. The resulting dissatisfaction gradually split the revolutionaries and spawned opposition groups. By September, 1912, the American consul at Acapulco observed that theater crowds no longer cheered Madero's picture, although photos of other leaders received loud acclaim.[3] Emiliano Zapata rebelled against Madero on November 23, 1911. In the same month, Angel Barrios and José F. "Che" Gómez revolted, but their uprisings proved short-lived. In February, 1912, Pascual Orozco, Jr., launched the most formidable insurrection to challenge the Madero regime. Orozco captured Ciudad Juárez and Chihuahua and defeated federal forces commanded by former Minister of War General José González Salas before General Victoriano Huerta put down the rebellion. In October, 1912, Félix Díaz, nephew of the former dictator, attempted a revolt in Veracruz. Another uprising in the north, headed by General Bernardo Reyes in November, 1912, was easily overwhelmed with the cooperation of United States border officials.[4]

Even the collapse of these insurrections failed to restore peace, for

[2] Ross, *Francisco I. Madero*, pp. 241–245; and Charles C. Cumberland, *Mexican Revolution: Genesis under Madero* (Austin, Texas: University of Texas Press, 1952), pp. 211–212.

[3] Clement Edwards (Acapulco), to Secretary of State Philander C. Knox, September 26, 1912/5213.

[4] For accounts of the early uprisings, see Cumberland, *Mexican Revolution*, pp. 185–188, and Ross, *Francisco I. Madero*, pp. 254–255; and for details of the Díaz revolt, see William Canada (Veracruz), to Knox, October 19, 1913/5287, and Ross, *Francisco I. Madero*, pp. 268–272.

numerous local bands kept the country in a turmoil. The American consul at San Luis Potosí reported:

> While the situation is ... almost intolerable, it must be stated that it affects the mass of the Mexican people in this district comparatively little; the main feature ... is not actual violence ... but is rather the insecurity, and this insecurity is not felt by a great majority of the population as they have nothing to lose and never have been devoted to public order.[5]

Only foreigners and the wealthy classes were affected. The Mexican army was hard pressed and proved unable to cope with such widespread rebellion. The United States military attaché warned: "Conditions are at the present time very uncertain and are growing more doubtful every day. There is absolutely no foundation on which to base a belief that Mexico can through its own efforts put down the present disturbances."[6] The resulting turmoil indicated the government's inability to control the country, and this stimulated discontent among the upper classes, who longed for the peaceful days of Díaz. The army, which had never strongly supported Madero, resented political interference with its operations and objected to Madero's frequent amnesties to rebels.

Hostility between the Mexican President and the American ambassador complicated Madero's relations with the United States. Henry Lane Wilson and Madero had incompatible outlooks and personalities. Wilson was a short man with a drooping stance that accentuated his small stature. His oval face had an owlish appearance with hard, clear eyes that usually squinted, peering out from under thick eyebrows. A jutting, almost pointed jaw, accented by a bushy mustache, completed a stubborn look that made him appear stiff and formal. He had a suave voice, except when he became excited—a frequent occurrence. Indeed, one of his principal weaknesses was his short temper, and he often found it necessary to deny highly undiplomatic statements uttered in a fit of anger. His clothes generally hung indifferently, and when addressing someone he invariably thrust his head forward and stared at his listener.

A lawyer, newspaper editor, and businessman, Wilson assumed his ambassadorial duties in Mexico in 1910, after serving as minister to Chile and Belgium. Since the American representative in Mexico was

---

[5] Wilbert Bonney (San Luis Potosí), to Knox, September 13, 1912/5017.
[6] Captain William Burnside to AGWAR, September 14, 1912, WD 5761–599.

the only ambassador accredited to that government, all other powers being represented by ministers, Wilson was automatically dean of the diplomatic corps. This apparently increased his natural vanity and inflated his ego, which was already considerably exaggerated.

Wilson regarded himself as an experienced diplomat representing the great American nation in a country that was unprepared for democracy, had an inexperienced government, and lagged far behind the United States in development. Accordingly, he considered himself a fount of knowledge that the new Mexican President should tap by requesting advice on all his problems. On his part, Madero saw no need to consult Wilson. With his practical, business outlook, the ambassador had little in common with the idealistic, visionary Madero.[7]

Wilson's primary objectives were promoting American business interests and assuring adequate protection for Americans and their property. This made him very popular with the American colony in Mexico. Those seeking concessions invariably received the ambassador's enthusiastic support. The Madero regime's inability to pacify the country irritated Wilson. In his view, an administration that could not maintain order was no government at all, for he considered this the principal responsibility of any regime. According to Wilson's reports, the Madero government was tottering almost from the moment it came to power and clung to office precariously on a day-to-day basis. He had no doubt that the President was to blame, and reported: "In the midst of this appalling situation . . . the Federal Government sits apathetic, ineffective and either cynically indifferent or stupidly optimistic. Its councils are divided and moved in contrary directions from one day to another." Because of the "character of the President," he was certain that government action "may be expected to be incoherent, spasmodic."[8] To the ambassador, Madero was "simply a man of disordered intellect." Wilson concluded: "The responsibilities of government shattered his [Madero's] reason completely . . . his mental qualities, always abnormal, developed all the characteristics of that

[7] For Wilson's views, see Henry Lane Wilson, *Diplomatic Episodes in Mexico, Belgium, and Chile* (Garden City, N.Y.: Doubleday, Page and Company, 1927), pp. 204, 333; Henry Lane Wilson, "How to Restore Peace in Mexico," in George H. Blakeslee, ed., *Mexico and the Caribbean* (New York: G. E. Stechert and Company, 1920), pp. 149–155; and Henry Lane Wilson, "Errors with Reference to Mexico," *Annals of the American Academy of Political and Social Science*, LIV (July, 1914), 159–161.

[8] Wilson to Knox, August 28, 1912/4899.

dangerous form of lunacy in which the best example in ancient times is Nero and in modern times a [Cipriano] Castro."[9]

Secretary of State Philander Knox considered the "increasing pessimism in the reports of the ambassador" as "unjustified, if not, indeed, misleading." Knox informed President William Howard Taft that the ambassador frequently adopted independent stands without consulting the Department of State and then attempted to cajole the Department into supporting his position.[10] For Wilson constantly outlined the type of instructions he desired. When Knox criticized his pessimism, the ambassador threatened to cease reporting entirely. The Secretary bowed to his bluster, expressing "regret" that his note was "misunderstood."[11] Knox disregarded Wilson's gloomy dispatches, and Washington continued to support Madero while its ambassador in Mexico opposed him.

Yet, the ambassador's pessimism, while greatly exaggerated, was not entirely unfounded, and numerous consular reports substantiated his analyses. The American consul at Saltillo, Philip Holland, believed that the "Mexican people . . . would welcome almost any solution," while the consul at Mazatlán concluded that Madero could retain power only by drastically reorganizing his administration.[12] Mexican newspapers constantly reported rebellions, raids, and battles, indicating widespread disorder and discontent. Indeed, the Assistant Chief of the State Department Latin American Division, Fred Morris Dearing, noted that the ambassador's reports closely paralleled those of the Mexican press, and Dearing suspected that Wilson derived his information exclusively from the newspapers delivered to the embassy.[13]

Pressures against Madero continued to mount in late 1912 and early 1913, as new rebellions occurred. Criticism in Congress increased, and the Mexican ambassador to the United States, Manuel Calero, resigned,

[9] Wilson to Bryan, March 12, 1913/6840.

[10] Knox to Taft, January 27, 1913/7229A.

[11] Knox to Wilson, January 21, 1913/5913A; Wilson to Knox, January 22/5916; and Knox to Wilson, January 24/5916.

[12] Philip Holland (Saltillo), to Knox, January 3, 1913/5825; and William Alger (Mazatlán), to Knox, January 25/6031. See also William Canada (Veracruz), to Knox, December 29, 1912/6025; and Thomas Bowman (Nogales), to Knox, December 20, 1912/5770.

[13] Fred Morris Dearing, Memorandum, January 21, 1913/5913A. Throughout December, 1912, and January, 1913, *El Pais*, *El Imparcial*, and the *Mexican Herald* were filled with reports of attacks by rebel bands.

declaring: "I lied to the American government for ten months telling them that the Mexican revolution would be over in six weeks. . . . The truth is that the situation is desperate."[14] The causes of the numerous revolts varied, but all contributed to the disorder and chaos in the country, and no government could survive this for very long. In December, 1912, Philip Holland at Saltillo predicted: "The revolution will continue . . . until at a critical and psychological moment a leader will rise and overthrow the present administration."[15] Time proved the astuteness of this prognosis. The leader who emerged was General Victoriano Huerta.

Much of Victoriano Huerta's character may be summed up briefly: he was an Indian and a soldier. A short, stocky man with square shoulders, he walked with the rolling gait common to those who spend much of their time in the saddle. His face was somewhat oval, with a high forehead and almost square chin. A thin mustache accented straight lips and a small mouth, while prominent cheekbones and dilating nostrils mirrored his Indian ancestry. His piercing, black eyes, resembling those of a defiant caged hawk, squinted from behind thick glasses, penetrating the person he addressed. His face was nearly always expressionless. An excellent orator, he used both hands while speaking, pounding the table or his chest with a fist to emphasize points. While addressing a small group, he frequently paced to and fro waving his arms. Healthy and robust, except for poor eyesight, he seldom showed fatigue.

Huerta had the stoicism, impassiveness, fatalism, and bravery of his Indian ancestors, and he was a born fighter. He was absolutely fearless: death meant nothing to him. At a time when few dared walk the streets of Mexico City without a pistol, he frequently went about unarmed. He could sit impassively in the midst of a battle or among soldiers celebrating a victory by firing wildly. According to one account of his fearlessness, perhaps apocryphal, Huerta was in a Cuernavaca hotel when a group passed in the street shouting, "Death to Huerta." The General "heard the cry, got up, and walked to the door—alone. 'Here is Huerta,' he said. 'Who wants him?'"[16] Stories of his bravery reached such proportions that some observers contend he refused anesthetics during surgery.

[14] Washington *Post*, February 5, 1913.

[15] Philip Holland (Saltillo), to Knox, December 13, 1912/5722.

[16] Mrs. Rosa King, *Tempest over Mexico: A Personal Chronicle* (Boston: Little, Brown and Company, 1935), pp. 82–83, 141.

His bravery led to an obverse quality: he had no concern for the lives of others. Joaquín Piña, the friend who wrote Huerta's so-called *Memoirs*, probably represented his thoughts quite accurately when he had Huerta state: "The death of a human being produces the same feeling in me as a leaf falling from a tree."[17] Huerta was also extremely ambitious and highly egotistical. He dominated his associates and commanded by sheer force of will power. A realist, he never wavered once he selected a course. One acquaintance observed: "When he comes to a knot he cuts it. To untie it would take too long."[18]

Huerta's addiction to alcohol was legendary, and his enemies sought to use this weakness to discredit him. Many contend he was almost never sober. The authors of these tales were mainly revolutionaries or people outside Mexico City who had little contact with Huerta. Nearly all his close associates maintain that they never saw him intoxicated. There is no question that he drank constantly: breakfast consisted of a beaten raw egg in a glass of cognac. Yet he had a great capacity for alcohol, and it scarcely affected him. Acquaintances report he imbibed cognac throughout the day, consuming without ill effects an amount that would fell most men. Although there were numerous photos taken during his presidency, he never appeared inebriated in any of them.[19] Certainly his actions were not those of an alcoholic, for he succeeded in retaining power for a considerable time against heavy odds.

Huerta was born in Colotán, Jalisco, and although there is some dispute about his age, official military records list 1852 as his birthdate. His early military career was devoted to staff work. Upon his graduation from the military academy at Chapultepec in 1875, he entered the army engineering corps. As a young captain, he helped organize the General Staff and served on it until 1901, reaching the rank of brigadier general. During these years, Huerta served as first engineer of the Commission of Geographic Exploration, which was preparing a military map of

[17] Joaquín Piña, *Memorias de Victoriano Huerta* (El Paso and Barcelona: Published by the author, 1915), p. 25.

[18] Hamilton Fyfe, *The Real Mexico: A Study on the Spot* (New York: McBride, Nast, and Company, 1914), pp. 120–121.

[19] *Ibid.*, pp. 122–123; Nemesio García Naranjo, *Memorias de Nemesio García Naranjo* (8 vols.; Monterrey: Ediciones de *El Porvenir*, 1956–1962), VII, 99; William L. Sherman and Richard E. Greenleaf, *Victoriano Huerta: A Reappraisal* (Mexico: Mexico City College Press, 1960), pp. 113–114; New York *Times*, December 12, 1913, and June 14 and July 22, 1914. René León to author, August 9, 1964; and Nemesio García Naranjo, Jr., to author in a personal conversation, September 29, 1964.

Mexico. The American Secretary of War, Lindley M. Garrison, praised the accuracy of the resulting map, describing it as comparable to United States army charts. Huerta also directed the astronomical work of the commission, for he had shown an aptitude for this science at Chapultepec.[20]

Huerta's combat experience began in 1901. After a brief tour fighting rebels in the state of Guerrero, the General spent two years commanding a battalion against rebellious Maya Indians in the steaming jungle of the Yucatan peninsula. Huerta put down the Maya revolt, but the terrain demanded some harsh tactics that first gave rise to his reputation for cruelty. He then returned to the General Staff. When Porfirio Díaz was forced into exile in 1911, Huerta commanded the escort that protected the aging dictator during the trip to Veracruz.

After Díaz' flight, Provisional President Francisco de la Barra sent Huerta to assume command in the state of Morelos where the General soon became embroiled in a controversy with Madero. President de la Barra ordered Huerta to suspend operations for five days and to cooperate with the revolutionary leader, who was attempting to negotiate an accord between Emiliano Zapata and the government. Zapatista raids continued during the conferences, and consequently Huerta led his small column of one thousand men from Cuernavaca immediately after the expiration of the five-day truce. When Madero and Zapata subsequently reached agreement, it was too late to recall Huerta's column. Despite Madero's appeal for another suspension of hostilities, President de la Barra affirmed that Huerta had acted on his orders, and the General pressed on. By September 18, he had placed garrisons in the six largest towns of the state, and he assured the Minister of War that he had "pacified" it.[21] In reality, the Zapatistas roamed at large, having merely been dislodged from the towns and defeated in several small, indecisive battles, but given the size of Huerta's force, little more was possible. Madero and Huerta subsequently blamed

[20] This account of Huerta's early career is based upon his official war record and an unpublished biographical sketch by Captain Edward Emerson, a reserve officer in the United States army and a war correspondent in Mexico. Emerson had Huerta's war record stolen from the Ministry of Defense and copied for him. Both the biography and the war record are WD 7422–10. Emerson wrote during Huerta's presidency and was highly anti-Huerta, but the factual information on Huerta's early career is accurate. Garrison's comment is Garrison to Colonel Edward M. House, House Diary, May 8, 1914.

[21] Huerta to Minister of War, October 31, 1911, Gobernación, 1911–1912. See also Cumberland, *Mexican Revolution*, pp. 178–181.

each other for their difficulties in Morelos. Madero and his supporters contended that the General's actions had frustrated the negotiations, and they charged that Huerta had disregarded orders to cooperate with Madero. Others alleged that only Madero's interference had allowed Zapata to escape, and Huerta attributed his subsequent recall to the intrigues of Madero.[22]

Despite their mutual mistrust, Madero, as President, was compelled to avail himself of Huerta's services when Pascual Orozco, Jr., one of Madero's chief lieutenants during the revolution, rose against his former chief. Orozco recruited a formidable force of ex-guerrillas during February, 1912, and by March 3 the Orozquistas had captured Ciudad Juárez and Chihuahua. Recognizing the seriousness of the situation, Madero's Minister of War, General José González Salas, resigned from the Cabinet to assume command of the troops opposing Orozco. His column was routed at Rellano on March 23. Humiliated by his defeat, González Salas committed suicide.

Searching desperately for someone strong enough to assume command, the Cabinet favored Huerta in spite of Madero's reticence.[23] While the forces in the north included some of the ablest officers in the Mexican army, Madero's government placed Huerta over them because of his experience commanding "large" forces, for he was one of the few Mexican officers who had taken the field at the head of a battalion-size force. Faced with a serious threat, Madero put aside his scruples and designated Huerta Commander of the Division of the North, placing the fate of his government in the hands of his old adversary. Huerta hastened north and began reorganizing the retreating army. He remained at Torreón throughout April, drilling his troops and recruiting.

Fortunately for the historian, the United States military attaché, Captain William Burnside, accompanied Huerta's column, and his reports provide a contemporary assessment of Huerta's strategy by a professional officer. Whereas the government claimed that Huerta had ten thousand men, Burnside reported that the entire force consisted of only six thousand troops. Later critics accepted the government figure and argued that Huerta's force vastly outnumbered Orozco's.

---

[22] New York *Times*, October 25, 26, and 27, 1911; Madero to Huerta, November 2, 1911, *Los Memorias y los mejores cartas de Francisco I. Madero* (Mexico: Libro Mexicana, 1956), pp. 202–205; Cumberland, *Mexican Revolution*, p. 181; and King, *Tempest over Mexico*, p. 87.

[23] Manuel Calero, *Un decenio de política Mexicana* (New York: Middleditch Company, 1920), pp. 131–132.

Burnside repeatedly confirmed the smaller figure, indicating that the contending forces were approximately equal.[24]

On May 12, the main forces met at Conejos where Huerta selected a strong defensive position. By frustrating Orozco's flanking movements, Huerta forced the *colorados* into a frontal assault. Although the forces engaged both numbered about five thousand men, the strong federal position and Huerta's skillful use of artillery proved decisive. The twelve-hour battle ended in a complete federal victory, and the Orozquistas retired from the field after losing about five hundred men and abandoning their supplies.[25] The defeated rebels retreated to Rellano, the site of their victory over González Salas, destroying the railroad. Huerta advanced cautiously, although not too hesitantly considering the job of rebuilding the railroad, for he covered the eighty miles to Rellano in twelve days. Orozco selected the battle-ground and constructed strong entrenchments. Again, the forces engaged were of equal size. Huerta employed a prolonged artillery bombardment to drive the Orozquistas from their positions before personally leading a general advance that carried the *colorado* trenches. Despite the fact that the insurgents succeeded in hastily withdrawing from the field after suffering only light casualties, they were in full retreat.[26]

The rebel leader fell back to Bachimba, tearing up one hundred and forty miles of railroad track. Huerta grew more cautious as the distance from his supply base at Torreón increased. Recruits augmented the

[24] Burnside to AGWAR, April 17, 1912, WD 5761–460, April 27, 5761–475, May 1, 5761–478, May 15, 5761–488, and May 22, 5761–498, all confirming the size of Huerta's force. For the size of Orozco's force, General Edgar Steever (Commander, Fort Bliss, Texas), to Adjutant General, May 13, 1912, WD AG 1875135 A/317, and New York *Times*, May 4 and 11, 1912.

[25] Burnside to AGWAR, May 13, 1912, 5761–487, and May 15, 1912, 5761–488. For Huerta's description of the battle, Huerta to Minister of Gobernación, May 11, AREM, L.E. 681, leg. 2 (R–39–2), f 33–34; and *El País*, January 25, 1913, for a reprint of a letter by Huerta to Nemesio García Naranjo, director of *La Tribuna*. The federal forces had 20 cannon, giving them a two-to-one superiority over the rebels in artillery. Throughout the campaign, Burnside's reports substantiate Huerta's accounts.

[26] Burnside to AGWAR, May 22, 1912, 5761–498, and May 25, 5761–502; and Huerta to Minister of Gobernación, May 13, 21, and 23 (two dispatches with the same date), AREM, L.E. 681, leg. 2 (R–39–2), f 51–52, 96–98, 113, and 117. Captain Edward Emerson's biography, previously cited, also contains some information on these battles, but Emerson accepted the government figures and sought to discredit Huerta. The military attaché's dispatches and press reports at the time refute his contentions.

victorious federal army, but troops were detached to protect the newly reconstructed railway. Huerta's army arrived at Bachimba Pass on July 2 to find that the rebels had chosen their position carefully, for Bachimba Pass and Canyon formed a natural fortress guarding the entrance to Chihuahua. The federals, who now enjoyed a numerical superiority over the depleted rebel force, were compelled to attack across level ground devoid of cover. Huerta prudently allowed his superiority in artillery to decide the battle, and the government forces took Bachimba Station on July 4. As in the previous encounters, the Orozquistas escaped on trains concealed in the pass beyond the range of the federal guns.[27] The battle of Bachimba effectively terminated the rebel threat by forcing Orozco to disperse his forces and resort to guerrilla warfare. He told the press: "It is useless for us to attempt to stand against Huerta's cannon."[28]

Huerta's campaign had destroyed the most serious rebellion that confronted President Madero. In putting down the uprising, however, Huerta had merely pushed the Orozquistas back and forced them to disperse. He had not destroyed the rebel army, which retreated after each encounter. The federals advanced only along the railroad and made no attempt to surround the enemy. Captain Burnside did not consider such a maneuver feasible, noting the risk entailed in dividing the small corps of adequately trained men and the need for supplies, which compelled operations to remain in proximity to the railroad.[29]

For his victories, Huerta received a promotion to General of Division, the army's highest rank. Many expected him to be appointed Minister of War, but Madero would not consider this.[30] Huerta postponed his return to the capital, and his hesitation sparked rumors of a rebellion.[31] The general was naturally suspect, for it was widely known that the army disliked Madero. In addition to commanding the strongest force in the country, Huerta had prestige as the "Hero of Bachimba." Finally, Huerta returned to Mexico City for a hero's welcome from the populace and a cold reception from the President. The General was

[27] Burnside to AGWAR, July 24, 1912, 5761–532 and 5761–533.

[28] New York *Times*, July 8, 1912.

[29] Burnside to AGWAR, July 24, 1912, 5761–534.

[30] *El País* reported that many generals favored Huerta for Minister of War on January 26, 1913.

[31] Reports of rumors of a Huerta revolt came from Consuls Alonzo Garrett (Nuevo Laredo), September 15, 1912/4633, and Marion Letcher (Chihuahua), September 15/5056; and General Edgar Steever (Commander, Fort Bliss), to Adjutant General, September 17, 1912, AG 1875135 A/589.

unable to render a detailed accounting of the one and a half million pesos given to him for army operations. Madero accordingly relieved him of his command, but granted him a leave to undergo an operation to remove cataracts in his eyes.

Huerta's army record was that of a loyal and dedicated soldier. He had fought for the governments of Díaz, de la Barra, and Madero and had won numerous decorations. One of the few generals who had experience commanding large forces, he had reached the highest rank in the army and put down the most formidable rebellion that threatened the Madero regime. In over forty-one years of military service, Huerta had applied for only two leaves.

Just as Huerta recovered from his eye surgery, a new uprising against the Madero government again swept him onto the national stage. At 3:00 A.M. on February 9, 1913, the regiments stationed at Tacubaya, a short distance outside the capital, rebelled under the leadership of General Manuel Mondragón, Mexico's leading artillery officer during the regime of Porfirio Díaz. Many cadets from the Tlalpan military school supported the rebellion. The *insurrectos* entered the city to release General Bernardo Reyes and Félix Díaz from prison, and they assumed command of the uprising. The insurgents then marched on the National Palace to join an advance party of cadets who had rushed ahead to seize it. These early morning maneuvers were not entirely unobserved, however, for Gustavo Madero received word of the uprising as soon as it began. After alerting General Lauro Villar, military commander of the Plaza, Gustavo rushed to the Palace with Minister of War General Angel García Peña, only to be seized by the cadets who had subverted the Palace Guard. General Villar summoned loyal troops and quickly restored control of the Palace to the government.[32] The rebels boldly marched to the Palace without taking precautions, ignoring warnings that loyal forces had recaptured the building. General Reyes fell in the resulting fusillade, and the insurgents fled from the Zócalo in disorder, milling about for an hour before Mondragón and Díaz reorganized them to capture the Ciudadela, the government arsenal.[33]

[32] Colonel Juan G. Morelos (Commander, Twentieth Battalion), to Military Commander of the Plaza, February 26, 1913, AHDN, XI/481.5/89, ff 13–14; and Manuel Bonilla, Jr., *El régimen Maderista* (Mexico: Talleres Linotipográficos de *El Universal*, 1922), pp. 128–135.

[33] Ramón Prida, *De la dictadura a la anarquía* (El Paso, Texas: Imprenta de El Paso del Norte, 1914), p. 475; and Burnside to AGWAR, February 25, 1913, 5761–669.

Ignoring the pleas of advisers, President Madero left Chapultepec and set out for the Palace immediately after receiving news of the uprising. Seemingly without fear, he rode up Avenida Cinco de Mayo, accompanied by friends, officials, and a guard of loyal cadets. Some people turned out to cheer him, and even opponents had to admire his bravery in rushing to the battle scene. His ride thus assumed the aura of a triumphant procession.

Huerta joined Madero en route, offering his services. Madero and his party reached the Zócalo after the rebels fled and discovered that Villar had suffered wounds in the successful defense of the Palace. The Minister of War suggested that Huerta assume command. Villar agreed, and Madero approved the order.[34] Madero distrusted Huerta, but the General had previously saved the government, and the situation seemed desperate. Consequently, Madero signed his own death warrant by placing the fate of the government in Huerta's hands. Villar requested Huerta to pledge to defend the administration to the last and then advised him: "Be very careful, Victoriano."[35] These words were indeed ironic.

When darkness halted the first day of combat, the rebels were clearly in the ascendancy. Their occupation of the Ciudadela gave them control of the government arms and ammunition reserves, and hence they were better equipped than Madero's troops. The Ciudadela was a veritable fort, with a low silhouette, thick walls, and a railing along the roof with rifle slits at the corners. This rebel position was so formidable that American newspapers reported that the fall of the government was imminent.[36] The rebels chose to remain on the defensive to gain the advantage of using machine-gun fire from fixed positions against troops advancing up streets. This constituted a reversal of traditional revolutionary tactics, but the government was compelled to attack, for its prestige suffered as long as the rebels retained control of any portion of the capital.

Huerta soon made arrangements with the insurgents. Like most army men, the General had little love for Madero, and perceiving that

[34] Bonilla, *El régimen Maderista*, pp. 146–156; and Prida, *De la dictadura a la anarquía*, p. 497.

[35] General Juan Gualberto Amaya, *Madero y los auténticos revolucionarios de 1910* (Mexico: Published by the author, 1946), p. 423.

[36] New York *Times*, February 10, New York *World*, February 10, Washington *Post*, February 10, Chicago *Daily Tribune*, February 10, and Los Angeles *Times*, February 10, 1913. Regarding the strength of the rebel position, Burnside to AGWAR, February 25, 1913, 5761–669; and personal observations of the Ciudadela by the author.

much of the populace was indifferent, he seized his opportunity to oust the President. On February 10, Enrique Cepeda, Huerta's nephew, met Félix Díaz at El Globo café. The next day Huerta and Díaz conferred at Cepeda's home.[37] What happened at these meetings is unknown, but certainly the two made plans to overthrow Madero. They undoubtedly agreed on prolonging the battle to increase public dissatisfaction with the government. It is also possible that Huerta indicated the locations of his future attacks to enable the rebels to slaughter loyal Maderista forces, although such an arrangement was hardly necessary, for Huerta could have eliminated these troops himself by sending them against impregnable positions.

Huerta's meetings with Díaz seemed to indicate that he made no effort to defeat the rebels. From this many observers concluded that Huerta could have easily put down the revolt had he desired to do so. This is not necessarily true. During the initial fighting the outnumbered federal troops were unable to mount a strong attack. The situation was so critical that Madero personally rushed to Cuernavaca to urge General Felipe Angeles to hasten to the capital with his detachment. The combat centered on a ten-day artillery duel at point-blank range, and Huerta found his forces severely handicapped in this phase of the fighting. Federal artillery proved ineffective against the Ciudadela, for torpedo shells were required to pierce its thick walls, and the government supply of this type of shell was stored in the Ciudadela. The units hastily recalled to the capital had only the ammunition they carried with them to the countryside—that is, shrapnel. Furthermore, the government forces experienced shortages of all types of ammunition, for the rebels held the supply.[38]

The American military attaché considered the Ciudadela a "very strong defensive position," and on February 13 he concluded that further government assaults would be futile.[39] Yet the federal attack was not well coordinated, and therefore strategy employed by Huerta

---

[37] Luís Liceaga, *Félix Díaz* (Mexico: Editorial Jus, 1958), p. 179; Ross, *Francisco I. Madero*, p. 291; Piña, *Memorias de Victoriano Huerta*, pp. 22–24; and Prida, *De la dictadura a la anarquía*, p. 505. Senator Jesús Ureta, Cepeda's neighbor, saw Huerta and Díaz enter the house for their meeting, and he informed Gustavo Madero, who arrested Huerta at gunpoint on February 17, 1913, but the General protested his loyalty and persuaded the President to restore him to his command, Bonilla, *El régimen Maderista*, pp. 204–211.

[38] Burnside to AGWAR, February 25, 1913, 5761–669, and June 5, 5761–761; and General Rubio Navarrete to Huerta, quoted in Amaya, *Madero*, pp. 429–430.

[39] Burnside to AGWAR, February 25, 1913, 5761–669, and June 5, 5761–761.

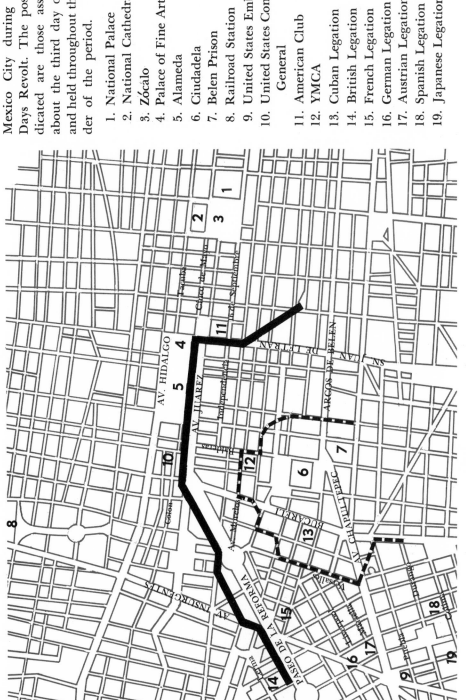

Mexico City during the Ten Days Revolt. The positions indicated are those assumed by about the third day of combat and held throughout the remainder of the period.

1. National Palace
2. National Cathedral
3. Zócalo
4. Palace of Fine Arts
5. Alameda
6. Ciudadela
7. Belen Prison
8. Railroad Station
9. United States Embassy
10. United States Consulate General
11. American Club
12. YMCA
13. Cuban Legation
14. British Legation
15. French Legation
16. German Legation
17. Austrian Legation
18. Spanish Legation
19. Japanese Legation

Federal lines ▬▬▬   Rebel lines ▬ ▬ ▬

was at least partially responsible for the government defeat. Units advanced singly, often without artillery cover. Nearly all the detachments sent forward in these charges were *rurales*, who loyally supported Madero. The attackers suffered appalling casualties. The United States military attaché noted that this piecemeal attack was not characteristic of Huerta, and he concluded that President Madero interfered with the General's operations and ordered daily advances.[40] It is far more likely that the strategy reflected Huerta's calculations. In addition, the Ciudadela was never completely surrounded. All attacks on the rebel position came from the Alameda, a park about twelve blocks from the arsenal. Only a few artillery pieces fired from the flanks. Huerta was unable to attack from the rear without endangering the embassy and the various legations, which were crowded with refugees.[41] Yet he should have covered it at a distance to sever the supply route.

The succeeding days of artillery fire caused extensive damage in the city, and Ambassador Wilson became involved in the political maneuvering to terminate the conflict. The ambassador demanded that all combatants respect American rights. Amid intervention pleas from the American and European press, President Taft halted arms shipments across the border.[42] The Secretary of State approved Wilson's demands for guarantees for foreigners, stressing that this action implied no recognition of Díaz. The Ambassador ignored Díaz' formal request for a recognition of belligerency.[43] Americans flocked to the embassy seeking sanctuary, converting the area adjoining the building into a refugee zone. The legations acted similarly. Since many of them were clustered together, the result was a huge international community under diplomatic protection. Naturally the American embassy, housing the dean of the diplomatic corps, was the focal point. The embassy hardly looked like the hub of a humanitarian effort, for it resembled a stone fortress, with battlements surmounting the roof and

[40] Burnside to AGWAR, February 25, 1913, 5761–669, and June 5, 5761–761.

[41] *Mexican Herald*, February 12, 1913; New York *Times*, February 12, 1913; and Manuel Márquez Sterling, *Los últimos días del Presidente Madero: mi gestión diplomática en México* (Habana: Imprenta El Siglo XX, 1917), pp. 425–426.

[42] Knox to Secretary of the Treasury, February 11, 1913, 812.113/1897A; Lieutenant Colonel J. S. Parkes (United States military attaché, Brussels), to AGWAR, February 21, 5761–656, quoting *L'Independence Belge* of February 15; and New York *Times*, February 13, 1913, reporting that the London *Daily Mail, Standard,* and *Daily Graphic* all called for American intervention.

[43] Wilson to Knox, February 9, 1913/6058; Knox to Wilson, February 10/6058; and Wilson to Félix Díaz, February 9, PR Mexico City, 1913, XXI, Cl. 800.

terraces. Towers projected upward irregularly, resembling the spires of a miniature castle, while rooms, dormers, and terraces jutted out in all directions. Fearing that injury to Americans would provide a pretext for intervention, the Mexican government offered to transfer the refugees to the suburbs, but the ambassador refused to abandon the embassy during this crucial period, despite its location adjacent to the combat zone.[44]

Ambassador Wilson decided to protect foreign interests by seeking a permanent solution to the problem—and in his view that meant obtaining a strong government for Mexico. In Wilson's opinion, this excluded the Madero regime. Wilson concluded that the rebellion was certain to topple Madero, and therefore the solution was not to aid the President, but to speed the fall of the government to terminate the combat. He told his colleagues: "Madero is crazy, a fool, a lunatic, and must be declared legally incapable of exercising his duties," adding: "This situation is intolerable . . . I am going to bring order."[45]

Instead of convening the entire diplomatic corps, the ambassador acted in concert with only the envoys whose views coincided with his own. He conferred with the British, Spanish, and German ministers, supposedly because they represented the countries with the largest colonies in Mexico City. Wilson subsequently attempted to justify his actions by citing Captain Burnside's opinion that the federal position was hopeless. The four diplomats initially requested a cease-fire. With the rejection of this proposal, they pressed for an agreement limiting the fighting to a specific zone.[46] Obviously, such an arrangement would seriously jeopardize the government's position.

Wilson urged Minister of Foreign Relations Pedro S. Lascuráin to "get some members of the Senate together" and "impose the resigna-

[44] Pedro S. Lascuráin to Knox, February 15, 1913, Isidro Fabela, ed., *Documentos históricos de la Revolución Mexicana* (12 vols.; Mexico: Fondo de Cultura Económica and Editoral Jus, 1960–1967), IX, 86. After the revolt, the organization of the American colony commended Wilson for his actions in protecting them, *Mexican Herald*, March 1, 1913; and Wilson to Knox, March 3, PR Mexico City, 1913, XXII, Cl. 800.

[45] Márquez Sterling, *Los últimos días*, pp. 415–416; and Bernardo J. de Cólogan, "Por la verdad" (declaración confidencial), AREM, L.E. 692, leg. 10 (R–44–15), f 1–7; and statement of Henry Lane Wilson on his return to Washington, July 26, 1913, Woodrow Wilson Papers, Box 37.

[46] Wilson to Knox, February 12, 1913/6112. The ambassador had previously suggested limitation of the zone of fighting, Wilson to Pedro Lascuráin, February 10, 1913, PR Mexico City, 1913, XXI, Cl. 800.

tion of President Madero."[47] British Minister Sir Francis Stronge approved Wilson's action. Like the ambassador, Stronge concluded that Madero's elimination was essential to peace, and he informed British Foreign Secretary Sir Edward Grey: "I can see no solution unless President [Madero] resigns." Despite Grey's warning that he was "doubtful of the wisdom of pressing resignation on Madero," Stronge continued to support Wilson.[48] The British minister informed Wilson that he considered Lascuráin a suitable president, but the ambassador demurred, contending that Lascuráin was "not strong enough." Wilson advised Stronge that he was "trying to meet with Huerta."[49] The ambassador informed Washington that the Cabinet advised Madero to resign, implying a vindication of his assessment, without indicating that this resulted from his suggestion. Due partly to Lascuráin's efforts, twenty-five senators called on Madero requesting him to retire, but the President ignored the demands.[50]

The ambassador decided to press Madero directly, and accordingly the Spanish minister, Bernardo J. de Cólogan, called at the Palace on February 15 to inform the President that the four diplomats believed he should abandon his office. Madero indignantly rejected this "advice."[51] This refusal only infuriated Wilson. To him, no duty was more important than protecting American interests, and he considered action to secure the installation of a government that would provide such protection as part of the process. Apparently, his three colleagues concurred. Madero was understandably alarmed by the diplomats' stance and feared that it foreshadowed American intervention. He immediately wired President Taft protesting the ambassador's course. Although the State Department denied any intention of intervening, Madero's anxiety was not unfounded.[52] Taft had held a midnight conference with military commanders on February 12 while American

---

[47] Sir Francis Stronge to Wilson, February 14, 1913, PR Mexico City, 1913, XXI, Cl. 800.

[48] Stronge to Grey, February 16, 1913, FO 371/1671; Grey to Stronge, February 19, FO 414/235; and Stronge to Grey, February 21, FO 414/235.

[49] Stronge to Wilson, February 14, 1913; and, undated (February 17), Wilson to Stronge, PR Mexico City, 1913, XXI, Cl. 800.

[50] Wilson to Knox, February 14, 1913/6173, and February 15/6175.

[51] Wilson to Knox, February 15, 1913/6175; Stronge to Grey, February 17, FO 414/235; and Bernardo J. de Cólogan, "Por la verdad" (declaración confidencial), AREM, L.E. 692, leg. 10 (R–44–15), f 1–7.

[52] Knox to Wilson, February 15, 1913/6172C. The United States announcement denying intervention appears in New York *Times*, February 17, 1913.

troops moved toward the border and transports with marines set sail for Guantanamo, Cuba.[53] Ambassador Wilson had recommended a "firm stand." He even proposed that all American naval vessels in Mexican waters and the marines aboard them be placed under his command and that he be empowered "to act without further instruction." Such an authorization could only have resulted in intervention, and Secretary of State Knox rejected this suggestion.[54]

The ambassador also attempted to approach General Huerta. On February 16, he informed the State Department: "General Huerta has indicated a desire to talk with me and I shall see him sometime during the day . . . I hope for good results of this." He subsequently reported that Huerta was unable to keep the appointment but had sent word that "he expected to take steps towards terminating the situation."[55] These dispatches clearly indicated that Wilson was in contact with the government commander, and his previously expressed view that Madero's resistance was futile suggested discussion of something other than the battle against the rebels. Yet the State Department made no effort to inquire about the implication. Apparently, the Department was not as concerned with Wilson's actions in Mexico as it was with the danger that he might provoke armed intervention.

The next day Wilson reported: "General Huerta has just sent his messenger to me again to say that I may anticipate some action which will remove Madero from power at any moment."[56] That morning, General Aureliano Blanquet, who had camped on the outskirts of Mexico City for some time, finally entered the capital and his troops assumed control of the Palace while the units previously guarding it advanced to the battle area. The ambassador noted that this comported with Huerta's indication that he would remove all Maderista troops from the Palace. Wilson told Cuban Minister Manuel Márquez

---

[53] Knox to Wilson, February 18, 1913, PR Mexico City, 1913, XXI, C1. 800; New York *Times*, February 16, New York *World*, February 12, and Washington *Post*, February 12, 1913. Records indicate that the army revised the existing "general plan . . . in case of armed intervention in Mexico" at this time, Admiral George Dewey to Secretary of War, February 13, WD AG 2011734.

[54] Wilson to Knox, February 11, 1913/6029; Knox to Wilson, February 12/6029; and Wilson to Knox, February 13/6149.

[55] Wilson to Knox, February 16, 1913/6180 and /6186.

[56] Wilson to Knox, February 17, 1913/6225, although the word "remove" was omitted in transmission, and the State Department thought the word was "retire." The original in the post records shows that the word was "remove," PR Mexico City, 1913, XXI, C1. 800.

Sterling: "Tomorrow all will be over."[57] The senators who appealed to Madero to resign formed a committee to approach Huerta and Díaz. They requested Huerta to depose Madero in order to forestall American intervention.[58] In a gesture designed to convince the senators that he had no personal ambitions, Huerta offered to install Supreme Court President Francisco Carbajal y Rojas in the presidency. The senators urged him to act himself, and Huerta, seeking to strengthen his position, requested and received the support of a majority of the Supreme Court.[59] Certainly, Huerta could have seized control at any time, but these conversations showed his concern for assuming power with legal sanction.

By February 18, Huerta had completed his preparation for a *coup d'état*. Since Gustavo Madero had thwarted the February 9 revolt, Huerta drew him from the Palace by arranging to dine with him at the Gambrinus Restaurant. At the Palace, General Aureliano Blanquet sent a small detachment under Colonel Jimenez Riveroll to seize the President. One of Madero's companions drew his revolver and shot Riveroll and his aide. In the confusion, Madero ran from the room only to encounter Blanquet, who informed him, "You are my prisoner," and then arrested the Cabinet members and officials.[60] Huerta seized Gustavo at the restaurant, after first receiving a message that presumably assured him of Blanquet's success. He feigned an emergency and disarmed Gustavo by borrowing his pistol before announcing his arrest.[61] Huerta then hurried to the railroad station to intercept General Rivera, who was arriving with reinforcements. He spirited Rivera away, under virtual arrest, but easily persuaded him to support the coup.[62] Rushing to the Palace, Huerta found Blanquet in firm control. On his arrival, Huerta greeted Madero as "Señor Presidente."

[57] Wilson to Knox, February 17, 1913/6235; and Márquez Sterling, *Los últimos días*, p. 488.

[58] Querido Moheno, *Mi actuación política después de la Decena Trágica* (Mexico: Ediciones Botas, 1939), pp. 12–13; and Senator José Diego Fernández in Jan Leander DeBekker, *De cómo vino Huerta y cómo se fué: apuntes para la historia de un régimen militar* (Mexico: Libreria General, 1914), pp. 122–125.

[59] Rafael Zayas Enrique, *The Case of Mexico and the Policy of President Wilson* (New York: A. & C. Boni, 1914), pp. 67–79; and Ross, *Francisco I. Madero*, pp. 305–306.

[60] Ross, *Francisco I. Madero*, pp. 308–309; and New York *Times*, February 19, 1913.

[61] Márquez Sterling, *Los últimos días*, pp. 464–465.

[62] Prida, *De la dictadura a la anarquía*, p. 526.

When Madero replied, "Ah, I am still President," Huerta corrected his statement to "Señor ex-Presidente." [63]

As soon as the coup was complete, Enrique Cepeda sprinted to the embassy with the news. He had accompanied Riveroll during the first abortive attempt to seize Madero and had suffered a hand wound during the scuffle. Cepeda dashed into the embassy, panting and bleeding, and shouted: "We got him! We got him!" [64] After recovering his breath, he explained that he rushed to keep his promise that the ambassador would receive the first report. Thus, Henry Lane Wilson informed the State Department of the coup two hours before the cathedral bells rang out the news in Mexico City. As soon as Huerta arrived at the Palace, he sent a note officially advising the ambassador, "The President of the Republic and his ministers are now in my power at the National Palace as prisoners," and requesting that Wilson notify the diplomatic corps and the rebels.[65]

At 5:10 P.M., the cathedral bells sounded and a large crowd assembled. After ten days of combat, the people were relieved at the end of the battle and wildly cheered Huerta. A general air of celebration prevailed. American papers reported that President Taft and his advisers showed "great relief." Washington officials expressed the opinion that Huerta was strong enough to govern Mexico successfully.[66] The *Mexican Herald* commented that Mexico "took her physic." [67] But while the residents of the capital rejoiced at the news, the rebels remained in their positions. Although Madero was a prisoner, Huerta and Díaz had agreed only on his overthrow. Each still coveted the presidency.

Ambassador Wilson, seeing his aspirations partially fulfilled, decided to assume the role of intermediary between Huerta and Díaz. He would do everything in his power to prevent the two would-be *caudillos* from destroying the stable government that now seemed within his grasp. Accordingly, he arranged a meeting between Díaz and Huerta on neutral ground—the United States embassy. Just why

---

[63] Miguel Alessio Robles, *Historia política de la Revolución* (Mexico: Ediciones Botas, 1938), p. 47; and Roberto Blanco Moheno, *Crónica de la Revolución Mexicana: de la Decena Trágica a los campos de Celaya* (Mexico: Libros Mexicana, 1957), p. 146.

[64] Alfonso Taracena, *Madero, víctima del imperialismo Yanqui* (Mexico: Editorial Jus, 1960), p. 237.

[65] Huerta to Wilson, February 18, 1913, PR Mexico City, 1913, XXI, Cl. 800; and Wilson to Knox, February 18/6244.

[66] New York *World* and New York *Times*, February 19, 1913.

[67] *Mexican Herald*, February 19, 1913.

neutral ground seemed necessary after the earlier Huerta-Díaz conferences will never be explained. Wilson probably felt he was demonstrating his power by summoning the two contenders to the embassy.

Huerta and Díaz remained closeted with Wilson for several hours after the coup. The ambassador intervened in the discussion three times to prevent the talks from collapsing. By 1:00 A.M., the two officers reached an agreement, which they signed and deposited in the embassy safe. This was the Pact of the Embassy, also known as the Pact of the Ciudadela. By this accord, Díaz recognized Huerta as provisional president, while Huerta allowed Díaz to select the Cabinet and pledged to support Díaz in the forthcoming elections. The Mexican Constitution required a vote within a year and prevented a provisional president from succeeding himself. At Wilson's insistence, Huerta and Díaz also pledged freedom of the press, joint action to maintain order in the capital, and the release of Madero's ministers.[68] This oral agreement involved only the Cabinet, conspicuously omitting the President and Vice President. There is no record of whether this was due to Wilson's failure to request their release or to the refusal of one or both of the *caudillos*. On completion of the talks, Ambassador Wilson presented Huerta and Díaz to the diplomatic corps, enthusiastically praising the new regime.

Thus the rebellion ended, and the two leaders agreed on a provisional government with the active participation of the American ambassador. This constituted interference in the internal affairs of Mexico. Wilson regarded this pact as the "most successful and far-reaching of all the difficult work I was called upon to perform during the revolution."[69] He informed the State Department: "I have been assuming considerable responsibility in proceeding without instructions in many important matters but no harm has been done, and I believe great benefits have been achieved."[70] Indeed, Wilson considered the success of the pact essential to Mexico's future and threatened American intervention when one of the designated ministers attempted to refuse the Cabinet appointment.[71]

Once the leaders of the two military factions came to terms, Huerta could have seized the presidency, but he refrained from doing so. He

[68] A copy of the pact is enclosed in Nelson J. O'Shaughnessy to Secretary of State William Jennings Bryan, April 15, 1914/11661; while the report of Wilson's three conditions is in Wilson to Knox, February 19, PR Mexico City, 1913, XXI, C1. 800.

[69] Wilson to Bryan, March 12, 1913/6840.

[70] Wilson to Knox, February 19, 1913/6264.

[71] Jorge Vera Estañol, *La Revolución Mexicana: orígenes y resultados* (Mexico: Editorial Porrua, 1957), pp. 282–283.

wished to follow constitutional forms and assume power legally—that is, according to the letter of the law. While Madero was a prisoner, he was technically still the President, since he had not resigned. Huerta, although in *de facto* control, cooperated with Congress and the Foreign Minister to secure legal title to the presidency. Referring to himself as the "general of division in charge of the Executive Power," Huerta requested the president of the Chamber of Deputies to convene the Congress to establish a new government. The general expressed a desire to "place himself in accord with the National Representation" to "find a legal solution" to the crisis.[72]

Francisco I. Madero and José María Pino Suárez signed their resignations on February 19 and placed them in the hands of Pedro Lascuráin, Minister of Foreign Relations, who would succeed to the presidency under the Constitution. Lascuráin pledged not to present the documents to Congress until Madero and Pino Suárez were safely out of the country, but he changed his mind once in possession of their resignations. Huerta apparently persuaded him to act earlier, either by warning that Félix Díaz threatened a new coup or by swearing on his scapular medal to protect Madero's life. The latter story sounds plausible, for Huerta had a flair for the dramatic and knew that such a gesture would impress the devoutly Catholic Lascuráin. Since Huerta was not very religious himself, he would have had few scruples about an oath, although it must be noted that reports use the word "protect" rather than guarantee.

Whatever the reason, Lascuráin submitted the resignations to the Chamber of Deputies that morning at 10:15. The Chamber, which was elected with Madero and had a Maderista majority, accepted the resignations by votes of 123–5 and 119–8. Minister of Foreign Relations Pedro Lascuráin, the constitutional successor, was proclaimed President at 10:34 A.M. His first and only act was to appoint General Victoriano Huerta Minister of Gobernación, thereby making Huerta his own constitutional successor. Lascuráin's term of office lasted less than one hour. At 11:15 A.M., the Chamber confirmed Huerta as constitutional President by a vote of 126–0.[73] Edith O'Shaughnessy, wife of an

[72] For Huerta's letter and statements, see Diego Arenas Guzman, ed., *Historia de la Cámara de Diputados de la XXVI legislatura Federal* (4 vols.; Mexico: Instituto Nacional de Estudios Históricos, 1963), IV, 333, excerpts from the congressional debates of February 19, 1913.

[73] Prida, *De la dictadura a la anarquía*, pp. 554–556; Márquez Sterling, *Los últimos días*, pp. 502–505; Wilson to Knox, February 19, 1913/6271; and *Mexican Herald*, February 20, 1913.

American diplomat, commented that Lascuráin's term was "a bit short, even for Latin America"; and the *Mexican Herald* observed: "Three presidents in one hour must be a national record." [74]

Thus, Huerta assumed the presidential office not at the time of the coup, but upon the resignations of Madero, Pino Suárez, and Lascuráin. This action was constitutional, and therefore, technically speaking, Huerta was the legitimate President of Mexico. Yet if the actions followed the letter of the Constitution, they were based on the existing power situation, which was the result of the coup. Congress, to be sure, could have refused to confirm Huerta, thereby removing his claim to constitutional succession, but in that event he would undoubtedly have seized the office and remained in control of the country. Yet he had rejected this course earlier and carefully followed constitutional forms.

With Huerta installed in the presidency, Henry Lane Wilson informed the State Department: "The revolution is now complete." [75] The ambassador was firmly convinced that his actions brought tranquillity to Mexico City. Nevertheless, turmoil continued in other parts of the country despite Huerta's announcement that peace was his sole objective. Little was complete—it was only the beginning.

[74] Edith O'Shaughnessy, *A Diplomat's Wife in Mexico* (New York: Harper and Brothers, 1916), p. 18; and *Mexican Herald*, February 20, 1913.
[75] Wilson to Knox, February 20, 1913/6227.

II

The First Reaction

On February 21, 1913, the rebel forces marched from the Ciudadela to the National Palace, where President Huerta reviewed them amidst great rejoicing. The revolutionists had triumphed, even though Huerta occupied the presidential chair instead of Félix Díaz. Despite numerous perplexing problems, the new regime seemed to be off to an auspicious start. The most pressing question was the disposition of the former President.

Madero remained a prisoner, and Cuban Minister Manuel Márquez Sterling took a particular interest in protecting his life. Although the Cuban minister had arrived in Mexico only a month earlier, he was an ardent Madero partisan. Immediately after Madero signed his resignation, Márquez Sterling proposed that the cruiser *Cuba*, dispatched to Veracruz during the revolt, convey Madero to exile in Havana. Madero accepted, and from that moment the Cuban minister worked tirelessly to protect the former President and secure his transfer to the vessel. The assassination of Gustavo Madero added urgency to these efforts. Yet the fact that Huerta had given assurances of Francisco's safety differentiated his case from that of his brother.

Ambassador Wilson did not share his Cuban colleague's concern for Madero's welfare. Wilson considered the activities of the new government of much greater significance than the fate of Madero. When Huerta inquired whether Wilson thought it more appropriate to exile Madero or to incarcerate him in a lunatic asylum, the ambassador advised the General to adopt whatever course was "best for the peace of Mexico."[1] Huerta may have interpreted this as a tacit consent to murder. At the least, it indicated that Wilson was unconcerned about

[1] Wilson to Knox, February 19, 1913/6271.

Madero's fate. Perhaps the ambassador could have saved the former President by utilizing Huerta's gratitude for the ambassador's role in the Pact of the Embassy. It is unlikely, however, that Huerta would have heeded any counsel in a matter that involved the survival of the government, and it cannot be denied that Madero was a menace to the Huerta regime.

One day after the coup, Madero's family petitioned the diplomatic corps to intercede to protect the former President's life. Instead of calling on Huerta personally, as dean of the diplomatic corps, the ambassador delegated the Spanish and Cuban ministers to convey the request to the government, instructing them to speak in the name of all chiefs of mission, but not in behalf of the diplomatic corps. The ministers encountered the Chilean envoy at the Palace, and the three diplomats discussed the matter with General Blanquet, new military commander in Mexico City.

Blanquet informed the ministers that Huerta planned to transfer Madero and Pino Suárez to Veracruz for exile that very evening. Blanquet also reportedly added that Huerta had pledged to retain the Maderista state governors, although a request for such an assurance constituted interference in internal Mexican affairs. Huerta granted the Cuban and Chilean envoys permission to accompany Madero to Veracruz.[2] That evening a train waited in the capital's depot with a full head of steam. At 10:00 P.M., a strong guard and the families of the former officials boarded the cars, but the prisoners failed to arrive.

Sending Madero into exile proved to be a complex undertaking because of the possibility of a pro-Madero counterrevolt by supporters of the ousted President. Since Huerta had just assumed power, conditions in some sectors remained unsettled, and in view of the political turmoil the attitude of many officials remained uncertain. Madero increased the government's fears, for when Huerta offered him the opportunity to select the commander of his escort, Madero requested General Felipe Angeles, who was one of his staunchest supporters.[3] Despite the fact that Angeles was already imprisoned with him, Madero refused to designate another officer.

The limited extent of existing Mexican railroads rendered Veracruz the only possible port of embarkation for Madero's voyage into

[2] Manuel Márquez Sterling, *Los últimos días del Presidente Madero: mi gestión diplomática en México* (Habana: Imprenta El Siglo XX, 1917), pp. 487–493.

[3] Ramón Prida, *De la dictadura a la anarquía* (El Paso, Texas: Imprenta de El Paso del Norte, 1914), pp. 552–553.

exile. The choice of any other port would necessitate a protracted, roundabout journey through a large portion of the country, which would greatly increase the opportunity for rebellion. But the very day Huerta assured the diplomats he would convey Madero to Veracruz, the military commander of that city, General José Refugio Velasco, telegraphed the capital requesting a clarification of the situation and implying that he would refuse to support the new government until he received additional information.[4]

Huerta naturally hesitated in view of the uncertain attitude of the commander at Veracruz, and he soon received messages that increased his anxiety. The United States consul at Veracruz, William Canada, informed the embassy at 1:00 A.M. that the military commander, the governor, and numerous other state officials declared that they had not recognized Huerta, and they ignored a government order to release all Felicista prisoners. Canada added that the military commander had begun recruiting Maderista volunteers in preparation for a rebellion upon Madero's arrival. Fearing renewed fighting, the consul warned: "Do not allow ex-President Madero to come here now."[5] This report served to confirm Huerta's own information, for the ambassador undoubtedly notified him of it. Throughout February and March, Wilson showed American consular reports to Díaz in order to apprise the government of their contents without having an official record in the Ministry of Foreign Relations.[6]

At 2:00 A.M., Lascuráin arrived at the railroad station with the news that Huerta had countermanded the orders and temporarily suspended the prisoners' departure for Veracruz.[7] Lascuráin brought renewed assurances of their safety. Subsequent reports from Veracruz confirmed the pro-Madero sentiments of its officials, and even after the commander declared his allegiance to the Huerta government on February 21, the President was understandably reluctant to risk sending Madero to that port.[8]

---

[4] General José Refugio Velasco to Huerta, quoted in Jan Leander DeBekker, *De cómo vino Huerta y cómo se fué: apuntes para la historia de un régimen militar* (Mexico: Librería General, 1914), pp. 172–173; and Márquez Sterling, *Los últimos días*, pp. 549–550.

[5] William Canada (Veracruz), to Wilson, February 20, 1913, PR Mexico City, 1913, XXI, C1. 800.

[6] Wilson to Bryan, March 9, 1913, PR Mexico City, 1913, XXII, C1. 800.

[7] *Mexican Herald*, February 21, 1913.

[8] Canada to Wilson, February 23 and March 26, 1913, PR Mexico City, 1913, XXVI, C1. 800.

Huerta's sudden decision to delay Madero's departure raised new concern for his safety. It so alarmed the Cuban minister that he spent the night at the Palace with the prisoners.[9] Madero's wife and mother again appealed for the intercession of the ambassador, and Wilson called on Huerta, in the company of German Minister Admiral Paul von Hintz, to request "utmost precautions" for Madero's safety.[10]

There were lengthy Cabinet sessions on February 21 and 22, and presumably the ministers discussed Madero's fate. The precise course of the debate cannot be determined, for both the Felicistas and Huertistas allege that the other faction compelled them to agree to Madero's assassination. Some even contend that Huerta himself opposed the assassination and never consented to it, the decision supposedly being reached while he was out of the room attending to other business.[11] This is extremely unlikely. Yet the fledgling government was not yet firmly established, and certainly Huerta could not risk a split in the Cabinet. Therefore, the Felicistas might possibly have forced him to agree to the execution against his will. It is interesting that the assassins were *rurales*, for unlike the regular army, which was directly under the orders of the President, *rurales* came under the authority of the Minister of Gobernación. Those who argue for Huerta's innocence make much of this.

It appears unlikely, however, that any single faction was innocent of the crime. Fear of a pro-Madero rebellion was the primary factor in the dilemma, and this applied equally to all members of the government. Accordingly, they undoubtedly all agreed on Madero's disposition. To imprison Madero permanently would entail a constant risk of his escape, while the possibility of exile was also fraught with danger because of doubts as to the loyalty of officials in the only logical port of embarkation. To the men considering his fate, there was only one other alternative.

[9] Márquez Sterling, *Los últimos días*, pp. 510–511.
[10] Wilson to Knox, February 20, 1913/6227.
[11] Cabinet members who blame Huerta include Jorge Vera Estañol, *La Revolución Mexicana: orígenes y resultados* (Mexico: Editorial Porrua, 1957), pp. 295–300, who also quotes Torbio Esquivel Obregón; and Rudolfo Reyes, *De mi vida, memorias políticas* (2 vols.; Madrid: Biblioteca Nueva, 1929–1930), pp. 93–121 and 166–169, who also quotes Francisco de la Barra and Alberto García Granados. Huertistas who blame the Felicistas include Querido Moheno, *Mi actuación política después de la Decena Trágica* (Mexico: Ediciones Botas, 1939), pp. 137–138; and Nemesio García Naranjo, *Memorias de Nemesio García Naranjo* (8 vols.; Monterrey: Ediciones de *El Porvenir*, 1956–1962), VI, 335–337, who quotes Dr. Aureliano Urrutia.

Huerta should have realized the potential effect this decision would have on public opinion in the United States, but he undoubtedly did not anticipate a significant reaction. The assassination of other Latin American political leaders had produced few complaints. Even if he had foreseen this problem it may not have altered his calculations. An outcry in the United States might be expected to diminish with time, and no threat seemed as serious as the immediate ones of a Madero-led revolt or a possible cleavage within the government over Madero's disposition. The immediate threat preoccupied Huerta—if he failed to maintain himself in power at this crucial juncture, subsequent protests would be irrelevant.

Ambassador Wilson was severely criticized for failing to intercede in behalf of Madero. Madero's mother subsequently claimed that she requested the personal intercession of President Taft and accused the ambassador of refusing to transmit it to Washington. Wilson contended the note bore no salutation. State Department records show that he did report her request, although not as addressed to the President.[12] The Cuban minister later charged that Wilson had ignored a suggestion for intercession by the diplomatic corps. A proposal to this effect by Márquez Sterling is indeed in the post records, but it bears an unsigned notation that the embassy received it April 23, after learning of attempts to sell it to Mexican newspapers as part of a campaign to embarrass the ambassador.[13] It appears that much of this criticism of the ambassador was unfounded, for he did take some measures to protect Madero. Yet it is true that he acted in a perfunctory manner and failed to press the matter. Wilson's earlier statement to Huerta suggests that he had little concern for Madero's fate. While his actions were clearly halfhearted, it is unlikely that vigorous efforts would have altered the course of events.

On February 22, shortly after Huerta and various members of his government had attended a Washington's Birthday reception at the embassy, Francisco Madero and José María Pino Suárez were assassinated while supposedly being transferred from the Palace to the penitentiary. At 10:00 P.M., Madero and Pino Suárez were placed in separate cars, each containing three *rurales*. Major Francisco Cárdenas and Lieutenant Rafael Pimienta commanded the detachment. The two

[12] Wilson to Knox, February 21, 1913/6320; Mercedes González de Madero to Taft, March 2, and John Bassett Moore to Mercedes González de Madero, April 30, PR Mexico City, 1913, XXVII, C1. 800.

[13] Márquez Sterling, *Los últimos días*, pp. 483–484; and PR Mexico City, 1913, XXV, C1. 800.

autos moved out of the Palace at high speed, but on arrival at the penitentiary they circled to the rear of the building, where the prisoners were shot.

Huerta announced the official government version, after a hasty Cabinet meeting, alleging that the convoy was attacked twice by groups seeking to rescue Madero and that the prisoners were caught in a crossfire while attempting to dash from the cars. The escort commander explained that the convoy attempted to elude the attackers by circling the penitentiary, which he said accounted for the fact that the prisoners died at the rear of the building rather than at the entrance.[14] Apparently the escort fired shots into the vehicles to substantiate this contention. The inadequacies of this cover story were readily apparent. While newspaper reports indicate that the government had announced its intention to transfer the prisoners to the penitentiary in advance, the convoy route remained secret and the event occurred one day after the indicated date.[15] The very idea of a rescue party firing on the moving convoy is absurd, for that would endanger the prisoners. A rescue party would inevitably have attempted to halt the cars before firing. Months later, Ambassador Wilson told the United States Senate Committee on Foreign Relations that relatives of persons killed on orders of Madero's government attacked the convoy, seeking revenge, but this far more plausible story came much too late to have any credibility.[16] The fact that General Angeles, imprisoned in the Palace with Madero and Pino Suárez, was left behind indicated advance planning, for a normal jail transfer should have included him. Years later, Major Cárdenas allegedly admitted that he had assassinated Madero and claimed that Blanquet, Mondragón, Díaz, and Huerta all ordered him to do it.[17]

News of the assassinations created a sensation in the United States, and most newspapers condemned the crime, discounting the official explanation. The New York *World* observed that the Ten Tragic Days

[14] New York *Times*, February 24 and 25, 1913; and Wilson to Knox, February 23/6321.

[15] The Washington *Post* reported the transfer February 23, making no mention of the assassinations, hence indicating an advance announcement of the transfer, since American papers carried stories of the assassinations only on February 24, Washington *Post*, February 23, 1913.

[16] New York *Times*, July 31, 1913.

[17] For Cárdenas' alleged confession, see R. Calixto Maldonado, *Los asesinatos de los Señores Madero y Pino Suárez* (Mexico: Published by the author, 1922), pp. 123–124, and Manuel Bonilla, Jr., *El régimen Maderista* (Mexico: Talleres Linotipográficos de *El Universal*, 1922), pp. 299–301.

had already proved that Mexico was incapable of ruling itself and dubbed the murders the "logical consequence of normal political conditions in Mexico."[18] American public opinion was aroused against the Huerta administration, and this bode ill for his relations with the United States. The widespread professions of horror prompted the Washington *Post* to inquire why those who attacked Huerta were not equally aroused against the former dictator of Venezuela, Cipriano Castro, who had committed numerous political assassinations but had just received permission to visit the United States.[19]

Despite these reactions, Ambassador Wilson accepted the government version "in the absence of other reliable information." He stated that the sincerity of Minister of Foreign Relations Francisco de la Barra convinced him of the veracity of the official explanation. The United States military attaché, however, considered the deaths murders.[20] British Minister Sir Francis Stronge reached the same conclusion, informing the Foreign Office: "there can be no doubt that the ex-President and Vice President were executed by order of the military revolutionary chiefs." Perhaps Wilson was merely yielding to his desires. He considered the event completely unimportant and believed that it was of no concern to the United States and should play no part in American-Mexican relations. Stronge, too, regarded the matter as an internal one and reported that the murders were simply considered as a "necessary and inevitable measure which is likely to facilitate the pacification of the country."[21] British diplomats clearly believed that the assassinations were none of their affair and that the crimes did not affect the desirability of maintaining friendly relations with the Mexican government. Huerta could not understand the uproar in the United States and often told American diplomats: "I did to Madero only what he wanted me to do to Díaz. How is my act worse than his?" [22]

The disposition of Francisco Madero was not the only dilemma facing the Huerta regime during its initial days in office—there was also the task of winning support within the country. While the government immediately initiated steps designed to conciliate the various revolution-

[18] New York *World*, February 25, 1913.

[19] Washington *Post*, February 26, 1913.

[20] Wilson press statement quoted in New York *Times*, February 25, 1913; and Burnside to AGWAR, February 25, 1913, 5761-669.

[21] Sir Francis Stronge to Grey, February 25, 1913, FO 371/1671.

[22] Edith O'Shaughnessy, *Intimate Pages of Mexican History* (New York: George H. Doran Company, 1920), p. 145.

ary groups, the principal task was securing the allegiance of the state governors. Naturally the army was safely united behind General Huerta. Almost as soon as he completed his coup on February 18, Huerta dispatched a telegram to all governors: "Authorized by the Senate, I have assumed the executive power, the President and his Cabinet being prisoners." [23] This first notice was so nebulous that it only confused many officials. Huerta's reference to the executive power, a product of his desire to await formal congressional action to install him as President, increased their uncertainty. Nonetheless, seven governors pledged their support immediately. By February 23, all but four states had recognized Huerta as President. [24]

Venustiano Carranza of Coahuila was one of these few governors refusing support. Carranza was a picturesque man with a flowing white beard, huge mustache, and smoked glasses. He was fifty-five years old, tall, and husky, with penetrating eyes and a ruddy complexion. An exceedingly cautious and suspicious individual, his mannerisms often indicated indecisiveness. Thoroughly honest and a stickler for regulations, he was also egotistical and domineering. In the words of one scholar, he was "bourgeois mediocrity incarnate." [25] Carranza was not the type of man who inspired traditional Mexican bravado. Although he launched his political career as a senator under Porfirio Díaz, Carranza joined the Madero revolution in 1911. He became governor of Coahuila during Madero's presidency, although the two later quarreled over the pay and control of Carranza's state troops. Some writers contend that this question drove a wedge between them and that Carranza was preparing to launch his own rebellion against Madero when the Huerta coup occurred, providing him with an opportunity to pose as the defender of Madero. [26] There is little substantial evidence, however, for this speculation. On the contrary, the United States military attaché believed that the Madero government was paying Carranza's state troops. [27]

[23] Huerta to state governors, February 18, 1913, quoted in Alfredo Braceda, *México Revolucionario: 1913–1917* (Mexico: Ediciones Botas, 1941), p. 142.

[24] Responses from governors appear in the *Diario Oficial*, CXXIV, 36, 415–416; and *La Nación*, February 23, 1913.

[25] Robert E. Quirk, *The Mexican Revolution: 1914–1915* (Bloomington, Indiana: Indiana University Press, 1960), p. 10.

[26] Braceda, *México Revolucionario*, pp. 93–95; and Stanley R. Ross, *Francisco I. Madero: Apostle of Mexican Democracy* (New York: Columbia University Press, 1955), p. 278.

[27] Burnside to AGWAR, March 3, 1913, WD 5761–666.

Carranza contended that the Constitution did not authorize the Senate to name a new President, and his state legislature promptly passed a resolution to this effect on February 19.[28] This was perfectly correct, but the Senate had not taken any such step, despite the implication to that effect in Huerta's telegram. Congress had merely accepted the resignations of the President, Vice President, and Foreign Minister and confirmed the ascension of the minister next in line. This followed the procedures stipulated in the Mexican Constitution.

Carranza vacillated for a considerable period before deciding to oppose Huerta. On February 21, he told Philip Holland, United States consul at Saltillo, that he had decided to "conform" to the Huerta government. After learning the details of Huerta's seizure of power, Carranza admitted that the resignations of Madero, Pino Suárez, and Lascuráin gave Huerta legal title to the presidency.[29] The governor dispatched a delegation to the capital to negotiate with Huerta on February 22, and the resulting exchanges continued for a considerable period. On February 23, the day after Madero's assassination, Holland informed the State Department that Carranza was in rebellion again. But Carranza did not cite the murders as justification for his revolt. Instead, the consul reported that the governor was enraged by the General's failure to reply to his bid for negotiations.[30]

The consul reported that "Carranza seemed very anxious for a while to conform with the new regime" and had appealed to Holland "to help him get in touch with Mexico City" on several occasions.[31] Holland diligently attempted to establish contacts between Huerta and Carranza that would facilitate negotiations. United States consuls throughout northern Mexico worked feverishly to secure an agreement, acting under orders from Ambassador Henry Lane Wilson, who directed them to "do all possible to bring about a general acceptance of the provisional government."[32]

On February 25, Carranza wired Minister of Gobernación Alberto

[28] Isidro Fabela, ed., *Documentos históricos de la Revolución Mexicana* (12 vols. to date; Mexico: Fondo de Cultura Económica and Editorial Jus, 1960–1967), I, 5.

[29] Holland (Saltillo), to Knox, February 19, 1913/6272, and February 21/6302 and /6472.

[30] Holland (Saltillo), to Knox, February 23, 1913, PR Mexico City, 1913, XXVI, C1. 800; Holland to Bryan, March 11/6968; Alfonso Junco, *Carranza y los orígines de su rebelión* (Mexico: Ediciones Botas, 1935), pp. 102–104; and Braceda, *México Revolucionario*, p. 163.

[31] Holland (Saltillo), to Bryan, March 5, 1913/6518; Holland to Knox, February 23 and 25, PR Mexico City, 1913, XXVI, C1. 800.

[32] Henry Lane Wilson to Knox, February 21, 1913/6319.

García Granados, proposing a telegraphic conference to regularize the relations between his state and the federal government.[33] The next day, the governor's brother Jesús informed United States Consul Luther Ellsworth at Ciudad Porfirio Díaz (now Piedras Negras), that the governor was definitely in rebellion, and when federal troops entered Coahuila that day, Venustiano Carranza wired President Taft declaring his opposition to Huerta.[34] This announcement came several days after Madero's death, and while Carranza cited the assassination in his proclamation, the immediate occasion of his revolt was the threat of federal troops deposing him as governor. Despite this telegram, Carranza's delegates continued their negotiations in Mexico City. All the discussions during this period reportedly concerned the very issue that had caused friction between Carranza and Madero—the pay and control of Carranza's state troops.[35]

Governor José Maytorena of Sonora had supported Carranza's stand and was also negotiating with the Huerta government. The grievances involved were the same, and again the death of Madero was never mentioned. Consul Louis Hostetter at Hermosillo reported that Maytorena demanded a guarantee of state sovereignty and payment of state troops by the federal government, as well as the withdrawal of federal troops from the state. Hostetter subsequently stated that Maytorena rebelled only because the "provisional government has never communicated directly with the state." Consul Thomas Bowman at Nogales corroborated Hostetter's account of the talks and the governor's demands, reporting that he had seen a telegram from the Huerta agent negotiating with Maytorena.[36]

American efforts to bring the parties to agreement proved fruitless. Reporting on the talks with Carranza, Consul Holland informed Consul General Philip Hanna in Monterrey disgustedly:

> you will understand how hard I tried to arrange for a settlement of affairs, and had to realize my complete failure in the end, which was

[33] Carranza's telegram was sent through the United States consulate's wires, Carranza to Alberto García Granados, February 25, 1913/21088, and since he used the minister's title he thereby implied recognition of the Huerta government.

[34] Luther Ellsworth (Cuidad Porfirio Díaz), to Knox, February 26, 1913/6385; Holland (Saltillo), to Knox, February 25/6402; and Carranza to Taft, February 26/6425.

[35] Junco, *Carranza y los orígines de su rebelión*, pp. 102–104 and 121–122; and Braceda, *México Revolucionario*, p. 163.

[36] Louis Hostetter (Hermosillo), to Knox, February 26, 1913/6498; Hostetter to Bryan, March 17/6855; and Thomas Bowman (Nogales), to Bryan, March 5, PR Mexico City, 1913, XXV, C1. 800.

due to cut wires and an obstinate governor. He is full of sentiment against Huerta because he would not communicate with him directly instead of by through [*sic*] intermediaries.[37]

Cut telegraph lines did hinder negotiations, for a dispatch from Henry Lane Wilson to Holland dated February 25 stating that Huerta gave "assurances of the best of intentions" toward Carranza did not reach Saltillo until March 13.[38] Despite the unpredictable service some messages did get through.

When his telegrams to the embassy failed to alleviate the situation, Consul Holland concluded that the ambassador had not contacted Huerta. Wilson stated that he handed the consular dispatches to the government daily.[39] The difficulty was that Huerta was too stubborn to accept Carranza's demands. The General had no patience for negotiations and simply demanded submission. As an army man he displayed contempt for civilian politicians and underestimated their strength. Having personally put down the Orozco uprising, Huerta assumed that the army could stamp out any new northern rebellion without excessive strain.

By March 1, Carranza reaffirmed his intention to revolt, and fighting began. On March 4, Ambassador Wilson made one last attempt to convince the rebel leader, instructing Holland to "assure the governor that he is rebelling against a legally constituted provisional government. . . . Urge upon him that his overthrow and defeat appear to the embassy to be inevitable. Urge upon him the necessity of immediately making terms with the provisional government." Holland informed the consul general in Monterrey on March 5 that Carranza had rejected Wilson's plea, accusing the ambassador of being "largely responsible for the present situation," and had prevented the consulate from transmitting further telegraph messages.[40] On March 4, federal troops entered Saltillo, and Carranza fled to the hills with his forces. With the beginning of fighting, all chance of negotiations ended. The revolution-

[37] Holland (Saltillo), to Consul General Philip Hanna (Monterrey), March 1, 1913, PR Saltillo, 1913, Pt. 2, Cl. 8.

[38] H. L. Wilson to Holland, February 25, 1913; and Holland, Memorandum, March 13, PR Saltillo, 1913, Pt. 2, Cl. 8.

[39] Holland (Saltillo), to Hanna (Monterrey), March 5, 1913, PR Saltillo, 1913, Pt. 2, Cl. 8; and Henry Lane Wilson to Bryan, March 9, PR Mexico City, 1913, XXII, Cl. 800.

[40] H. L. Wilson to Holland (Saltillo), March 4, 1913, PR Mexico City, 1913, XXII, Cl. 800, and PR Saltillo, 1913, Pt. 2, Cl. 8; Holland to Hanna (Monterrey), March 5, PR Monterrey, Cl. 8.

ary position was officially confirmed by Carranza's announcement of the Plan of Guadalupe on March 26.

Thus, despite Carranza's later contention that he had never recognized Huerta, American consular reports written at the time tell a very different story, for he had expressed a willingness to do so many times. John Silliman, vice consul at Saltillo, who later served as President Wilson's agent to Carranza and whose sympathies were strongly prorevolutionary, stated that he was certain Carranza really desired an arrangement with Huerta. Silliman felt the governor was "entirely sincere" in his negotiations with the government, and he attributed the break to Huerta's rigid stance.[41]

In addition, throughout the negotiations, all the consuls involved reported that the matters in dispute concerned relations between the state and federal governments. The assassination of Madero was never mentioned as a cause of discontent, and the negotiations continued beyond it. Apparently, Huerta could have reached an agreement with Carranza had he made an effort to do so. But because of his rigid and domineering attitude, his failure to take the rebellion seriously, and his sheer neglect of this particular uprising at a time when he was negotiating with numerous rebels, Huerta lost his chance to conciliate Carranza. This was certainly a grave error. Carranza may have rebelled anyway at a later date when he felt in a stronger position, but he would have lost the claim of following Madero.

Carranza boldly proclaimed himself Madero's heir and called his movement one for constitutionalism. Whatever one might think about Huerta's seizure of power, certainly Carranza had no legitimate claim to the presidency, for the Constitution provided only for succession to the ranking minister. Yet Carranza posed as the defender of Madero. Many Americans were enchanted by the name of his movement— the Constitutionalists. The announced aim of avenging Madero proved highly useful as a propaganda device, successfully rallying supporters in both the United States and Mexico.

In other sections of Mexico, reports indicated rapid pacification of the country, as numerous rebel leaders announced support for the government and surrendered to join the new regime.[42] In spite of these gains, the United States military attaché did not anticipate complete

---

[41] John Silliman (Saltillo), to Bryan, August 4, 1913, PR Mexico City, 1913, XXVI, C1. 800.

[42] Wilson to Knox, February 27, 1913/6412; Theodore Hamm (Durango), to Knox, February 27/6413, and February 28/6734; and New York *Times*, February 28, 1913.

pacification, noting that the administration lacked funds to "pay off the alleged revolutionary patriots."[43]

The primary diplomatic problem confronting the Huerta administration was that of obtaining recognition. Huerta dispatched a letter announcing his presidency to the heads of all governments maintaining relations with Mexico, and many immediately indicated their intention to reply, thereby recognizing his regime.

Ambassador Wilson urged prompt United States recognition. On February 21, he convened the diplomatic corps to discuss the situation and reported that nearly all the envoys in Mexico City concurred that Huerta had assumed power constitutionally and therefore would be recognized. They believed prompt action would aid the government and hence speed the return of peace and stability.[44] Secretary of State Philander Knox informed Wilson: "The Department is disposed from the statements and tenor of your recent telegrams to consider the new provisional government as being legally established." But Knox added that recognition would be contingent upon satisfactory settlement of the outstanding questions between the two countries. He listed the Tlahualilo controversy, Chamizal tract, Colorado River water distribution dispute, and various minor claims.[45] Knox had long maintained that the United States had "no concern whatsoever with the internal machinery" of the Mexican government and "no other feeling than that of absolute impartiality as between contending factions," as long as American citizens and their interests received protection.[46] The Secretary considered the complaints against the Huerta coup irrelevant, insofar as American policy was concerned, and devoted all his attention to the claims questions.

The Taft administration clearly intended to recognize Huerta and assumed that its successor would pursue a similar course. Taft failed to act only because the time between Huerta's rise to power and the end of Taft's term was insufficient to allow completion of negotiations.[47]

[43] Burnside to AGWAR, March 3, 1913, 5761–666.

[44] Wilson to Knox, February 21, 1913/6319.

[45] Knox to Wilson, February 21, 1913/6325A.

[46] Knox to John D. Archibold, May 10, 1911, JD 90755–863.

[47] In a Philadelphia speech, Knox stated that recognition was withheld only pending settlement of disputes, New York *Times*, April 28, 1915, while the former President expressed the same view in a letter, Taft to W. V. Backus, Taft Papers, July 10, 1916. Knox subsequently informed the ambassador that he would have extended recognition to Huerta as late as March 4 if the Mexican government had agreed to the proposals, Henry Lane Wilson, *Diplomatic Episodes in Mexico, Belgium, and Chile* (Garden City, N.Y.: Doubleday, Page and Company, 1927), p. 297.

Certainly the Huerta administration was willing to concede the American claims to obtain recognition; and had Taft continued in office, Huerta would undoubtedly have given the Chamizal to the United States, settled the other outstanding questions, and then received recognition. The ambassador informed the State Department that he was certain of a favorable settlement of these matters, noting that the Mexican administration was "grateful to the embassy for its good offices to bring about termination of the conflict." [48]

Ambassador Wilson continued to advocate immediate action, stressing that the Huerta regime was pro-American and would meet American requests promptly. [49] But Knox refused to extend recognition prior to a formal agreement on the claims. Huerta attempted to press the matter by requesting United States consent to the appointment of Emilio Rabasa, noted international law expert, as ambassador. [50] Washington ignored this note, since the government certainly could find no objection to Rabasa but was not yet ready to recognize the Huerta government by receiving a new envoy. The British government indicated that it would delay recognition of Huerta temporarily. American newspapers, continuing their campaign against the assassination of Madero, reported that this British decision represented a protest against the crime. The British, however, delayed only because they considered recognition unnecessary. The Foreign Office regarded recognition of a provisional government as "contrary to normal practice" and proposed to await Huerta's inauguration as permanent President before acting. [51] British diplomats assumed that Huerta would be elected permanent President at the subsequent elections. Stronge advocated immediate recognition, noting that the Constitution prohibited the provisional President from being a candidate for re-election; and British citizens with interests in Mexico also pressed the government to accord formal recognition to Huerta. Sir Edward Grey therefore decided that British interests in Mexico required the stability that Huerta could bring. Accordingly, the British reticence proved short-lived and recognition soon followed. [52]

As the Taft administration ended, it appeared that recognition was only a matter of time. In the view of the New York *Times*, only the

[48] Wilson to Knox, February 22, 1913/6326.

[49] Wilson to Knox, February 25, 1913/6373, and February 26/6394.

[50] Wilson to Knox, February 27, 1913, 701.1211/127.

[51] Grey to Stronge, February 25, 1913, FO 371/1671.

[52] Stronge to Grey (undated, received March 1), 1913, FO 414/235; Foreign Office Minutes dated March 1, FO 371/1671; Stronge to Grey, March 6, FO 371/1671; and Sir Louis Mallet to Grey, March 12, FO 371/1671.

"formality of political recognition" was left to the incoming administration. The New York *World*, which had condemned Madero's assassination, noted: "If a government is a fact and there is reason to believe that it can maintain itself, good form does not permit annoying questions as to the methods by which it was set up." The editor concluded that recognition would be the "best for all concerned."

Before he left office in March, 1913, Taft prophetically told friends that he "realized what a difficult thing it would be for a new administration to gather up the reins of government and understand the conditions in the southern republic in a few weeks or a few months," and that he believed "it would take at least six months for Mr. Wilson and his cabinet to grasp details of diplomatic negotiations of troop and battleship movements and of international niceties. . . ."[53] Yet even with this foresight, he could not have imagined the changes of policy the inauguration of Woodrow Wilson would bring.

[53] Washington *Post*, February 18, 1913.

III

The Advent of Woodrow Wilson

On March 4, 1913, less than a month after Huerta's rise to power in Mexico, Woodrow Wilson assumed his duties as President of the United States. The two men, whose rise nearly coincided, had little else in common. Their divergent backgrounds and conflicting ideologies contributed to the deteriorating relations between the two countries, which soon assumed the aspect of a personal duel.

Woodrow Wilson was a slender, frail-looking, and unsmiling man, who contrasted sharply with his contemporaries in politics. His narrow, almost rectangular face, with high cheekbones and jutting jaw, was gaunt and drawn. His lively blue-gray eyes narrowed when he spoke, penetrating the person addressed, and gave him the stern appearance of his Calvinist forebears. Receding iron-gray hair, arched eyebrows, and nose glasses completed his austere figure. An excellent orator with a resonant voice, he spoke sincerely, employing carefully selected phrases to create a mood which enveloped his audience.

Wilson had entered politics after an academic career by winning the election for governor of the state of New Jersey. Thus he began political life in a high-level position instead of the usual rise through minor offices. Lacking practical experience in the rough world of politics, his outlook differed from that of his colleagues. Because of this and the fact that he was the first Democrat to occupy the White House in sixteen years, his inauguration indicated significant changes in American policy.

Wilson's strong religious beliefs made him an ardent moralist. A Calvinist, he believed moral law governed the actions of mankind, and hence that everyone had a duty to uphold the law. In viewing world events, Wilson concluded that a lack of morality was the source of all difficulties. To him moral rectitude superseded law and government, and consequently he often based his decisions on what he considered ethical reasons, reducing foreign affairs to purely moral issues.[1] As a result, intuition played a major role in determining his policy. "With him it was a matter of conviction formed without weighing evidence and going through the process of rational deduction," wrote Robert Lansing. "His judgments were always right in his own mind, because he knew they were right. . . . He knew it and that was the best reason in the world—no other was necessary."[2] Compromise was out of the question, for there could be no concessions to evil. An acquaintance reported that Wilson frequently exclaimed, "God save us from compromise."[3]

The consequent feeling of self-righteousness combined with the natural egotism of the expert-become-executive caused Wilson to reject advice that did not correspond with his own views. As a professor he was accustomed to having students accept his every word, and it seemed only natural to utilize the presidency to carry out the ideas he had expounded in the classroom. Because of his moral convictions, he demanded absolute loyalty from his supporters, and his willingness to end a long friendship over a minor dispute made him an extraordinarily poor judge of men. Consequently, his advisers often told him only what they knew he wanted to hear.[4] Yet Wilson's inability to tolerate opposition stemmed from beliefs so ingrained, so much a part of him, that he was unable to perceive the resulting dogmatism. He resembled a crusader who, convinced of his own righteousness and expecting violent opposition from the forces of evil, closes his mind to everything and presses forward with grim determination, certain that his cause will triumph.

[1] Arthur S. Link, *Wilson the Diplomatist* (Baltimore: Johns Hopkins University Press, 1957), pp. 16–18; Harley Notter, *The Origins of the Foreign Policy of Woodrow Wilson* (Baltimore: Johns Hopkins University Press, 1957), pp. 8–10 and 269–270; and Samuel Flagg Bemis, "Woodrow Wilson and Latin America," in Edward H. Buehrig, ed., *Wilson's Foreign Policy in Perspective* (Bloomington, Indiana: Indiana University Press, 1957), pp. 108–109.

[2] Diary of Robert Lansing, November 20, 1921, Lansing Papers.

[3] Raymond Fosdick, "Personal Recollections of Woodrow Wilson," in *Lecture and Seminar at the University of Chicago in Celebration of the Centennial of Woodrow Wilson: 1856–1956* (Chicago: University of Chicago Press, 1958), p. 4, hereinafter cited as *Centennial of Woodrow Wilson.*

[4] Arthur S. Link, *Woodrow Wilson and the Progressive Era: 1910–1917* (New York: Harper and Brothers, 1954), p. 32; Arthur S. Link, *Wilson: The Road to the White House* (Princeton, N.J.: Princeton University Press, 1947), pp. 94–95; John Morton Blum, *Woodrow Wilson and the Politics of Morality* (Boston: Little, Brown and Company, 1956), p. 4.

Despite his academic background, Wilson had a limited outlook and possessed little knowledge of foreign affairs. Domestic matters and the mechanics of government constituted his major interests, and his studies of British government were his only contacts with politics abroad. His published works scarcely touched diplomacy. Although his early publications showed considerable research, this was not true of his later works, and in 1916 he stated, "I haven't read a serious book through for fourteen years." [5] He preferred reflection to research, and his popularity on the campus was the result of his oratorical ability rather than of any fresh intellectual content in his lectures. For Woodrow Wilson was a teacher rather than an intellectual, interested in general ideas but bored by details.

Wilson's convictions led him to base his foreign policy on a single word—democracy—and to adopt a program of moral imperialism that entailed abandoning the traditional policies of national interest and assuming the stance of a universal authority. He sought to help mankind by spreading democracy, instead of soliciting advantages or privileges for the United States. Accordingly, he abandoned the promotion of national interest abroad and ceased protecting Americans and their property overseas. [6]

European chancelleries, accustomed not only to protecting their interests everywhere but actively seeking to extend them, found the American President's methods incomprehensible. His actions did not seem plausible to experienced diplomats, who could not consider him naive enough to believe his own statements and accordingly assumed that he had seized upon these ideas as a pretext for expanding American influence. Wilson was equally unable to understand the traditional methods, for in his view he was merely preventing the country from being dragged into war to preserve the holdings of the few. He told a friend: "I sometimes have to pause and remind myself that I am President of the whole United States and not merely of a few property holders in the Republic of Mexico." [7] He would never have paused to ponder whether Americans abroad were part of the "whole United States."

[5] Ida Tarbell, "A talk with the President of the United States," *Colliers*, LVIII (October 28, 1916), 37.

[6] Link, *Wilson the Diplomatist*, pp. 13–15; and Notter, *Origins of the Foreign Policy of Woodrow Wilson*, pp. 112, 118–119, and 197–198.

[7] Rear Admiral Cary T. Grayson, *Woodrow Wilson: An Intimate Memoir* (New York: Holt, Rinehart and Winston, 1960), p. 30.

Since the Mexican situation was the first diplomatic problem Wilson confronted, these new policies received their initial test there, although the President knew little about Latin America. His historical studies had not touched this area, and in his *History of the American People*, he devoted a mere three pages to the Spanish and Portuguese background to discovery.[8] Convinced as he was of Anglo-Saxon superiority, he regarded Latin Americans as inferior people. Accordingly, Wilson intended to provide them with lessons in government and democracy.

The President despised the military despots who ruled much of Latin America, for he considered them as outmoded as absolute monarchs. He regarded the recurring revolutions as a scourge that stifled developing democracy.[9] Indeed, he considered the frequent uprisings as something of a joke and referred to his stomach upsets as "turmoil in Central America."[10] Yet if at times he seemed to forget that the democracy he loved stemmed from revolutions in England and the United States, he did differentiate between "acceptable" revolutions, which opposed dictators, and those that installed despots in power, even if the distinction was not always clear.

Wilson assumed that Mexico faced problems similar to those of the United States, despite its different history and traditions, and therefore was convinced that the solutions he employed domestically could be applied to Mexico. Unaware of the divergent background of the peoples, he assumed that the outlook and attitudes of Mexicans were identical to those of Americans. Therefore, he believed that if the United States swept the current *caudillo* away, the Mexican people would rejoice at his removal, establish an elective government, and be eternally grateful to the United States. Not only was this view based on false assumptions, but it ignored such fundamental attitudes as nationalism. Mexicans did not intend to take lessons from the United States. Yet Wilson, viewing the entire situation on a moral plane, regarded all other considerations as subsidiary. He failed to realize that people who have never experienced democracy cannot understand its advantages.

Wilson viewed Mexican events through rose-tinted glasses, which screened out all derogatory information and admitted only what agreed with his preconceived notions. To him the issue was clear. He regarded Madero as "an idealist" who "was trying hard to uplift the Mexican people" and who accordingly deserved American "sympathy

[8] Bemis, in Buehrig, ed., *Wilson's Foreign Policy in Perspective*, pp. 112–113.
[9] *Ibid.*, pp. 115–116.
[10] Grayson, *Woodrow Wilson*, p. 2.

and support."[11] Madero's assassination profoundly shocked him, and an emotional account by Mrs. Madero during a visit to the White House helped arouse him against Huerta.[12]

To Wilson, Huerta was the symbol of all Latin American problems —a hated dictator who seized power in a military coup against a supposedly democratic regime and imposed his rule on a people thirsting for democracy. The President would treat this villain much as he would a recalcitrant student in one of his classes—he would chastise him so severely that his reprimand would not merely terminate his antics, but serve as a warning to others contemplating similar action. Wilson therefore proposed to employ the power of the United States to oust the despot as a service to mankind, and in so doing, save all Latin America from its historic problem of dictatorship.

The first instrument of Wilson's opposition to Huerta in March, 1913, was nonrecognition. By adopting this stance, Wilson reversed traditional American policy. Historically, the United States had always recognized *de facto* regimes, and such statesmen as John Quincy Adams and James Buchanan had affirmed this doctrine. Recognition did nothing more than the word implied: by it one government acknowledged the existence of another, thereby enabling normal relations between them to continue on an established basis. But to Woodrow Wilson, recognition constituted approval, and he would have nothing to do with dictators. He therefore disregarded the normal diplomatic distinction between *de facto* and *de jure* recognition, for according to established practice, it was possible to express his disapproval by withholding the latter while continuing normal relations through *de facto* recognition. Wilson apparently felt that nonrecognition would topple the offending government and that its collapse would inevitably lead to a democratic regime. His idealism would prove to be lacking *savoir-faire* in a world of harsh realities.

Yet nonrecognition can constitute intervention, and Wilson soon found that his unequivocal opposition to Huerta drew him further into the Mexican imbroglio. For Huerta continued in power despite Wilson's refusal to extend recognition, and his regime was not the first Mexican government that failed to receive immediate United States recognition. In the past, however, the delay was due to a normal waiting policy. Wilson opposed Huerta, and accordingly nonrecognition was

[11] House Diary, January 18, 1913.
[12] New York *World*, May 26, 1914, for a report of Mrs. Madero's visit to the White House.

accompanied by other overt actions directed against the Mexican government.

Wilson's policy would have been more understandable if he had consistently applied it to other revolutionary regimes. But in February, 1914, when a military junta seized power in Peru, he recognized it almost instantly, with no inquiry as to its democratic outlook or origins.[13] This occurred despite a confusing situation in which the Congress and the military, after jointly ousting the Chief Executive, split over the choice of a successor, with the result that Peru momentarily had two "presidents." The London *Times* observed: "President Wilson, if he lives up to his declared policy against unconstitutional government may be unable to recognize the new regime."[14] Wilson also extended recognition to a Chinese government whose president was accused of murdering a rival.[15] Just how this differed from the charges against Huerta regarding Madero's death was known only to the President. When a Cabinet member inquired whether the Chinese regime was really democratic, the President replied that "after years of study he had only one final conviction in government, and that was that the same sort of government was not suitable for all nations."[16] The same philosophy, if applied to Mexico, would have reversed American policy. Clearly, the President employed a double standard, a strange paradox for a man who based his stands on moralism. Yet China was remote, and even Peru lay beyond the traditional sphere of American influence in the Caribbean—the area most closely connected with national security and the site of most American armed intervention. Hence, by recognizing these regimes while opposing Huerta, Wilson was in reality pursuing the traditional American policy of dominance in the Caribbean. His actions against Huerta were partially aimed at discouraging rebellions in Central America and thereby protecting the Panama Canal, then under construction. Thus, while the President's methods were unorthodox and his objectives idealistic and universal, his policy unwittingly followed the traditional outline, at least in its sphere of application. Wilson himself would never have admitted this.

[13] Bryan to Benton McMillin (Lima), February 12, 1914, SD 823.00/127a. For reports of the coup in Peru, McMillin to Bryan, February 4, 1914, 823.00/116, and February 5, 823.00/117.

[14] London *Times*, February 6, 1914.

[15] E. David Cronon, ed., *The Cabinet Diaries of Josephus Daniels, 1913–1921* (Lincoln, Nebr.: University of Nebraska Press, 1963), pp. 23–26.

[16] David Franklin Houston, *Eight Years with Wilson's Cabinet, 1913–1920* (2 vols.; Garden City, N.Y.: Doubleday, Page and Company, 1926), I, 49, for the President's comment.

If false notions formed the basis of Wilson's actions in Mexico, this was due to his refusal to heed advice from those familiar with the Mexican situation. The President had formed his attitudes about Mexico before consulting the facts, and he examined reports only to seek information that substantiated his preconceived notion. He distrusted State Department and Foreign Service personnel who understood Mexican events. Because of low salaries and many years of Republican rule, these branches were staffed by numerous wealthy Republicans. In addition, these diplomats had no sympathy with Wilson's plans, and repudiating the old policy necessarily entailed rejecting the counsels that guided it. Principally, however, the difficulty stemmed from Wilson's unwillingness to listen to realistic counsel that did not comport with his own idealistic view. His closest intimate, Colonel Edward M. House, wrote that the most effective method of dealing with Wilson was to "discover a common hate, and exploit it, get the President warmed up, and then start on your business."[17] These factors, along with the President's customary aloof and impersonal attitude, made him rather rigid and doctrinaire in matters that required open-mindedness and flexibility.

The cabinet was no more qualified to decide foreign policy questions than the President, and this was particularly true of Secretary of State William Jennings Bryan, a pacifist with no experience in diplomacy. Wilson named him to the post solely because of the necessity of guaranteeing his support in Congress. The top position in the Cabinet was the only suitable place for a three-time presidential candidate. Thus, domestic politics superseded foreign affairs even in the selection of the Secretary of State. Wilson himself did not consider Bryan the most suitable man for the office, but in this instance he was compelled to bow to political necessity.[18] Bryan, a power in the Democratic party for many years, was an accomplished political tactician. A superb orator, he was a crusader who, like Wilson, thought in terms of moral issues. To him the problems of society revolved around phrases like "people bearing burdens" and "the wicked in high places."[19] British Ambassador Lord Bryce reported that Bryan was inclined to "rash generalizations which are prompted by his ignorance of conditions

---

[17] House Diary, November 22, 1915.

[18] Lind, *Wilson the Diplomatist*, pp. 25, 113; and Ray Stannard Baker, *Woodrow Wilson: Life and Letters* (7 vols.; Garden City, N.Y.: Doubleday, Doran and Company, 1931), III, 440.

[19] William G. McAdoo, *Crowded Years* (Boston: Houghton Mifflin Company, 1931), pp. 337–338.

abroad." The British diplomat was particularly alarmed by Bryan's "most childlike proneness to accept the statements made to him by people who talk the current democratic jargon."[20] Like the President, Bryan clung tenaciously to these views. Bryce's successor in Washington, Sir Cecil Spring-Rice, concluded in exasperation: "Talking to Mr. Bryan is like writing on ice."[21] Truthful himself and loyal to his friends, Bryan assumed that they would reciprocate that loyalty, and accordingly he was a poor judge of men. His eternal optimism caused him to misinterpret situations. Although he had visited Mexico three times, these were pleasure trips, and he had not sought information about the country or its political traditions and customs.

Bryan's main concern as Secretary of State was finding places for deserving Democrats starved for patronage during sixteen years of Republican rule. The numerous State Department civil service posts irritated him, and he spent considerable time searching for openings his friends might fill in other departments. He constantly recommended candidates for positions throughout the government. In making appointments to the diplomatic service, Bryan again thought primarily in terms of domestic politics. He endeavored to distribute the posts according to political expediency, and he spoke not of an individual's qualifications, but of "candidates for appointment from New England." He was always prepared to replace a career diplomat with a new appointee exclusively on the basis of party affiliation.[22] This technique was fine for party loyalty but devastating for American diplomacy.

Bryan treated his responsibilities as Secretary of State somewhat cavalierly and spent considerable time away from his post. Each day he did the family marketing, becoming a familiar sight strolling around Washington stores carrying a large basket on his arm, fighting crowds to reach the counters, and searching for his favorite white radishes. In addition, he did not consider affairs of state sufficiently pressing to prevent him from leaving Washington to continue lecturing on the Chautauqua circuit. The Great Commoner contended that his salary of twelve thousand dollars a year was inadequate, although he had amassed a small fortune in landholdings, which he insisted on retaining as security for his old age. European diplomats roared with laughter at the

20 Bryce to Grey, March 11, 1913, FO 414/235.

21 Spring-Rice to Grey, February 17, 1914, quoted in Stephen Gwynn, *The Letters and Friendships of Sir Cecil Spring-Rice: A Record* (2 vols.; Boston: Houghton Mifflin Company, 1929), II, 202.

22 Bryan to Wilson, May 24, 1913, Bryan-Wilson Correspondence, I, 5 and *passim.*

spectacle of an American Secretary of State abandoning Washington to lecture under a tent in some rural town. The New York *Times* reported that Bryan spent thirty-seven of his first 134 days in office away from Washington and thus devoted only three-fourths of his time to his post.[23] Ambassador Walter Hines Page in London complained, "Washington is a deep hole of silence toward ambassadors." Spring-Rice informed his government: "Bryan is an ardent advocate of peace. In fact, the time that he devotes to the public advocacy of this great cause leaves him hardly any leisure time to attend to the business of his office."[24] Bryan's prolonged absences from Washington accented his lack of knowledge of world affairs. For example, on March 21, 1913, he wrote to Wilson from Lincoln, Nebraska, reporting that he had just "secured authentic information" that Madero had resigned before his assassination.[25] He could have made the same "startling" discovery by consulting the records of his own Department of State or by reading the newspapers of the pertinent dates.

While Wilson's reluctance to delegate authority would probably have caused him to retain most of the decision-making power in any event, Bryan's presence in the Cabinet obliged Wilson to be his own Secretary of State. The President composed diplomatic notes on his portable typewriter without consulting anyone and often cautioned Bryan to pay special attention to dispatches written on "his pen."[26] All of the accumulated experience of veteran diplomats in the State Department was thus ignored and bypassed.

Yet Wilson and Bryan agreed on a missionary diplomacy toward Mexico. Both employed zealous moralistic criteria, and both viewed Huerta as a bloody dictator who was obstructing democracy. While Wilson made the decisions, Bryan invariably provided the kind of counsel the President desired and enthusiastically and faithfully implemented the policy of his Chief. Bryan had devoted most of his political career to a crusade against the abuses of big business, and consequently he shared the President's view that Americans abroad had left home only in search of excessive profits and hence did not deserve protection. When a committee of Americans from Mexico visited Secretary Bryan to request protection for their property,

[23] New York *Times*, July 17, 1913.

[24] Page to House, November 23, 1913, Burton J. Hendrick, *The Life and Letters of Walter H. Page* (3 vols.; Garden City, N.Y.: Doubleday, Page and Company, 1922–1923), I, 212; Spring-Rice to Grey, May 19, 1913, FO 414/235.

[25] Bryan to Wilson, March 21, 1913, Wilson Papers, File II.

[26] Bryan-Wilson Correspondence, *passim*.

Bryan rejected their plea, merely advising them to leave Mexico. The Secretary of State simply did not understand that many of these people had invested everything they owned in Mexico and were small businessmen, not large corporations seeking a profit. In his opinion:

> Americans who go from our country into another country for the purpose of making money, must leave their country to decide the conditions under which they remain if they would claim their country's protection. . . . If any American citizen having property in Mexico refuses to leave Mexico because he is afraid that his property will suffer, he puts his property interests above his own welfare, but he cannot rightly ask this Government to put his property in another country above the lives of American citizens who may be sacrificed in the attempt to protect that property.[27]

Bryan advocated ordering all Americans to leave Mexico as a method of pressuring Huerta. He naively supposed that such an announcement would relieve the government of the responsibility to protect its citizens and remove all possibility of entanglement with Mexico over harm to Americans. In his opinion, sending troops to protect the property of Americans in Mexico would be to "allow such Americans to declare war."[28]

Other members of the administration also lacked basic qualifications to provide advice on the Mexican question whenever the President was inclined to seek it. Josephus Daniels, who as Secretary of the Navy would have a major role in any military action in Mexico, was also a pacifist. Like the President and the Secretary of State, he was almost totally ignorant of diplomatic procedures, and he shared their naiveté. Another Cabinet member who frequently expressed opinions on Mexico was Postmaster General Albert S. Burleson. A Texan, Burleson had very definite views about Mexico, and he reflected Texas sentiment, which favored the revolutionaries.

Wilson only consulted his Cabinet about Mexican matters during the early months of his administration. Once he reached his decision, he no longer sought advice and grew tired of the endless discussions. By September, 1913, Colonel House found Cabinet members complaining that the President "confers with none of them excepting in matters concerning their particular departments." House discovered, "Not one of them has been able to tell me a single thing regarding what the

---

[27] Bryan to Wilson, undated, received July 20, 1913, Wilson Papers, File II.
[28] *Ibid.*

President has in mind for Mexico." [29] Washington reporter Charles W. Thompson commented:

> Nobody who was competent to tell him [Wilson] the truth about Mexico could get his ear, could even get to his presence. It soon became a stock joke among the people who came to Washington, eager to lay their knowledge of Mexican conditions before him, that the only way to get to him was to tell Tumulty that you had never been in Mexico. [30]

The problem of molding policy for the Mexican imbroglio was compounded by pressing domestic matters. For the President had come to office with his eyes riveted on internal events rather than foreign affairs, and throughout the early days of his administration his gaze remained firmly fixed on the home front. He told a friend: "It would be the irony of fate if my administration had to deal chiefly with foreign affairs." [31] Thus, the Mexican situation commanded only a small portion of the President's time at the outset, and this contributed to his errors there. Wilson made his basic policy decision while burdened with domestic matters and began to devote more attention to Mexico only when it became apparent that mere nonrecognition was insufficient to achieve his objectives.

Wilson entered the White House convinced that the most urgent problem facing the United States was tariff revision. He at once set out to rectify what he considered an injustice by summoning a special session of Congress on the day of his inauguration. The President was immediately submerged in numerous conferences with party leaders engaged in drafting the bill, even before Congress assembled. He then dramatized his proposals by breaking tradition to address Congress personally on April 8, 1913. As Congress debated throughout the spring and summer, the President followed the tariff struggle closely and frequently conferred with legislative leaders.

During the congressional debates on the bill, Wilson turned his attention to his second objective—the regulation of banking and currency. He began conferring with advisers and congressional leaders to shape the proposal during the early days of his administration, and the sessions continued until June 23, when the President again appeared

[29] House Diary, September 25, 1913.

[30] Charles W. Thompson, *Presidents I've Known and Two Near Presidents* (Indianapolis: Bobbs-Merrill Company, 1929), p. 261.

[31] Wilson to E. G. Conklin, cited in Baker, *Woodrow Wilson: Life and Letters*, IV, 55.

on Capitol Hill to lay the Federal Reserve Act before the legislature. The resulting congressional flurry dragged on until December, and the President carefully followed the debates, intervening when necessary to aid the bill's progress.

Thus, throughout the spring and summer of 1913, Wilson was occupied on the domestic scene securing passage of his two most important pieces of legislation. These matters absorbed most of his time and energy. In addition, the President hoped to prevent any other issues from arising to distract Congress until it had enacted this legislation, and consequently he allowed all foreign policy questions to slide until the passage of these bills was certain. During the same period, the President had to deal with cries for legislation forbidding interlocking directorates and exempting labor unions from antitrust laws. Although these measures did not bear fruit until the following year, much of the preliminary planning took place during the initial months of Wilson's administration, for the President found it necessary to formulate proposals to prevent overzealous legislators from attaching controversial amendments to the tariff and the Federal Reserve Act. Although the tariff was not enacted until October and the banking bill until December, most of the key maneuvering on both bills was completed by the end of June. By that time the basic decisions had been made and passage of the tariff was all but assured, although the banking bill, while drawn up, still had to be shepherded through Congress.

Therefore, Wilson's initial blunders in Mexico may have been due in part to his lack of attention to the problem. For it was not until August that he really moved against Huerta, and by then the crucial stage in the domestic legislation had passed.

Surrounded by incompetent advisers, whose opinions he did not wish to hear, and preoccupied by domestic events, Wilson molded his foreign policy according to his own beliefs. The result of the first test of this policy in Mexico was a series of blunders. The fact that the President did not understand the situation in Mexico compounded the problem and contributed to the veritable comedy of errors that characterized his first actions.

IV

The Huerta Regime:
Government and Battlefield

The diplomatic confrontation between Mexico and the United States was inextricably intertwined with domestic Mexican events, for the Wilson administration was intervening in Mexican internal affairs. Naturally, the nature and strength of the Huerta regime and the activity of the revolutionaries determined the context in which the diplomatic struggle was conducted.

Victoriano Huerta sincerely wished to help his people and considered further economic development the most effective method. The General failed to perceive that the necessary protection of foreign interests antagonized the poverty-stricken peons who comprised the overwhelming majority of the Mexican population. Huerta was firmly convinced that Mexico was not prepared for democracy, and in his view it might never succeed there. The General felt that only a strong government could control the country sufficiently to promote its development. He told the American chargé that Mexico was "not ready for any government save a dictatorship."[1]

It is hardly surprising that an egotist like Huerta considered himself the only man capable of improving the country. Thus he believed that maintaining himself in power was in the best interests of the nation. This became his primary objective, merging with his passion for pacification. Inevitably Huerta depended mainly on the army and old army comrades such as General Aureliano Blanquet, for support. To broaden his base, he embraced several anti-Madero factions. Many of those who supported him were more antirevolutionary than pro-Huerta, for the wealthy, business, and foreign classes regarded him as the defender

---

[1] Nelson O'Shaughnessy to Bryan, December 24, 1913/10405.

of law and order. His alliance with the Catholic party originated in this manner. While seeking support from these elements, Huerta nonetheless tried to concentrate all power in his own hands.

Whatever his aims and good intentions, Huerta was a dictator. As might be expected from his crassness and lack of concern for human life, even his own, he had no compunctions about executing opponents. Yet nearly all *caudillos* resort to executions, and while this hardly makes the practice acceptable, it means that Huerta was no worse than his contemporaries. Indeed, the very revolutionaries who opposed the dictator employed the same methods. Huerta trusted no one, and although he had several confidants among his Cabinet members, he eliminated each when he decided that the person was becoming too powerful. He concentrated on the stronger men whom he regarded as potential rivals. Since these men were well known, they could not simply be executed. The task required greater finesse and Huerta became an expert at this. The pattern was repeated many times. There was a sudden "important mission" abroad, which required an individual of great prestige. The mission was always urgent, and the person involved invariably left the country within twenty-four hours after Huerta informed him of this great duty. Often the emissary departed before the government had sufficient time to decide exactly what "important mission" he was to fulfill. Huerta and the Cabinet would appear at the railroad station to bid a "sad and reluctant" farewell to their "esteemed colleague," praising his service to the nation while hurrying him aboard the waiting train.

Huerta's tastes were simple and even as President he did not alter his private life. Instead of occupying Chapultepec Castle, the presidential residence that overlooked the city from a hilltop, he continued to reside in his home on Calle Alfonso Herrera and also maintained a small retreat in another part of the city. When reporters inquired about his obvious distaste for the mansion at Chapultepec, he jokingly replied: "It isn't proper for a man as bad as they say I am to venture so near heaven."[2] Although the revolutionaries would have one believe that Huerta was universally hated, he moved about the capital practically unguarded much of the time and occasionally even walked through the streets alone.[3] The General rarely appeared at the National Palace,

[2] New York *World*, November 17, 1913.

[3] In the last month of his administration, as opposition increased, Huerta was closely guarded, but until then he went about with only a few aides and at times even alone.

preferring to spend his days at military barracks and his evenings in various cantinas. His drinking increased with his failure to pacify the country. The General conducted much of his business from various taverns, and in the later days of his administration, he spent considerable time in his automobile. Anyone wishing to confer with him was compelled to search the city until finding the President, either in his car or in a cantina. Huerta received petitioners in his auto and transacted business while driving about the capital dictating to a stenographer who accompanied him.

Immediately after his seizure of the presidency, Huerta moved to terminate the various rebellions disrupting the country and sought to secure the cooperation of anti-Madero insurgent groups. As his initial act, Huerta declared a nationwide amnesty.[4] Numerous rebel leaders immediately flocked to the new government's banner, pledging support and placing their forces under its command.[5] The President's old adversary, Pascual Orozco, Jr., announced his adherence to the new regime, and his father journeyed to Morelos to attempt to negotiate with Zapata. The federal forces dispatched to Coahuila routed the rebels at nearly every encounter, hastily capturing the state capital of Saltillo and forcing Carranza and his legislature to flee. Despite Mexican press claims that Carranza had sought refuge in the United States and abandoned his revolt, the revolutionists captured Nogales.[6] Carranza, though in retreat, defiantly issued his Plan of Guadalupe to formalize his revolt on March 26. Quite naturally, the varying conditions in different sectors of the country produced conflicting reports. Consul Philip Holland at Saltillo, center of the Carranza rebellion, inevitably viewed this movement more seriously than did observers in other areas of Mexico. His vice consul, John Silliman, concurred, and as Silliman was a former classmate from Woodrow Wilson's Princeton days, the President paid particular attention to his reports. By contrast, Consul Theodore Hamm at Durango considered the rebels mere bandits without any unified purpose.[7]

4 Huerta's order is dated March 4, 1913, General Manuel Mondragón to all Generals, AHDN, XI/481.5/80–82.

5 Reports of rebels declaring support for the government include Wilson to Bryan, April 9, 1913/7066, O'Shaughnessy to Bryan, March 18/6769, and Philip Holland (Saltillo), to Bryan, March 25/7023.

6 Reports that Carranza fled to the United States appeared in *La Nación*, March 15, 1913, and *Mexican Herald*, March 13, 1913.

7 Philip Holland (Saltillo), to Bryan, March 14, 1913/6719; and Theodore Hamm (Durango), to Bryan, April 5/7358.

The Huerta government inadvertently contributed to the strength of the rebel movement while seeking to stamp it out. Huerta distrusted the men elected with Madero and foolishly replaced many state governors with military officers. This ill-conceived policy merely drove the local followings of the ousted executives to join the revolt. Huerta could have promoted peace more effectively by seeking to reconcile these governors to his rule. The General, however, had little patience for protracted negotiations and frequently antagonized local authorities. In one bizarre instance, General Jacinto B. Treviño was summarily dismissed as governor of Nuevo León and rushed aboard a train for Mexico City. Realizing his error, Huerta met Treviño at the station, conducted him to a hastily arranged fiesta in his honor, and then returned him to his post. A short time later, the performance was repeated with the military commander of the state.[8] Changes continued as the rebel movement persisted, for Huerta believed military governors could impose pacification. By May, only half the Madero governors remained in office.

Huerta immediately inaugurated a program to reorganize and strengthen the army. The president was undoubtedly confident that he could remold the army into an effective pacifying force, just as he had once retrained the Division of the North. Some of his plans were well conceived, but applying them to the entire military service from the presidential chair proved more difficult than dealing with a single segment personally. The nature of the Mexican army also presented formidable obstacles, for recruits were invariably obtained through seizure by a press gang under the *leva*, or taken from jail. Once the recruit was uniformed and armed, the military considered him a soldier, with no training necessary. These troops proved highly unreliable and the overwhelming majority wished only to flee at the first sign of battle. In this situation, even a well-planned army reorganization had little prospect of success. Huerta began by restructuring the command into ten regional divisions. On May 30, he issued a decree increasing the strength of the army to eighty thousand men, and one month later he even attempted to institute universal military training.[9] Despite these efforts, the United States military attaché

[8] Philip Hanna (Monterrey), to H. L. Wilson, March 28, 1913, and April 10, PR Monterrey, C1. 8.

[9] The order on the military zones is April 10, 1913, Huerta to Mondragón, AHDN, XI/481.5/88 ff 129–130; the decree increasing the army is dated May 30, AHDN, XI/481.5/88 ff 295–296; and the compulsory training was announced in *El Imparcial*, June 2, 1913.

estimated the actual strength of the army at twenty to twenty-five thousand men.[10]

Army strategy was not suited to guerrilla warfare. Federal columns traveled in large bodies along the railroads. With untrained conscript forces, commanders could not risk dividing the troops into small detachments to pursue guerrillas, for this would increase the opportunity for desertion. The strategy of the high command was entirely defensive. Army officers equated victory with control of the cities and communications networks, and consequently the army was fragmented in an attempt to place a force in every city. These detachments were too small to win major battles, yet too large to pursue guerrillas effectively. This fragmentation enabled the insurgents to defeat the army piecemeal. In addition, the predisposition to ignore the rural areas allowed the revolutionists to regroup and move throughout most of the nation unhindered. This in turn enabled the rebels to concentrate their forces at will and seize the initiative. Federally held cities became isolated pockets, whose garrisons were unable to venture beyond the immediate environs of the city. Furthermore, the army was hobbled by incompetent officers who owed their rank to age, revolution, or influence. The problem was compounded by the excessive number of officers, for the Mexican army had 139 generals to command its twenty thousand men. Yet Huerta was powerless to remove many of these officers, for some units were fiercely loyal to their commanders.

Huerta's preoccupation with maintaining power prevented him from taking the field personally. Given the condition of the army, it is unlikely that the old warrior could have defeated the rebels, but certainly he was the general most likely to succeed. His experience and leadership ability might have enabled him to train and inspire one segment of the troops if he took the field at their head. The same inadequacies of strategy would still have hobbled him had the revolutionaries elected to ignore him and continue harassing tactics. Yet, had Huerta assumed personal command, it would undoubtedly have tempted the revolutionaries to seek to kill him and destroy his army in one grand battle, and if they attempted this, Huerta might well have emerged victorious.

In his first address to Congress on April 2, Huerta stressed that he had assumed office by its authority, pledged to respect state sovereignty, and appealed for peace. His plea for pacification evoked delirious

[10] Burnside to AGWAR, June 10, 1913, 5761–762.

cheering and drew lavish praise from capital newspapers.[11] Shortly thereafter, Huerta addressed the Jockey Club seeking support from society. Huerta brought the audience to its feet with an appeal: "I am not a man of government; I understand not those things. I love and understand soldiering. When I see a train with . . . all the paraphernalia of war I feel a keen impulse to go along. . . . I, gentlemen, have never been afraid. . . . But now I am afraid, because grave responsibilities weigh upon me."[12]

The Mexican President proposed that Congress schedule elections for July, but a Chamber committee recommended postponing the vote until the country was pacified.[13] Félix Díaz had announced his candidacy on March 6, and the Maderista deputies preferred retaining Huerta in office as provisional President rather than calling an election that would install Díaz in the presidency for the duration of Madero's term. Many of them considered Huerta less likely to restore Porfirianism than Félix. The Catholic party also opposed early elections, for it sought time to organize its campaign and let Díaz' popularity wane. Díaz supporters vociferously protested any postponement of the ballot, with Minister of Gobernación Alberto García Granados submitting his resignation to register his objection. Díaz angrily renounced his candidacy. Huerta averted a major crisis by offering Díaz the post of Minister of Gobernación.[14] This was a shrewd maneuver, for while this ministry supervised the voting, Cabinet members were ineligible to stand for election, and hence Díaz was compelled to refuse the office. Realizing the impossibility of convincing Congress to call July elections, Huerta selected October 26, and at length Congress agreed.[15] Since the delay provided Huerta with time to strengthen his position, what appeared to be opposition actually facilitated his plans.

Huerta continued his efforts to purge the Díaz men from his Cabinet. On June 12, Minister of War Manuel Mondragón resigned in the face of newspaper criticism of his conduct of the campaign against the

[11] For the speech to Congress, Wilson to Bryan, April 2, 1913, 812.032/14; and *Diario Oficial*, CXXV, 27, April 1, 283–292; for newspaper comments, *El País*, April 2 and 3, 1913; and *Mexican Herald*, April 2, 1913.

[12] *Mexican Herald*, April 23, 1913.

[13] For the congressional refusal to act, *El Imparcial*, April 20 and 23, 1913; *La Nación*, April 24, 1913; and Nemesio García Naranjo, *Memorias de Nemesio García Naranjo* (8 vols.; Monterrey: Ediciones de *El Porvenir*, 1956–1962), VII, 125.

[14] Wilson to Bryan, April 24, 1913/7250; and *Mexican Herald*, May 8, 1913.

[15] Wilson to Bryan, May 1, 1913/7335, and *Diario Oficial*, CXXVI, 27, May 31, 1913, 375, 386–390.

revolutionaries.[16] At a banquet on June 22, Huerta suddenly announced that he was saddened by Mondragón's imminent departure for Paris. Mondragón, who was completely unaware of his impending assignment, exclaimed in amazement, "Why—a—you mistake." Huerta replied, "Yes, my dear General, yes, you are, an important mission." When Mondragón protested that he was unprepared and had no trunks, Huerta assured him, "Don't worry, I'll send you trunks." Early the next morning a government truck delivered thirty trunks to Mondragón's residence, and the General departed that evening following a "sad" farewell at the railroad station, attended by Huerta, Blanquet, and Díaz. The day after he left the government decided the nature of the "important mission" that required his hasty departure: Mondragón would serve as Mexican delegate to the Universal Exposition in Belgium.[17] Huerta also secured the resignation of the Secretary of Public Instruction, Jorge Vera Estañol. The President moved his own supporters into the Cabinet, naming Dr. Aureliano Urrutia Minister of Gobernación, General Aureliano Blanquet Minister of War, and Manuel Garza Aldape Minister of Public Instruction. At the height of the crisis, Huerta, Díaz, and Rudolfo Reyes caucused, and after the tense confrontation, Reyes announced cancellation of the Pact of the Embassy, attempting to mask the split by stating that setting the election date fulfilled the pact.[18]

A short time later, Huerta continued his consolidation of power by appointing Félix Díaz special ambassador to Japan. The diplomatic mission effectively prevented Díaz from campaigning for the presidency. It could also serve to eliminate him from the contest entirely, for once abroad he could return only if recalled by the President. The electoral law required all candidates to be in the country on election day. Huerta assured Díaz that his official mission endowed him with extraterritorial status, which would guarantee his candidacy despite the requirement, but some doubt regarding his legal status persisted.[19] Even if the legal question was resolved, it was obvious that a prolonged sojourn abroad would seriously diminish his electoral possibilities.

Having solidified his position, Huerta once again pledged peace at all costs, although his problems mounted. Relations between Congress

---

[16] *El País*, June 10, 1913, for the editorial attacking Mondragón.

[17] New York *Times*, June 14, 1914, for the story of the banquet, while the railroad station scene and announcement of the mission appear in *El Imparcial*, June 23 and 24, 1913, and *El País*, June 24, 1913.

[18] *El País*, June 13, 1913.

[19] Minister of Foreign Relations Federico Gamboa to Díaz, September 23, 1913, AREM, L.E. 847, leg. 9 (115–R–12), f 9.

and the President were strained by the arrest of several deputies on charges of plotting against the government. There were frequent rumors of conspiracies, resulting in numerous arrests in the capital, although many of these stories proved baseless.[20]

In the north, the revolutionaries registered substantial gains on the battlefield. They captured Naco on April 14, 1913, and took Parral and Ciudad Juárez in May. June witnessed the fall of Matamoros, Zacatecas, and Durango. The latter was lost only after the federals repulsed several attacks during a prolonged siege, while the insurgents held Zacatecas a mere five days. Nonetheless, the revolutionaries had demonstrated their ability to seize important cities. Elsewhere, the federals parried insurgent attacks on Guaymas and Saltillo, and captured Monclova. In an effort to counter rebel activities in Sonora, the government sent the gunboat *Morelos* around South America to the Pacific Coast to convey reinforcements by sea. Despite heavy federal reinforcements rushed north during May and June, American consuls continued to report that the government's position was deteriorating. Captain Burnside observed: "The government is in the worst possible position."[21] He noted that the revolutionaries had disrupted more than half the railroads in the country, stressing that this hobbled the army, which lacked sufficient horses and wagons and had to depend entirely on the railroad for supplies and movement.[22]

Seeking to mask the situation, Mexican newspapers reported all battles as federal triumphs. Government forces were never vanquished in their columns, and each city fell to the revolutionaries after a long series of federal victories. Yet even with this biased reporting, the problem was obvious. The press fanned support for the government by charging that the rebels planned to sell part of Mexico to the United States.[23]

News of revolutionary victories reaching the United States was accompanied by reports of atrocities. The rebels repeatedly sacked cities, detained civilians for ransom, and refused to respect foreign

[20] *El País*, April 18, 1913, reported the arrest of the governor of Morelos and the state deputies; *El Imparcial*, April 28, reported the arrest of Deputy Valentín Del Llano, who allegedly had Zapatista propaganda in his home; and *El Imparcial*, May 6, reported the arrest of Deputy Enrique Bordes Manuel by the governor of San Luis Potosí. Plot rumors appeared in *El País*, June 9, and *El Imparcial*, July 14, 1913.

[21] Burnside to AGWAR, April 16, 1913, 5761–728.

[22] Burnside to AGWAR, July 8, 1913, 5761–784.

[23] Articles alleging revolutionary willingness to sell land to the United States appeared in *El Imparcial*, May 13, and *El País*, June 2, 1913.

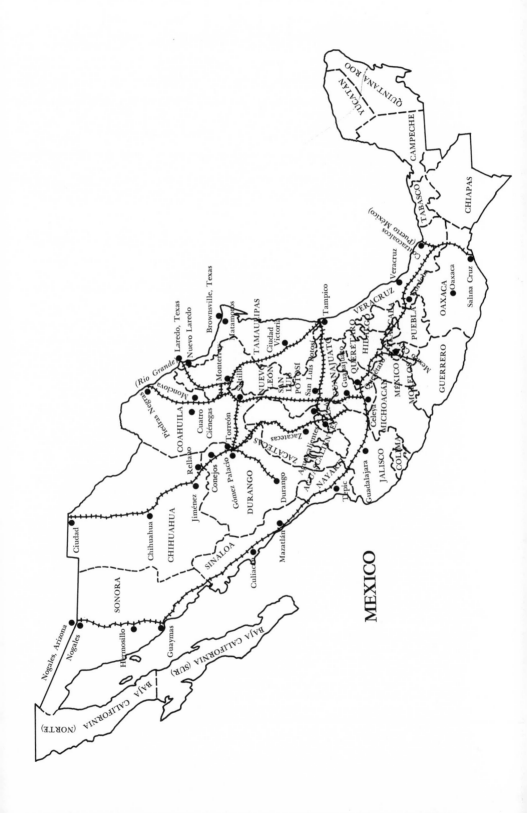

flags. American consuls described the situation as absolute anarchy.[24] These actions, particularly by General Francisco Villa, attracted considerable attention in the United States, causing Mr. Dooley to characterize the origins of the revolution:

> ... wan day while he [Villa] was peacefully engaged in changin' th' brand on a consignment iv steers that had just arrived, a message came to him that made ivry dhrop iv pathriotic blood in his veins bile with passyn. He heerd that th' hated government, th' oppressors iv his people, had just deposited fifty thousah' dollars in a bank in Chihoohoo. This outrage stirred him as nawthin' else cud. Sthrappin' a jimmy, a brace an' bit, an' a pound iv dynnymite to his belt, he put spurs to his horse an' jined th' rivylootionry forces an' soon rose, through vacancies caused be death, to th' chief command.[25]

Despite the rebel advances, there were some encouraging signs for the government. The consul at Durango reported that five hundred volunteers aided in the defense of the city during a rebel attack, a unique occurrence.[26] In a desperate attempt to control the Zapatistas, the government adopted the *reconcentrado* policy employed by the Spanish in Cuba. The Government claimed that fifteen thousand suspected Zapatistas were shipped out of Morelos by the end of June. Although this policy alienated everyone in the state, the immediate effect was a considerable gain for the Huerta regime, and for a time it appeared that the Zapatista threat might be controlled. In the north, rallying federal forces repulsed an assault on Torreón in early August, 1913, after retaking Matamoros with a naval bombardment. But the United States military attaché noted that government gains were chimerical, for the rebels invariably destroyed the railroad behind the advancing federals.[27] Application of the *leva* among Indian tribes provoked local revolts, and Burnside predicted further outbreaks if the government failed to secure funds to meet the army payroll.

[24] Reports of revolutionaries seizing property, obtaining forced loans, sacking cities, detaining people for ransom, and committing other excesses came from Consuls Luther Ellsworth (Ciudad Porfirio Díaz), May 8, 1913/7472, and May 9 /7474; Wilbert Bonney (San Luis Potosí), June 23/8013; and Theodore Hamm (Durango), June 21/7919, July 7, PR Mexico City, 1913, XXIV, Cl. 800, July 13/8075, and July 14/8450.

[25] New York *Times*, March 15, 1914.

[26] Theodore Hamm (Durango), to Bryan, May 14, 1913/7720.

[27] Burnside to AGWAR, July 8, 1913, 5761–784.

The success of the Carranza rebellion in the north was possible only because large quantities of arms and ammunition crossed the border from the United States. The overwhelming majority of the population along the American side of the frontier sympathized with the Carranza rebellion.[28] Some of these individuals simply aided every Mexican revolt, preferring the profits of smuggling. A substantial portion of those residing near the border were originally from northern Mexico and accordingly supported the northern revolt.

Smuggling was easy and profitable. The Rio Grande was shallow and readily fordable during much of the year, and in Arizona only monuments marked the border. Restrictions presented little difficulty, for with sentiment overwhelmingly favoring the rebels, elected officials and law enforcement officers were understandably hesitant to apprehend arms smugglers. Often law officers shared the prevailing prorebel sentiment and even aided smugglers. In one bizarre instance, a United States cavalry patrol arrested the town marshal of Nogales, Arizona, in the act of carrying arms into Mexico.[29] The Mexican consul in Naco, Arizona, reported that the local rebel leaders regularly conducted meetings in a tavern owned by the town's deputy sheriff and used the officer's ranch as the base for arms smuggling.[30] In another case, a United States deputy marshal seized a plane that a French pilot attempted to smuggle into Mexico, only to have the plane and the guard he placed on it both disappear across the frontier.[31] The United States attorney for the border district reported that local law officers warned smugglers of impending raids and investigations in time to allow their escape into Mexico.[32]

Enforcement of the neutrality laws and the embargo depended exclusively upon federal officers, whose actions were also somewhat

[28] For comments on the sentiments of the border population and actions of law officers, Luther Ellsworth (Ciudad Porfirio Díaz), to Bryan, April 5, 1913/7029, and July 2/7944; General Tasker H. Bliss to Adjutant General, April 19, Bliss Papers; and Bliss to Secretary of War, April 28, SD/7289.

[29] C. S. Hamlin (Assistant Secretary of the Treasury), to Bryan, August 2, 1913, PR Mexico City, 1913, XXIII, Cl. 800; and L. W. Mix (mayor of Nogales), to Major J. L. Fleming (commander at Nogales), July 23, JD 1057013-Sect. 12 – 579.

[30] Miguel E. Diebold (Mexican inspector of consuls, El Paso), to Ministry of Relaciones Exteriores, repeating a message from Enrique de la Sierra (Mexican consul, Naco), September 25, 1913, AREM, L.E. 765, leg. 5 (77–R–13), f 1–6.

[31] Statement of U.S. Deputy Marshal L. D. Johnson, May 6, 1913, JD 157013-Sect. 10-548.

[32] Dudly W. Norbinson (assistant United States attorney, Southern District of California), to Attorney General, June 13, 1913, JD 157013–Sect. 10-464.

timid. Some officials hesitated in the face of vague directives from Washington. The Wilson administration did not desire strict enforcement. General Tasker H. Bliss, commander of the Southern Department, noted that the army received no specific instructions.[33] The only orders were to "enforce the neutrality laws." Despite a ruling by the Attorney General's Office prohibiting shipment of arms to Mexico without special permission from the President, federal officers were aware that the absence of specific directives indicated that Washington was at least unconcerned about the matter.[34]

Smugglers circumvented the law by operating through legitimate arms dealers near the border. Once the munitions reached the border area, the shipments were broken down into small units and easily concealed in all kinds of goods normally shipped to Mexico. With large numbers of sympathetic residents willing to assist, the arms could constantly be carried across the border in small quantities. It proved almost impossible to intercept the shipments, since they originated from ranches or stores within a few feet of the frontier, and the difficulty of detecting numerous small shipments carried by individuals is readily apparent. Customs officials could scarcely be expected to police every inch of the long border, and hence if they could not intercept the arms en route to the dealers, they often found themselves powerless to do anything but stop the few large shipments that arrived in food containers. Agents reported seeing men on the Mexican side of the line hauling boxes of ammunition stenciled with the names of border firms. The United States attorney in Phoenix noted that the Douglas Hardware and Phelps Dodge companies, with warehouses in Naco, had received one hundred thousand rounds of ammunition in September alone. Another check revealed that firms along the border had over two million rounds of ammunition in stock. The Phelps Dodge warehouse, located less than one hundred feet from the frontier, received particularly large shipments. Observing that the caliber of the ammunition stocked was the same as that used by the Carrancistas, and pointing out the "absence of any big game near the border," the United States attorney in Phoenix concluded: "The great part of such large shipments of arms and ammunition . . . could only be reasonably intended for sale to

[33] Bliss to General Hugh Scott, May 5, 1913, Scott Papers, Box 15.

[34] *U.S. v. José Mesa* (overturning a decision in *U.S. v. Arunflo Chavez*), was reported in Winfred T. Denison (Assistant Attorney General) to Charles R. Beatie (United States attorney, New Orleans), March 26, 1913, JD 90755–G–21, and sent to all United States attorneys on the border by Jesse C. Adkins (Assistant Attorney General), May 10, 1913, JD 157013–Sect. 10-412–423.

parties who might be expected to take them to Mexico."[35] But such evidence was insufficient to secure conviction, and agents were faced with the task of attempting to apprehend smugglers in the act of crossing the frontier. The government did briefly place a guard on the Douglas Hardware warehouse after catching a shipment leaving it for Mexico, but this proved short-lived.[36] When Secretary of War Garrison visited the frontier in July, he recommended that the Attorney General "liven up his men" to curtail smuggling.[37] The Attorney General noted the impossibility of policing the entire border, blamed the shortage of manpower, and contended that appropriations did not permit the hiring of additional men. General Bliss observed that efforts were so lax that there was no customs inspector on duty at the El Paso bridge after 4:00 P.M., making it possible for carloads of ammunition to cross at night.[38] Mexican consuls attempted to compensate for the lax American effort by maintaining their own Secret Service to trace arms shipments. Given the difficulty of policing the entire border, federal officials often were dependent on the Mexican consuls for indications of shipping points, and many of those apprehended along the border were seized on the complaints of Mexican consuls. While this effort did bring about the interception of some shipments, its effect was minimal in view of the extent of the smuggling operations. Even arrest often proved futile. United States commissioners who set bail for captured smugglers were Texans and shared the prevailing border sentiment. They mandated only minimal bonds, enabling the smugglers to resume operations the next night. Texas juries and judges proved reluctant to convict those arrested.[39]

Arms smuggling was not the only advantage that accrued to the revolutionaries from their easy access to the border. Well-known revolutionary leaders frequently crossed the frontier to conduct meetings and strategy sessions within the United States. Propagandists operated freely on the American side, and rebel agencies were established

[35] Judge J. E. Morrison (United States attorney, Phoenix), to Attorney General, September 26, 1913, WD AG 2080816B.

[36] Colonel John F. Guilfoyle (Ninth Cavalry), to Garrison, August 28, 1913, JD 157013–Sect. 12-560, reports the arrest of a merchant next door to the Douglas Hardware Company who was caught packing ammunition in barrels, which led to the brief guard on the warehouse.

[37] Garrison to Wilson, July 24, 1913, Wilson Papers, File VI.

[38] Bliss to Adjutant General, September 11, 1913, JD 157013–Sect. 12-577.

[39] Judge J. E. Morrison to Attorney General, December 13 and 22, 1913, JD 157013–Sect. 13-639 and 643.

in almost every border town. Rebel envoys conferred with Texas Governor O. B. Colquitt, who openly indicated his sympathy with their cause. In one instance, Carranza himself traveled to Austin to confer with the governor. United States consular reports note that officers of the revolutionary army regularly traveled on American trains in plain clothes, transferring from one garrison to another. Telegraph business in the frontier districts showed a considerable increase during the revolutionary period, for Carranza transmitted his orders via lines in the United States.[40]

The United States consul in Ciudad Porfirio Díaz, Luther Ellsworth, continually reported arms smuggling and neutrality violations. Citing the numerous crossings by revolutionary leaders, Ellsworth noted that the neutrality laws prohibited conspiring in the United States to aid a revolution. He observed: "If they are not conspiring in our country . . . they are fit to be saints."[41] Justice Department agents confirmed Ellsworth's reports. The consul stressed that the absence of specific directives caused many border officials to conclude that the government did not wish enforcement. Wilbur Carr, head of the consular service, gave some indication of the administration's views, instructing Ellsworth to confine his reports to political conditions in Mexico and leave neutrality violations to the Justice and War departments.[42] Obviously, Washington had little interest in the matter. Ellsworth's observations caused Carranza to instruct his agent in Washington, Sherbourne G. Hopkins, to request Ellsworth's recall.[43] Hopkins, an American attorney associated with oil companies, made a career of aiding revolutionists. He was regarded as an expert on methods of circumventing United States neutrality laws and had previously assisted Madero, as well as numerous Central American rebels. A Latin American Division

[40] Luther Ellsworth (Ciudad Porfirio Díaz), to Bryan, April 24, 1913/7297, April 25/7266, May 1/7334, May 22/7611, and June 9 and 23, PR Piedras Negras (Ciudad Porfirio Díaz), C1. 8. For Mexican consular reports of these activities, Ricardo S. Bravo (Mexican consul, Eagle Pass), to Ministry of Relaciones Exteriores, April 8, AREM, L.E. 758, leg. 1 (75–R–1), f 26. An undated memorandum of a conversation between a Carrancista envoy and Governor Colquitt appears in AREM, L.E. 861, leg. 2 (121–R–5), f 40–49, and the filing location indicates that the conversation took place during the summer of 1913.

[41] Ellsworth to Bryan, May 22, 1913/7611.

[42] Wilbur Carr to Ellsworth, May 8, 1913/7331.

[43] Carranza to Hopkins, May 18, 1913, Isidro Fabela, ed., *Documentos históricos de la Revolución Mexicana* (12 vols. to date; Mexico: Fondo de Cultura Económica and Editorial Jus, 1960–1967), I, 49–50; and Hopkins to Bryan, May 30, SD 123. E1–51/128.

memorandum noted: "There seems to be no doubt that Hopkins has been adviser and confidential agent of practically any Mexican or Central American revolutionist or plotter who had sufficient money to pay for his services."[44]

Despite the flow to the Carrancistas, the Wilson administration carefully investigated the sources of Huerta's arms. While exerting little effort to curtail smuggling to the revolutionaries, Wilson and Bryan delayed export permits for arms previously purchased by the Mexican government.[45]

Thus the Carranza revolution owed much of its success to the availability of American arms, and while it may have proved impossible to halt the flow entirely, clearly the major portion could have been cut off if the Wilson administration desired to do so. The administration stance on smuggling caused Mr. Dooley to comment:

> In their [Mexico's] domestic throubles we presarved a careful nootrality an' put it on th' shelf in th' pantry. We took no sides on'y askin' cash in advance f'r arms an' ammynition an' insistin' that both parties shoot south whin near th' Rio Grande, so as not to disthurb th' Sunday School picnic parties watchin' th' rivolution from th' Texas shoores.[46]

Indeed, the Wilson administration went to considerable lengths to indicate its sympathy for the Carrancistas. On December 27, the Constitutionalist commanders in Sinaloa dined abroad the U.S.S. *Pittsburgh*, which fired a sixteen-gun salute as they boarded. European diplomats considered this an insult to Huerta and regarded it as an attempt to provoke him to secure a pretext for armed intervention.[47]

Yet despite the aid from Washington, the revolutionaries insisted on employing their own methods in their struggle, frequently alarming

[44] E. Bell to Boaz Long, Memorandum on Sherbourne G. Hopkins, June 14, 1913, 811.44H77.

[45] Bryan to Wilson, August 2, 1913, and Wilson to Bryan, August 4, Bryan-Wilson Correspondence, I, 113–114.

[46] New York *Times*, March 15, 1914.

[47] New York *Times*, December 27 and 28, 1913. The revolutionaries also received aid in the form of sanctuary for smuggling operations from the dictator of Guatemala, Manuel Estrada Cabrera. The Huerta government frequently unsuccessfully protested against revolutionary activities in Guatemala. Noting the dictator's tight control of his country, the Mexican minister concluded that such activities could hardly be carried out without his concurrence. Luis Pérez Verdía (Mexican minister in Guatemala), to Ministry of Relaciones Exteriores, January 24, 1914, AREM, L.E. 787, leg. 15 (86–R–15), f 25, and February 5 and 6, AREM, L.E. 787, leg. 12 (86–R–12), f 1–7 and 8–10.

world opinion. A London *Times* correspondent reported an interview with Carranza that astounded Europe, quoting Carranza's statement: "We Constitutionalists shall execute anyone who recognizes a president unconstitutionally elected." The Constitutionalist leader repeated his statement at the reporter's request, speaking "as calmly as if he were making a perfectly normal remark." Summing up his impressions, the reporter commented:

> To hear this amiable, scholarly old gentleman define so bloodthirsty and to us utterly unreasonable a line of action made me feel as if I were dreaming. It threw a strange light upon his profession of belief in democracy. I have no doubt that he sincerely imagines himself a believer in that creed. I am sure that the best of his followers are equally sincere. . . . But the discrepancy between their professions and their avowed policy shows how far the mentality of Mexico is distant from that of Europe and the United States.[48]

The military situation in Mexico ebbed and flowed in confusing fashion as both the government and the revolutionists scored victories. In the south, government forces made substantial gains in late summer, defeating the Zapatistas in several encounters. During August, Zapata's headquarters was captured, complete with his archives and arms cache. The federal commander in Morelos declared the campaign completed August 19.[49] Becoming overconfident, the government announced that the Revolution was crushed. The hollowness of this boast was soon apparent when Zapatistas attacked and robbed a trainload of reporters en route to the captured command post. Government forces also advanced in the north, retaking Ciudad Porfirio Díaz in October.

The fall of Torreón on October 8 after a long siege indicated the strength and also the character of the revolutionaries. General Francisco Villa's atrocities in the city shocked American public opinion. Villa ordered the execution of 125 captured federal soldiers, including a general, along with a large number of Spaniards.[50] George Carothers, the United States consul at Torreón, who subsequently became an ardent Villa partisan while serving as Wilson's agent to him, reported, "The rebels neither fear nor respect God, man or devil, their only idea appears to be destroy."[51] The London *Times* noted: "Each side

[48] London *Times*, October 27, 1913.

[49] *El Imparcial*, August 20, 1913.

[50] John Silliman (Saltillo), to Bryan, October 9, 1913/9125, October 10/11190, and October 16, PR Saltillo, Cl. 8.

[51] George Carothers (Torreón), to Bryan, August 16, 1913/8538.

calls the other side 'traitors,' and the only course to take with a 'traitor' —that is, a man who differs from your views—is to shoot him." [52] When foreign governments protested the massacre and criticized the Wilson administration for aiding its perpetrators, Mr. Dooley observed:

> Our relations with Panch is most corjal an' just what y'd want th' relations iv a gr-reat civilizes republic with wan iv th' most notorious burlairs in public lif to be. We give him th' gun, he shoots th' prisoner, an' we apoligize to th' powers. It's wan iv th' pleasantest alliances this counthry had conthracted since it took in th' mickrobe iv inflovinsy. . . .[53]

Desperately seeking to strengthen his position, Huerta militarized the entire administration. He ordered all government employees into the army, placing the women in the Red Cross or White Cross and requiring all to wear their uniforms at work. All Cabinet members became brigadier generals.[54]

The revolutionists continued to advance throughout the north in late 1913 and early 1914. The federals recaptured Chihuahua in November, but the garrison was merely an isolated pocket in rebel territory and was starved out within a few weeks. The revolutionaries seized Ciudad Porfirio Díaz, Ojinaga, and Ciudad Juárez the same month, and although government forces repulsed thrusts at Zacatecas and Tampico, the federals were clearly under heavy pressure in the north. The government did manage to counterattack by recapturing Torreón in December and rallied to score victories at Monterrey and Mazatlán. But Villa besieged Torreón again late that month, and it soon became apparent that this city was the key to the north. Both sides claimed victory frequently, causing the Brooklyn *Daily Eagle* to comment: "The result of a great battle in Mexico depends upon which side gets to the telegraph line first." [55] As conflicting reports from Torreón continued, the *Daily Eagle* quipped:

> Torreón will soon be taken
> (If General Villa's not mistaken).
> He's repulsed on every side
> (If Huerta's tale is not denied).[56]

[52] London *Times*, October 27, 1913.
[53] New York *Times*, March 15, 1914.
[54] Huerta's order, dated March 15, 1914, is in Gobernación, 1913–1914.
[55] Brooklyn *Daily Eagle*, March 22, 1913.
[56] Brooklyn *Daily Eagle*, March 26, 1913.

Torreón fell on April 2 when the federals evacuated after exhausting their supplies. Casualties were heavy on both sides, but the capture was a serious loss to the government. While the Huerta administration remained in control of the Mexican heartland, the revolutionists held most of the north.

Villa's executions after his capture of Juárez and Ojinaga again provoked vigorous protests as they were witnessed from the American side of the border. In the words of the London *Times*: "General Villa is not a man whose humanity can be the subject of enthusiasm." [57] American papers compared Villa and Huerta, the Washington *Post* calling Villa: "The man of the hour—Half Indian, half beast, the Robin Hood of Mexico, the Mexican equivalent of our own Jesse James. . . . If the removal of one man whose crimes make him detestable signifies nothing but the elevation to power of a man of deeds still more abhorrent in our estimation, where is the victory?" [58] The New York *Times* said of Huerta: "For a whole year he has maintained a rule which was not expected to last more than a few months, and has met all opposition with audacity, tact, and remarkable self-control. That he is an extraordinary man . . . the world must recognize." [59] Although this praise of Huerta was excessive, the contrast between the two Mexican leaders was obvious.

Interned troops from both sides presented a perplexing problem to United States authorities. Detachments that crossed the border were detained by the United States army. As the number increased, the army wished to release them so as to be relieved of the responsibility of guarding and feeding them. The Taft administration had always permitted repatriation. In April, 1913, the Secretary of War directed that the men be allowed to "filter back" to their own forces. [60] All interned revolutionaries were released immediately, and since the insurgents controlled nearly the entire border, they were able to rejoin their forces without fanfare. As Ciudad Juárez was the only federally controlled point on the border, the army prepared to send the interned federals to that city via El Paso. Governor Colquitt of Texas immediately protested. A storm ensued, and the Wilson administration decided that repatriation in a body would constitute reinforcement of the

[57] London *Times*, May 22, 1914.
[58] Washington *Post*, January 13, 1914.
[59] New York *Times*, February 11, 1914.
[60] Lindley M. Garrison to General Tasker H. Bliss, April 17, 1913, AG 2008188–A44.

besieged federal garrison.[61] Accordingly, the United States detained the federals, while continuing to release insurgents who subsequently crossed the border.

Thus, the Wilson administration was heavily involved in the military situation in northern Mexico, but this involvement entailed only covert support. While the administration was obviously making no attempt to shut off the flow of arms to the revolutionists, it still maintained the fiction of an embargo and did not publicly support the Carrancistas. For Wilson had to grope his way about during the initial months of his presidency before openly taking a stand. He revealed his objective slowly and acted overtly only as he was drawn into Mexican affairs. Consequently, his initial efforts were quite clumsy.

[61] Bliss to Garrison, April 22, 1913, AG 2008188–A48; Adjutant General to Bliss, April 25, AG 2008188–A53, and April 26, AG 2008188–A55; Governor O. B. Colquitt to Bryan, April 26, 812.2311/91, and April 28, 812.2311/96; and Colquitt to W. Wilson, April 29, 812.2311/99. Bryan proposed returning the interned federals to Veracruz, solely to "get rid of them," but Wilson opposed any semblance of "cooperation" with Huerta, Bryan to Wilson, August 31, Wilson Papers, File VI, and Wilson to Bryan, September 1/10495.

V

First Friction and Fumbling Policy

Woodrow Wilson's first presidential act regarding Latin America revealed the extreme naiveté that caused numerous errors in his policy toward Mexico. On March 11, 1913, he advised the Cabinet that he would issue a statement denouncing revolutions and dictatorships, which would be handed to all Latin American envoys to discourage radicals from using his administration as an excuse to launch rebellions. The President apparently believed that a declaration to the governments of these countries would affect antigovernment elements. When he released the declaration, the reference to dictatorships was widely interpreted as encouragement to the anti-Huerta rebels in Mexico.[1]

While Wilson had a firm conviction that Huerta's government was morally objectionable, he hesitated, deliberating what form his opposition would take. Observers erroneously concluded that the President was debating the advisability of recognizing Huerta.

Ambassador Wilson in Mexico City continued to advocate recognition, stressing that Huerta had assumed power in a legal manner. He contended that contradictory statements by the alleged eyewitnesses rendered a judgment on Madero's death impossible. The ambassador emphasized that conditions in Mexico demanded a strong government and that Huerta was the strongest individual on the horizon.[2] Fred Morris Dearing, Assistant Chief of the State Department Latin American Division, seconded the ambassador's recommendations. Dearing viewed the Huerta revolt as an expression of widespread national

[1] David Franklin Houston, *Eight Years with Wilson's Cabinet: 1913–1920* (2 vols.; Garden City, N.Y.: Doubleday, Page and Company, 1926), pp. 43–44; Bryan to all United States legations and embassies in Latin America, March 12, 1913, SD 710.11/102A; and New York *Times*, March 12, 1913.

[2] Wilson to Bryan, March 12, 1913/6840, April 9/7066, and May 15/7652.

disgust with Madero's incompetence. He absolved Huerta of blame for Madero's death, noting, "Huerta and his advisers are not so stupid that they could not have foreseen the effect of permitting this to occur," and stressed that Madero's death "has nothing whatever to do with the expediency" of recognizing Huerta.[3]

In urging recognition, the ambassador often stressed the drawbacks of nonrecognition in order to emphasize the need for prompt action. He did not realize that the President opposed Huerta and that some of his arguments for recognition undoubtedly appealed to Wilson as reasons for adopting the opposite course. Thus, the ambassador indicated that delay would weaken the government and that in view of the financial crisis and the reluctance of American bankers to extend loans prior to recognition by the United States, nonrecognition might cause the government to collapse. Since the President hoped to force Huerta from power, these arguments helped convince him to withhold recognition. The ambassador's pleas that Huerta would protect American interests if supported also had a reverse effect.

In Mexico, Huerta continued negotiations with the ambassador and displayed a willingness to pay a high price for recognition. Having received no instructions, the ambassador assumed the new administration would continue the Taft policies. Accordingly, Wilson pressed American claims, believing recognition would be delayed only until satisfactory arrangement of these matters. He reported on March 13 that Huerta had agreed to the American position on all outstanding disputes.[4] This would have meant surrender of the Chamizal territory to the United States, despite an arbitration decision to the contrary, payment of the damage claims of the Tlahualilo Company, and a guarantee of full compensation for all damages suffered by Americans during the Revolution. Thus, Huerta clearly made the maximum possible concessions in an effort to court United States recognition and went to great lengths to show his friendship with the ambassador. President Wilson, however, was not interested in friendly gestures or in a settlement of claims. Wilson ignored another Huerta request to assent to the appointment of Emilio Rabasa as Mexican ambassador.

The announcement that the British would extend recognition to Huerta despite previous indications to the contrary aroused concern in Washington. Coupled with Wilson's as yet undeclared policy, it

[3] Fred Morris Dearing, Memorandum, April 16, 1913/8070.
[4] Wilson to Bryan, March 13, 1913/6681.

indicated that Britain and the United States had reversed positions. Diplomats such as Henry Lane Wilson, who thought in terms of traditional diplomacy aimed at securing concessions and advantages, were appalled at the prospect of America's leading competitor in Mexico recognizing the Huerta government first. The ambassador stressed the importance of acting in advance of Britain.[5] President Wilson was not disturbed by this prospect but only by British recognition of a government that came to power by force.

While the administration hesitated, the evident delay could not escape the attention of Mexicans or their government. The administration ignored notes from the Mexican chargé protesting the legality of the Huerta government and studiously avoided any action that might be construed as recognition. When Bryan distributed a presidential announcement of the recognition of China to the diplomatic corps, he cautioned the Mexican chargé that his inclusion did not constitute recognition.[6] Wilson even allowed the Mexican-American arbitration agreement to lapse in June, since extending the treaty would have meant recognizing Huerta. By June 1, all European governments represented in Mexico had recognized Huerta. Of the Latin American nations represented in Mexico, only Argentina, Brazil, Chile, and Cuba delayed. The ABC powers notified the United States that they would be guided by its action. Ambassador Wilson reported that nonrecognition increased anti-Americanism in Mexico.[7] Huerta now refused to conclude any agreements on United States-Mexican disputes in advance of recognition. Mexican newspapers fanned anti-American opinion, with one even advocating a boycott of American goods, although others immediately cautioned that this was foolhardy in view of Mexico's favorable balance of trade with the United States.[8]

In May, Huerta's Minister of Foreign Relations, Francisco de la Barra, informed the ambassador that pending recognition the Mexican government would deal with the embassy only on routine matters and suspend any important business.[9] Ambassador Wilson considered this an insult, noting that if such a policy continued the embassy would be useless. The Assistant Chief of the Latin American Division and State

[5] Wilson to Bryan, March 31, 1913/6957.

[6] Bryan to W. Wilson, April 24, 1913, Wilson Papers, File VI.

[7] Wilson to Bryan, April 25, 1913/7273.

[8] The boycott was announced by *El Imparcial*, May 15, 1913, and opposed by *La Nación*, May 21, and *El País*, May 23, 1913.

[9] Wilson to Bryan, May 10, 1913/7454.

Department Counselor John Bassett Moore supported the ambassador's views and advised immediate recognition. Moore, number-two man in the State Department, noted "serious inconveniences" resulting from President Wilson's policy and added:

> The government of the United States having originally set itself up by revolution has always acted upon the *de facto* principle. We regard governments as existing or not existing. . . . Our depreciation of the political methods which may prevail in certain countries can not relieve us of the necessity of dealing with the governments of those countries. . . . We cannot become the censors of the morals or conduct of other nations and make our approval or disapproval of their methods the test of our recognition of their governments without intervening in their affairs.

Noting that "recognition is purely and simply the avowal of an apparent state of fact," Moore concluded: "There would appear to be incongruity in keeping an ambassador at a post, not for the purpose of transacting important business, but merely for the purpose of receiving and transmitting complaints against the attitude of his own government, with which attitude he does not himself agree."[10] On the other hand, Boaz W. Long, newly appointed Chief of the Latin American Division, stressed that American public opinion was hostile to Huerta. Long, a former resident of Mexico, was an admirer of Porfirio Díaz, detested Madero, and regarded the Mexican people as political "infants." Yet while disparaging the Revolution, he noted that recognition of Huerta would bring only temporary advantages.[11] Perhaps his equivocal stand was an attempt to please the President without breaking completely with his own beliefs.

Americans residing in or having interests in Mexico favored support of Huerta, and the President received numerous missives from the business community advocating recognition. But Wilson undoubtedly viewed the advice as merely an outgrowth of corporation admonitions against domestic regulation.[12] E. N. Brown, president of the National Railways of Mexico, and New York banker James Speyer approached presidential advisers to urge contacts with Huerta.[13] Brown told Colonel

---

[10] Dearing, Memorandum, May 12, 1913/12767; and Moore, Memorandum, May 14/8378.

[11] Boaz Long to Bryan, Memorandum, May 25, 1913/17177.

[12] William Haven (American Bible Society), to Bryan, March 17, 1913/6779; and Oscar J. Braniff to A. B. Farhuhar to Joseph Tumulty, April 22/7258.

[13] James Speyer to William McAdoo, May 7, 1913/7473; and House Diary, March 27, 1913.

House that while Madero's death was undoubtedly "intentional" it was the "only solution." He urged retention of Ambassador Henry Lane Wilson until the Mexican elections, adding, "if this government could not maintain itself, no other could." Colonel House relayed what he called this "interesting information" to the President and supported Brown's recommendations.[14]

The Cabinet also examined the question of recognition during the early months of the new administration. Secretary of War Lindley M. Garrison continually advocated recognizing "a brute like Huerta," since he doubted "whether the Mexicans could ever organize a government" if the Huerta regime crumbled. Garrison believed this was Mexico's "last chance" and opposed intervention even though he thought many Mexicans desired it. The Postmaster General was under the impression that the northern insurgents desired American intervention, although Secretary Lane disagreed. When Burleson related an incident in which a band of rebels beheaded a prisoner, Secretary Daniels reported, "This horrible and murderous thing shocked the Cabinet."[15] Obviously, the Cabinet lacked information about Mexico, for few Mexicans desired intervention and atrocities were common. These Cabinet discussions, however, did not affect American policy, for despite his preoccupation with the tariff controversy, the President had already decided that he would "not recognize a government of butchers."[16]

Colonel House continued to urge recognition of Huerta, and on May 6 he sent the President a plan submitted by Delbert J. Haff, approved by various American companies with holdings in Mexico. Haff, a lawyer with experience in Mexico, regarded the Madero revolution as a revolt of the proletariat and viewed Huerta as the only hope for stability. He proposed that the United States recognize Huerta on condition that he guarantee an early election and that both government and rebels suspend hostilities and bind themselves to accept the election results. Colonel House accepted this recommendation.[17]

The President was so impressed with the plan that he nearly reversed his position. He drafted a dispatch to Henry Lane Wilson stating: "We

[14] House Diary, March 27 and April 1, 1913.

[15] Daniels Diary, April 18, 1913.

[16] Arthur S. Link, *Woodrow Wilson and the Progressive Era: 1910–1917* (New York: Harper and Brothers, 1954), p. 109.

[17] House to Wilson, May 6, 1913, Wilson Papers, File II; and Delbert J. Haff to Wilson, May 12/7576.

are ready to recognize him [*i.e.*, Huerta] now on condition that all hostilities cease, that he call an election at an early date, the twenty-sixth of October now mentioned being, in our judgment, too remote, and that he absolutely pledge himself . . . [to] a free and fair election. . . ." [18] The President expected to send a "special agent" to seek the assent of the revolutionaries. But Wilson reconsidered and never transmitted this dispatch. In view of his firm hostility to Huerta, it is surprising that he even contemplated the proposal. Sensing the administration's reticence, Julius Kruttschnitt, chairman of the board of the Southern Pacific Railroad and one of the plan's strongest advocates, proposed that the United States promise only to recognize the election victor. Bryan felt this offered "a way out," while the President considered the proposal "most interesting" and "important," although he did not accept the plan. [19]

Having decided against recognition, Wilson apparently considered armed intervention. He discussed the question with Colonel House in May, and both believed that it could be accomplished successfully with only fifty thousand men. [20] Army commanders began checking maps of the area between Veracruz and Mexico City, even employing them for map problems to familiarize officers with the terrain. The Secretary of the Navy requested the Army War College to prepare data on Mexican coastal defenses and military strength. The Wilson administration also continued to maintain a sizeable naval squadron in Mexican waters as a symbol of disagreement with the Huerta regime. Although the navy would have preferred that these ships return home for target practice, the President insisted that they remain on station along the Mexican coasts.

A loan to the Huerta regime by a Franco-British banking syndicate in May produced the first official indication of the administration's attitude. Bryan summoned the British and French ambassadors to formally voice the United States government's objections to the loan. Both envoys assured him that this was a transaction of private bankers undertaken without the knowledge or approval of their governments. [21] Yet Bryan was unable to prevent a United States

[18] Wilson, Memorandum and draft dispatch addressed to Henry Lane Wilson, undated, Wilson Papers, File II.

[19] Julius Kruttschnitt to Bryan, May 26, 1913, Wilson Papers, File II; Bryan to Wilson, May 27, Bryan-Wilson Correspondence, I, 28; Wilson to Bryan, May 28, *ibid.*, *I, 28*.

[20] House Diary, May 2, 1913.

[21] Bryan, Memorandum, May 23, 1913, 812.51/76.

banking syndicate from extending a loan to the Mexican National Railroad.

The attitude of the Wilson administration was accordingly apparent to all close observers, despite the absence of a formal announcement, although the President had not yet determined the precise means to employ in attempting to oust Huerta. This decision was complicated by the President's preoccupation with domestic affairs and the complex maneuvering in Congress over the tariff bill. There were also other foreign policy matters that required his attention, such as the preparations for the June visit of Brazilian Foreign Minister Dr. Lauro Muller and the crisis over the passage of an alien land law in California. The latter provoked a protest and public reaction in Japan which alarmed Wilson. Huerta's intention to send a special emissary to Japan seemed to indicate a possible *rapprochement* between Japan and Mexico directed against the United States. Wilson hastily dispatched Bryan to California in an effort to prevent passage of the land law, but even this desperate step proved futile. The Japanese protests created military as well as diplomatic problems and absorbed a considerable amount of the President's time. European events also required observation, for although the United States was not directly involved, developments such as the Balkan conflict and later negotiations, the expansion of the German and French armies, the dispatch of a German military mission to Turkey, and the crisis caused by the demonstrations in Ireland by advocates of home rule all created tension that affected United States diplomatic activities in Europe.

The decision regarding the methods to be employed against Huerta was rendered even more difficult by a conflict between the American President and his ambassador to Mexico. The Wilson administration had inherited Henry Lane Wilson from its predecessor. President Wilson would gladly have dismissed the ambassador but for the fact that sending a replacement would constitute recognition of the Huerta government. This was a prospect even more distasteful to the President than retaining the envoy. The ambassador's continued attempts to write his own instructions accented his disagreement with administration policy. Well aware that he had experience in Mexico while the administration was confronting its first foreign policy decision, the envoy did not hesitate to provide the benefit of his knowledge. His advice was highly unwelcome since it clashed with the President's intentions. It was apparent that the diplomat was not a suitable instrument for a policy aimed at pressuring Huerta from power. The President and

Secretary of State studiously ignored the ambassador, who frequently complained that he was not informed of policy decisions or of exchanges with the Mexican chargé in Washington. State Department officials rarely forwarded the ambassador's dispatches to the White House.

The administration revealed its attitude toward the ambassador at once. In the confusion of the early days of transition, the new Secretary of State inadvertently signed a commendation praising the ambassador's actions during the Ten Days Revolt.[22] The Assistant Chief of the Latin American Division had prepared the telegram according to standard departmental procedure, lauding the ambassador's protection of Americans during the revolt. Apparently, the red "important" tag slipped off before the dispatch reached Bryan's desk, and the Secretary signed it without reading it.[23] Upon discovering his error, Bryan angrily telegraphed the embassy canceling the commendation.[24]

Henry Lane Wilson had many enemies who seized this opportunity to discredit him, although the majority of the American colony in Mexico continued to support him. The colony's organization sent a memorial and a committee to Washington urging his retention, but his opponents were also active.[25] Robert H. Murray, an old antagonist who served as Mexican correspondent to the New York *World*, launched the attack the moment Woodrow Wilson assumed office, and the *World* soon mounted a veritable crusade against the ambassador. On March 7, the *World* charged that the ambassador helped arrange and plot Huerta's coup, and called for his replacement. The *World* followed with claims that Bryan was investigating the situation.[26] The New York *Times* responded with an editorial praising the ambassador's protection of Americans during the revolt.[27]

As this furor raged, Luís Manuel Rojas, Grand Master Mason of the

22 Bryan to Wilson, March 6, 1913, 124.126/25.

23 Dearing to Bryan, March 18, 1913, 124.126/32.

24 Bryan to Wilson, March 7, 1913, 124.126/28A.

25 American colony to Woodrow Wilson, March 4, 1913, SD 123.W691/111. This file, the personnel file on Henry Lane Wilson, shows that the President and Secretary of State were deluged with letters from Americans in Mexico praising the ambassador, and also that others who disliked him wrote urging his recall, 123.W691, *passim*. The committee of the American colony visited Bryan on April 5, 1913, New York *Times*, April 6, and presented a leaflet, George W. Cook *et al.*, *Facts Submitted by the American Colony to President Wilson* (Mexico: Printed by the committee, 1913), praising the ambassador and urging his retention.

26 New York *World*, March 7, 8, 9, 10, and 11, 1913. The ambassador had once thrown Murray out of the embassy after a dispute.

27 New York *Times*, March 8, 1913.

Great Lodge of the Valley of Mexico and a member of the Mexican Chamber of Deputies, released a statement charging Ambassador Wilson with total responsibility for Huerta's coup and moral responsibility for Madero's death. Rojas alleged that Wilson threatened Madero with American intervention, and he attributed Madero's assassination to Wilson's failure to demand protection for the late President.[28] The ambassador noted that Madero had never requested asylum in the embassy, as Rojas contended. The envoy transmitted an affidavit signed by the entire embassy staff, attesting that one of them was present at or party to all Wilson's acts during the revolt, and that they could state positively that he had no discussions with Huerta or Díaz regarding the coup.[29] Huerta and Díaz also immediately took issue with Rojas' charges. Huerta stated that his only meeting with the ambassador prior to the coup occurred when Wilson had protested the placing of a battery of artillery close to the embassy.[30] The Mexican government initiated court action against Rojas, but dropped the charges when the Chamber of Deputies disapproved, for Rojas enjoyed immunity as a member of that body. The New York *World* headlined this story: "Mexicans refuse whitewash coat for H. L. Wilson."[31] This was deliberately misleading, for the Chamber had debated only the immunity of one of its members. While it is true that the ambassador refrained from attempting to protect Madero, Rojas' charges were plainly exaggerations. Madero's widow, who by this time had agreed to support Carranza's revolt, promptly seconded the accusations, thus contradicting an earlier statement by Ernesto Madero, who had absolved the ambassador.[32]

[28] Luís Manuel Rojas to Bryan, March 25, 1913, 123.W691/278. Rojas' statement was published in *El País*, April 15, 1913.

[29] Wilson denied the charges and stated that Rojas was of "unsound mind," Wilson to Bryan, April 7, 1913, 123.W691/162; and the affidavit by the embassy staff is Wilson to Bryan, April 15, 123.W691/189. The charges caused so much bitterness in Mexico that when Warden Wilson, the ambassador's son, requested assignment to Mexico years later while serving in the Foreign Service, the State Department decided not to send him to avoid reviving memories of the ambassador.

[30] Huerta's statement appeared in *El Imparcial*, April 8, 1913, and Díaz' statement appeared in *El País*, April 9, 1913.

[31] New York *World*, April 16, 1913.

[32] Ernesto Madero's statement, "I do not charge Ambassador Wilson with aiding in the overthrow of the Madero Government," appeared in the New York *Times*, March 9, 1913; and the statement by Sara Pérez de Madero appeared in Alfredo Braceda, *México Revolucionario: 1913–1917* (2 vols.; Mexico: Ediciones Botas, 1941), pp. 249–253 and 241–242, which also includes letters between Señora Madero and Luis G. Garfias, the Carranza envoy who successfully sought her support.

While President Wilson already distrusted the ambassador because of their different views, these charges now caused him to associate Ambassador Wilson at least in part with the fall of Madero. The President's ire was further aroused by a Guatemalan government statement attributing that country's recognition of Huerta to the ambassador's calling on him as dean of the diplomatic corps, which caused the government to conclude that United States recognition was imminent.[33]

By this time it was obvious that Wilson retained the ambassador only because replacing him would entail recognition of Huerta, and accordingly Henry Lane Wilson demanded that the Department deny rumors that it was investigating the charges against him.[34] A week later, on May 16, he submitted his resignation. This presented the administration with a problem it was not prepared for, and Bryan immediately requested the ambassador to withdraw his resignation, promising a press statement denying the investigation. He explained that he was out of town when the first telegram arrived.[35] While the administration had lost confidence in the ambassador, it was not yet ready to withdraw him, although rumors that the President sought a new envoy persisted. State Department Counselor John Bassett Moore noted the incongruity of a situation in which the "United States has been represented at the city of Mexico by an ambassador whose conduct apparently is not approved and whose recommendations have been ignored."[36] Yet the only alternative to recognition by replacement was to leave a chargé in office. Fred Dearing of the Latin American Division cautioned that First Secretary Nelson J. O'Shaughnessy's "qualifications are such that we could not expect so successful a conduct of the embassy's business as under the ambassador."[37]

Because of its distrust of Henry Lane Wilson, the administration felt it lacked accurate information on Mexico, and Wilson and Bryan decided to send "special agents" to "investigate" the situation. Bryan had suggested this as early as April 18 and had dispatched William H. Sawtelle, a Tucson attorney, on a brief mission to report sentiment in the state of Sonora.[38] The President had previously employed a special

[33] Guatemalan minister in Washington to Bryan, June 28 and July 1, 1913/27425.

[34] Wilson to Bryan, May 10, 1913, 123.W691/194.

[35] Wilson to Bryan, May 16, 1913, 123.W691/201; and Bryan to Wilson, May 17, 123.W691/201.

[36] Moore, Memorandum, May 14, 1913/8378.

[37] Dearing, Memorandum, May 12, 1913/12767.

[38] William H. Sawtelle to Bryan, undated, apparently May, 1913, Wilson Papers, File II.

agent in the Philippines. Wilson and Bryan selected the agents primarily for their loyalty, and they invariably agreed with Wilson's policy before departing for Mexico. The administration considered friendship with the President a more important qualification than knowledge of Mexico.

At the end of May, 1913, Bryan dispatched Reginald Del Valle, an American citizen of Mexican extraction, to northern Mexico. Del Valle was an excellent choice. In addition to being friendly with Bryan, he was thoroughly familiar with Mexican politics and problems, and he spoke Spanish fluently. Bryan instructed him to pay particular attention to the sources of the dissatisfaction with the government, the causes of the Madero revolution, and the system of land tenure.[39]

Del Valle conferred with rebel leaders and other exiles in Tucson and then visited Hermosillo. He reported that the Carrancistas contended that the government of Huerta was illegal and demanded his resignation. They claimed to be fighting for liberty and attributed all the trouble to Huerta. Other refugees charged that the Constitutionalists were at fault.[40] Del Valle reported that all business in the Carrancista-controlled area was paralyzed because the revolutionists levied forced loans and seized private property.[41] After interviewing rebel leaders, Del Valle concluded that the Constitutionalists merely sought personal power. He met Carranza and described him as having "personally a good appearance, little ability, narrow, inordinate stubbornness, inclined to severity, not liked." He noted that the first chief "did not wish to be tied down to any agreement" and "seemed to fear that I had some proposition to which I would insist on binding him."[42] Bryan disregarded Del Valle's unfavorable impression of Carranza, suggesting that perhaps American refusal to allow open arms shipments "irritated" the revolutionary leader.[43] Despite his disappointment with Del

[39] Bryan to Del Valle, May 31, 1913/20446. When the Mexican chargé in Washington queried Bryan about press reports of Del Valle's mission, Bryan, while refusing to confirm that Del Valle was acting as Wilson's confidential agent, stated that "he and President Wilson were personal friends of Del Valle" and characterized Del Valle as "one of the probable candidates for ambassador in Mexico," de la Cueva to Ministry of Relaciones Exteriores, AREM, L.E. 786, leg. 1 (85–R–28), f 1–2.

[40] In an effort to maintain the secrecy of his mission, Del Valle sent his reports to Ben G. Davis, chief clerk of the State Department, apparently relaying them through a friend in New York. Del Valle to Davis, June 8, 1913/23641, and June 9/23642.

[41] Del Valle to Davis, June 17, 1913/23644.

[42] Del Valle to Davis, June 23, 1913/23646, and June 27/23648.

[43] Bryan to W. Wilson, June 25, 1913, Bryan-Wilson Correspondence, I, 79.

Valle's negative view of the insurgents, Bryan instructed him to confer with Zapata and visit state capitals near Mexico City when he arrived there.[44]

Wilson and Bryan desired Del Valle's mission to remain secret and became annoyed when Mexico City papers reported his arrival and activities. Yet obviously it was necessary for him to identify himself to those he interviewed. Del Valle did become careless with the press, however, admitting that he was commissioned by the President while denying any official capacity. Bryan directed him to "avoid newspapers," but the Mexican press reported that Del Valle conferred with Francisco de la Barra and had requested an appointment with Huerta.[45] Bryan then abruptly ordered Del Valle to return "at once" to "report personally on the situation."[46]

Upon his arrival in Washington, Del Valle reported that his investigation had convinced him that the revolutionaries were mainly bandits. Noting that Huerta was establishing a military regime, he stressed the impossibility of conducting free elections if the military controlled the ballot boxes. Del Valle concluded that compromise was out of the question and predicted that conditions would deteriorate because of the lack of discipline among the revolutionaries.[47]

Late in May, while Del Valle was still in Mexico, President Wilson dispatched yet another "confidential agent," William Bayard Hale, to Mexico City. A former Episcopal clergyman-turned-journalist, Hale authored Wilson's campaign biography and became a close friend of the President. Because of this, Wilson selected him for the mission to Mexico, even though Hale knew nothing about the country. Bryan apparently instructed Hale to investigate Ambassador Wilson's conduct during the Ten Days Revolt.

Hale had come to Mexico as a staunch advocate of the President's policy of opposing Huerta and was fully convinced that Henry Lane Wilson was unsatisfactory. The new special agent avoided diplomats and government officials, seeking only individuals who could provide information that corroborated his own convictions. Those having grievances against the ambassador flocked around Hale. Boaz W. Long, head of the Latin American Division learned that New York *World* reporter Robert H. Murray had become Hale's constant companion

---

[44] Bryan to American legation in Cuba (for Del Valle), June 28, 1913/23649a.

[45] Davis to Del Valle, July 8, 1913/23650a; and *El País*, July 10, 1913.

[46] Davis to Del Valle, July 15, 1913/23650b.

[47] Del Valle to Bryan, July, 1913 (no day), Wilson Papers, File II.

and confidant. Long noted that Murray had accompanied Ernesto Madero on his flight into exile and that it was widely believed that the Madero family subsidized Murray's prorevolutionary writing. A member of the American colony who had lost a legal battle with one of the ambassador's associates also befriended Hale. Long concluded: "It seems to me almost incredible that Mr. Hale could go in search of information and immediately ally himself with any one given man or set of men, expecting thereby to receive an absolutely impartial view." Yet the special agent did not question the accuracy of the information he received from these sources.[48]

Hale viewed the struggle as one "between surviving medievalism . . . and modern civilization." This was the beginning of the administration's fascination with revolutionary objectives which caused the United States government to overlook the differences between the revolutionaries' pronouncements and their conduct. The special agent described the ambassador as a "vain busybody, highly nervous temperament increased by indulgence, not scandalous, which slight frame is not equal to, good fighter for American interests . . . but totally lacks judgment, self control, is swayed by trivial fancies, vanity, temper."[49] Hale reported that the ambassador had invited Huerta to dine at the embassy. The following exchange between Bryan and Wilson is penciled on this report:

What do you think of Huerta dining with Wilson?
W. J. B.

Think it most seriously unwise. Probably make it worse to interfere. I think Wilson should be recalled.
W. W.[50]

On June 18, a few weeks after he arrived in Mexico, Hale prepared a lengthy analysis of the ambassador's actions during the Ten Days Revolt, which resembled an indictment. His tone was that of an oracle certain that he, and only he, knew the truth. After admitting that

[48] Long, Memorandum, August 22, 1913/17669. Even after his return to the United States, Hale continued to receive information from Murray, R. H. M. to Hale, September 27, 1913, Wilson Papers, File II. Hale told Bryan, "This is from a man in whose judgment I have confidence."

[49] Hale also sent his messages addressed to Ben G. Davis, via F. A. Muschenheim in New York City. Hale to Davis, June 3, 1913/23616.

[50] Hale to Davis, June 25, 1913/23621 reports the invitation to Huerta, and a copy of it in the Wilson Papers contains the penciled exchange between Bryan and Wilson, Wilson Papers, File II.

Madero had proved incapable of the responsibilities of the presidency, that his regime had become unpopular, and that he had resorted to repressive methods, Hale attributed Madero's fall exclusively to the actions of Henry Lane Wilson. He contended that the Huerta coup occurred only because of the ambassador's support. He cited the ambassador's known dislike for Madero and brushed off the British minister's support with the comment, "Mr. Stronge is a silly, stuttering imbecile." After attributing Huerta's coup to the ambassador, Hale stated that Huerta and Díaz reached agreement before they met the envoy, ignoring the obvious contradiction. He correctly noted that the ambassador consulted only those ministers who were inclined to support his views. The special agent repeated previous unfounded charges that the ambassador refused to grant Madero asylum. Having lamented Madero's failure to have Reyes and Díaz shot "according to the prevailing Mexican custom," Hale attacked the assassination of Madero and Pino Suárez as a horrendous crime. He accused the ambassador of having "delivered the men to death." Hale admitted that Henry Lane Wilson sincerely believed that Madero was harming the country and that the revolt against him was popular, adding: "Taking that view, a great deal can be said in justification of many of Mr. Wilson's acts and in extenuation of others," although Hale carefully refrained from examining this aspect. Having described the ambassador as the cause of the entire coup, he stated, "It is in my judgment absurd to picture Mr. Wilson as a malicious plotter." He concluded, "It cannot but be a cause of grief that what is probably the most dramatic story in which an American diplomatic officer has ever been involved, should be a story of sympathy with treason, perfidy and assassination in an assault on constitutional government." [51]

Despite the contradictions and errors in Hale's recital of "the facts" and the unreliability of his sources, the President and the Secretary of State accepted his conclusions. Certainly there was much that Henry Lane Wilson could be criticized for, but to accuse him of total responsibility for the plot and the death of Madero was absurd. Naturally, Hale's report astounded the President and confirmed all his suspicions. He wrote Bryan: "The document from Hale is indeed extraordinary. I should like, upon my return from a little outing, to discuss with you very seriously the necessity of recalling Henry Lane Wilson in one way

[51] Hale to W. Wilson, June 18, 1913/7798½. Hale had earlier condemned the ambassador's actions in a brief telegram, Hale to Davis, June 12, Wilson Papers, File II.

or another, perhaps merely 'for consultation' until we have had a talk with the man himself."[52] Bryan agreed that Henry Lane Wilson should be recalled.[53] Despite his shock, Wilson did not allow the matter to interfere with his outing, for he needed relief after the exhausting conferences that shaped the Federal Reserve Act. But the mere recall of the ambassador would not solve the Mexican problem, for it had grown increasingly complex.

Numerous envoys made informal representations requesting at least a clarification of the American position, for all diplomats in Mexico urged their governments to press the Wilson administration to recognize Huerta.[54] This increased the necessity of a determination of American policy, for the Wilson administration had merely withheld recognition, but had not decided whether to take additional steps.

Pressures also increased within the United States. Senator Albert Fall, Republican from New Mexico, advocated repeal of the arms embargo and open aid to the revolutionaries. When Senator Henry Cabot Lodge called for armed intervention, Senator Fall quickly supported this proposal.[55] Such statements rendered it imperative that the President announce his stand to prevent senators from endangering the American position. Senator Augustus O. Bacon, chairman of the Senate Committee on Foreign Relations, signaled the administration's future course after a White House visit, stating that the United States definitely would not recognize Huerta.[56]

Henry Lane Wilson continued to complain that the administration had never informed him of its policy, and at length Bryan telegraphed the "President's personal statement of his position":

This government does not feel that the provisional government of Mexico is moving towards conditions of settled peace, authority and justice . . . . If the present provisional government of Mexico will give the Government of the United States satisfactory assurances that an early election will be held, free from coercion or restraint, that Huerta will observe his original promise and not be a candidate at that

[52] Wilson to Bryan, July 1, 1913/7864½.

[53] Bryan to Wilson, July 3, 1913, Bryan-Wilson Correspondence, I, 94; and Bryan to Wilson, July 8, Wilson Papers, File VI.

[54] H. L. Wilson to Bryan, July 8, 1913; and Moore to W. Wilson, July 10/7992.

[55] New York *Times*, June 28 and July 23, 1913; and New York *World*, July 21, 1913.

[56] New York *World*, June 20, 1913.

election, and that an absolute amnesty will follow, the Government
of the United States will exercise its good offices to secure a genuine
armistice.[57]

This dispatch, by indicating that the United States would consider
recognizing Huerta's successor, was the first official statement that
bluntly expressed refusal to recognize Huerta. Although the ambassador
had gone so far as to state that he had "no preconceived views" in
conflict with the faithful representation of the President's policy, he
replied that United States interests could be protected only by recognizing Huerta or by withdrawing the embassy personnel as a protest
against existing conditions.[58]

The "President's personal statement" revealed a serious misinterpretation of the Mexican situation. In the portion of the statement
referring to Huerta's candidacy, the phrase "observe his original
promise" was inserted in the original draft, apparently by the President.
Huerta had never made any pledge that he would not be a candidate,
but Wilson believed that he had. President Wilson contended that the
Pact of the Embassy committed Huerta to stand aside and allow Díaz to
be elected to the presidency, and that since the pact was signed in the
American embassy with the mediation of the ambassador, the United
States was a party to the agreement and hence could hold Huerta to his
pledge.[59] Obviously such a promise was not binding, especially since
the United States was not a party to the pact. Even if the American
ambassador had signed the pact, the fact that the United States had not
extended recognition to the Huerta government would have negated
any other provisions, for recognition would logically have flowed from
such a commitment. In either event, Wilson's contention involved
considerable exaggeration. But the American President apparently
believed that he could accept those portions of the "agreement" that
he found convenient and demand adherence to them while rejecting the
rest of the document.

Hale continued his barrage of pessimistic reports from Mexico. He
observed that the government's financial position was deteriorating, and
he believed Huerta was considering resigning in order to become a legal
candidate in the forthcoming elections. After meeting Del Valle and

[57] Bryan to Wilson, June 15, 1913/7743.

[58] H. L. Wilson to Bryan, June 9, 1913/7743, and July 9/7999.

[59] The explanation of the President's view and his contentions in regard to Huerta's
promise not to be a candidate were subsequently revealed to British Minister Sir
Francis Stronge by John Lind, Stronge to Grey, August 20, 1913, FO 204/419.

discovering that this agent did not agree with his views, Hale advised Bryan: "I fear he cannot be taken seriously as a reporter." [60] Interestingly, Del Valle, who visited northern Mexico and met with rebel leaders, opposed the revolutionaries, while Hale, who visited the capital, opposed the government.

The ambassador complained, "The presence here in Mexico of persons claiming to be representatives of the President are lowering the dignity of the embassy and detracting from the respect and deference with which the Mexican people have been taught to regard it." [61] Henry Lane Wilson reported that Félix Díaz' secretary gave him a copy of his interview with Hale and informed him that Hale's evident hostility displeased the government. Hale had stated that he did not believe the United States would ever recognize Huerta, but that it would be glad to extend recognition to his successor and seemed well disposed toward Díaz. This was a strange attitude, since Díaz bore as much responsibility as Huerta for Madero's fall and death. The ambassador said he was transmitting this to the President so that he would not be "misled" by Hale's statements. Ambassador Wilson considered the special agent "unfit to form a just and clear idea of the situation here." [62] Since the administration never formally notified him of the agents' missions, the ambassador feigned ignorance of their official status in order to criticize them. Since he was aware that they possessed State Department codes, his reports on their activities were really desperate attempts to diminish their influence.

Realizing that the administration had rejected his recommendations, the ambassador displayed his disgust in his dispatches. The envoy became increasingly exasperated and argued desperately for the policy he sincerely believed was correct. Sensing that his reports were ignored, he frequently demanded that they be shown to the President. On July 11, he angrily stated, "The President should understand that in dealing with this situation he is now face to face with grave responsibilities which cannot be avoided by a halting or uncertain policy." [63] Certainly this statement did not endear him to the President, although Wilson had already decided on his recall.

On July 16, 1913, Bryan recalled Henry Lane Wilson for "consultations." He instructed the ambassador to depart as soon as possible,

[60] Hale to Davis, July 9, 1913/8203.
[61] Wilson to Bryan, July 8, 1913/7990.
[62] H. L. Wilson to W. Wilson, July 1, 1913, Wilson Papers, File II.
[63] Wilson to Bryan, July 11, 1913/8027.

and Wilson sailed that evening on the Ward liner *Mexico*.[64] American papers freely predicted that he would not return to Mexico. While the ambassador was at sea, Alfonso Madero issued his first press statement since the former President's death, a move obviously timed to influence the White House meeting. Alfonso announced that the Madero family supported Carranza and charged that the ambassador was "morally responsible" for the overthrow and assassination of his brother.[65] Upon landing in New York, Henry Lane Wilson ignited new controversies with his press statements. The Boston *Herald* quoted him as saying: "I have always striven to keep down factions opposed to Huerta. My motive in aiding the federal government of Mexico has been to protect the lives of Americans." The New York *Times* noted that the ambassador had the air of "a man who was entirely satisfied with the course of action he had pursued and who was confident that the future would justify every move that he had made."[66] Upon discovering that the State Department had failed to send a message directing him to come to Washington, Ambassador Wilson peevishly announced that he would remain in New York until the Chief Executive requested his presence in the capital.[67]

On July 26, the ambassador conferred briefly with Bryan and then dictated a report on the Mexican situation. The President was golfing during this conference. In his statement, the ambassador charged that Madero had violated all his promises and had proven to be anti-American. Wilson reviewed the Ten Days Revolt, with several inaccuracies, and contended that he participated in the Pact of the Embassy only on humanitarian grounds. The ambassador advised recognition of the Huerta government, but cautioned that unconditional recognition at this late date would be interpreted as surrender. He therefore advocated recognition by means of a protocol requiring Mexican guarantee of favorable settlement of American claims, agreement to the American position in disputes with Mexico, and an election in October. He considered intervention the only alternative.[68]

The two Wilsons confronted each other for fifty minutes on July 28, and the obvious delay between the ambassador's arrival and the meeting indicated the President's feelings. The President did most the talking and refrained from asking the ambassador for advice. Henry

64 Bryan to Wilson, July 15, 1913, PR Mexico City, 1913, XXIII, Cl. 800.
65 New York *World*, July 20, 1913.
66 Boston *Herald* and New York *Times*, July 26, 1913.
67 New York *Tribune*, July 26, 1913.
68 Memorandum by H. L. Wilson, July 26, 1913, Woodrow Wilson Papers, File II.

Lane Wilson angrily concluded that the President had already reached a decision without reading his report.[69] The Washington *Post* and New York *Times* continued to support the ambassador editorially, the *Post* hailing him as "unquestionably the best informed American on Mexican affairs," while the New York *World* increased its attacks on the envoy.[70]

Shortly thereafter, the ambassador appeared before the Senate Committee on Foreign Relations, which invited him despite White House disapproval. Newspapers noted that he made an excellent impression and many senators were amazed at his knowledge of Mexico. His testimony increased committee sentiment for intervention and produced charges that the State Department had withheld information from the Senate.[71] The President forced cancellation of a scheduled appearance before the House Committee on Foreign Relations.

Bryan requested Henry Lane Wilson's resignation, which was formally submitted on August 5, 1913. The Secretary informed the embassy: "The part which he felt it his duty to take in the earlier stages of the recent revolution in Mexico would make it difficult for him to present the views of the present administration in view of the situation which now exists." [72] President Huerta at once thanked the ambassador for his services to the Mexican nation.[73] Wilson's resignation did not take effect until October 14, to allow him to complete his vacation. On August 13, the British government announced that it had recognized Huerta only because of Henry Lane Wilson's laudatory speech after the conclusion of the revolt. The ambassador told reporters that he spoke as dean of the diplomatic corps rather than as American ambassador and that the Spanish minister wrote his speech. This statement aroused Bryan and Wilson, who immediately apologized to the British government, dumfounding the British, who considered this unnecessary. The Spanish minister informed the press that he did indeed write the speech for Wilson, a fact which the British minister substantiated.[74] Secretary of State Bryan, annoyed by "embarrassing questions" from reporters throughout this period, announced that he would no

[69] H. L. Wilson to Bryan, August 28, 1913, 123.W691/277.

[70] New York *Times* and New York *World*, July 28, 1913; and Washington *Post*, July 28 and 31, 1913.

[71] New York *Times*, July 31 and August 2, 1913; and Washington *Post*, July 31 and August 1, 1913.

[72] Bryan to O'Shaughnessy, August 14, 1913/8379A.

[73] Huerta to H. L. Wilson, *El Imparcial*, August 12, 1913.

[74] New York *Times*, August 14, 15, and 16, 1913; and Sir Francis Stronge (British minister in Mexico), to Sir Edward Grey, August 19, FO 204/419. The Ambassador later served as adviser to Charles Evans Hughes in his bid to oust Wilson in 1916.

longer reply to queries, but would release statements whenever he deemed it necessary.[75]

With the removal of the ambassador, the first secretary of the embassy, Nelson J. O'Shaughnessy, became chargé d'affaires. O'Shaughnessy, who had assumed his duties as first secretary only on March 3, was associated with the patrician Republican class. His father was one of the chief promoters of the Nicaraguan Canal, and he himself was friendly with the Roosevelts and Vanderbilts. President Wilson was not pleased with placing him in charge of the embassy in Mexico, but the Chief Executive so distrusted the ambassador that he regarded O'Shaughnessy as a lesser evil. There was no alternative, for sending another ambassador or chargé would require approval of the Mexican government and hence would constitute recognition of Huerta. Indeed, O'Shaughnessy was instructed that he was accredited to the Minister of Foreign Relations, rather than to Huerta, and was directed not to pay a courtesy call on the President upon assuming his duties as chargé.

Nelson O'Shaughnessy had not desired the Mexican post, for its duties were strenuous. His tastes were European, and he preferred the short workdays in unimportant European embassies. Yet there were compensations, for the American representative in Mexico was the most important diplomat in the country, and President Huerta went to great lengths to cultivate the friendship of the O'Shaughnessys. Huerta always greeted the chargé with an *abrazo* and called him son. He invariably took Mrs. O'Shaughnessy's arm at diplomatic receptions and gave her a place of honor. The O'Shaughnessys were fond of Huerta and like the ambassador, the chargé considered recognition of his government in the best interests of the United States. But he had learned from the ambassador's recall and accordingly did not urge recognition on Wilson. On the contrary, he cautiously requested frequent instructions and reported his every act. He followed instructions carefully, even if he considered them absurd. O'Shaughnessy attempted to employ his friendship with Huerta to enable smoother handling of minor problems and stressed this relationship in his dispatches. This only increased Wilson's distrust of him.

Thus the Wilson administration had cleared the way for action. The ambassador who opposed its policies was removed, and there was now ample information from the special agents. With the tariff bill virtually assured of passage and only the Federal Reserve Act requiring attention,

[75] Bryan to Wilson, July 30, 1913, Bryan-Wilson Correspondence, I, 98–99.

the President had more time to consider the Mexican situation. In late July he reached his decision, finally perceiving that it would require more than mere nonrecognition to oust Huerta. He would have to announce his position and seek to pressure Huerta out. But the method he chose again proved inadequate.

VI

Confrontation and Rebuff The Lind Mission

President Wilson decided to "mediate" the Mexican dispute by offering a plan to transfer it from the battlefield to the ballot box in true democratic fashion. Stating that the government of the United States "does not feel at liberty any longer to stand inactively by," the President proffered his good offices. He outlined a "satisfactory settlement" that would require an armistice, a pledge of an early election, Huerta's promise not to be a candidate, and agreement by all parties to accept the election results. Wilson promised to recognize a government chosen under these conditions.[1]

Since the President's proposal dealt with domestic problems and thus constituted intervention in the internal affairs of Mexico, it had no possibility of success. No government could consent to an armistice with rebels, for this would imply recognition of their belligerency. The United States had consistently rejected similar proposals during its own Civil War. Further, Wilson assumed that the only opposition to an armistice came from the Huerta government, which he regarded as the source of all Mexican problems. In this he erred, for the Constitutionalists also refused to accept an armistice, preferring to seek complete military victory. The demand that Huerta renounce his candidacy was shortsighted and unnecessary. National integrity would not allow a Mexican leader to be selected by a United States President. In addition, the Mexican Constitution barred consecutive terms, and this prevented a provisional president from becoming a candidate to succeed himself. Instead of seeking a guarantee that Huerta would not declare his candidacy, and thus providing an opportunity to reject foreign interference in Mexican internal affairs, Wilson could have expressed

[1] Woodrow Wilson, address to Congress, August 27, 1913, SD 812.00/8614A.

90

confidence that Huerta would respect the limitation of the Mexican Constitution—a phraseology the Mexican President could not have easily rejected. Naturally Huerta could not admit that foreign pressure barred his candidacy.

Wilson should have perceived that his "mediation" plan was doomed at the outset. A similar proposal by Bryan and Hale "leaked" a few weeks earlier, and newspapers revealed complete details.[2] The Washington *Post* commented that both sides in Mexico would surely reject it, while Ambassador Henry Lane Wilson reported that Huerta would certainly spurn mediation.[3] Although the President paid scant attention to an ambassador he distrusted or to an antiadministration newspaper, he should have heeded the advice of Secretary of War Garrison and Senator Bacon, who reached the same conclusions. Hale had also reported that Huerta dismissed his Minister of Hacienda for suggesting an early election.[4] Obviously, if Huerta felt that strongly about the matter, he would react similarly to an identical American proposition. Even if Wilson doubted these indications, he certainly could have realized the futility of his plan when both Carranza and Huerta publicly announced on July 30 that they would reject any mediation proposal. Indeed, Carranza's agents in Washington issued a similar statement several days earlier.[5]

Confident that his plan advanced Mexican interests, Wilson rigidly persevered in his course, feeling certain that anyone who studied the plan would perceive its altruism. It apparently never occurred to him that Huerta might not agree that his own elimination served the best interests of Mexico. Wilson did not regard his action as intervention—was he not merely pointing out the only ethical solution? Wilson's determination to bar Huerta's candidacy contradicted his conviction that the majority of the Mexican people supported Carranza, for if this were true Huerta had no prospect of victory in a fair election. If the government controlled the election, its candidate—Huerta or someone else—would be certain to triumph. In either event, Huerta's candidacy was irrelevant.

[2] New York *World*, July 24, 1913. The suggestions are Bryan to Wilson, undated (received July 20, 1913), Wilson Papers, File II; and Hale to Davis, July 17/23629.

[3] Washington *Post*, July 25, 1913; and New York *World* (quoting Henry Lane Wilson), July 27, 1913.

[4] Garrison to Wilson, July 24, 1913, Wilson Papers, File VI; Washington *Post*, July 25, 1913 (quoting Senator Bacon); and Hale to Davis, July 28/23633.

[5] New York *Times*, July 25 and 26, 1913 (quoting Carranza's agent in Washington); and New York *World*, July 30, 1913, referring to the statements by Huerta and Carranza.

The man Wilson selected to deliver his plan was the former governor of Minnesota, John Lind. Lind was a Swede who came to America as a youth. A tall, gaunt, hard-looking man, he had the blue eyes and sandy hair of the ancient Norsemen. When excited he emphasized his words by tapping his right hand on the stump of his left wrist, all that remained after an accidental shotgun blast forced amputation of his left hand. Assuredly he was a man of controversy. He inspired devotion among his supporters and hatred among those he opposed, and he reciprocated these feelings. Lind had initiated his political career as a silver Republican in Congress, won election as governor on the fusion ticket in 1898, and later returned to Congress as a Democrat. A close friend and supporter of William Jennings Bryan, he had aided the drive to nominate Woodrow Wilson for the presidency in 1912. Bryan therefore recommended him for the mission to Mexico.

Lind was singularly unqualified. His only previous contact with Mexican matters was a telegram to Bryan advising the recall of Henry Lane Wilson, based on information he received from a former army officer, and his own unfavorable opinion of the ambassador's brother, whom Lind had known in Congress.[6] Lind had no diplomatic experience and could not speak Spanish. He was a rabid anti-Catholic, who later proposed that the United States take an option on the Cathedral in Mexico City, which he considered a suitable site for a new embassy.[7] He disliked minority groups, especially Irish Catholics, which of course estranged him from Chargé Nelson O'Shaughnessy in Mexico City.

But the President and Secretary of State placed their confidence in him and considered these inadequacies as assets. In their view he had no prejudices about Mexico based on former contacts and had no connection with State Department personnel whose ideas differed from those of the President. Wilson sought a faithful lieutenant who would be devoted only to his own policy, and Lind's friendship with Bryan assured his loyalty. In addition, Lind's anti-imperialist and anti-big-business views, so prevalent among progressives, guaranteed that he would not advocate a return to the policies of Henry Lane Wilson.

[6] Lind to Bryan, March 16, 1913, SD 123.W691/126; and statement of John Lind regarding his lack of preparation and knowledge of Mexico, 66th Congress, 2d session, United States Senate Committee on Foreign Relations, *Investigation of Mexican Affairs* (Washington: U.S. Government Printing Office, 1920), testimony of John Lind, April 27, 1920, pp. 2317–2318.

[7] Lind to Bryan, December 18, 1913/10256. Bryan replied bluntly: "Do not understand your reference to option on the Cathedral," December 19/10256. Lind contended that he had been joking, Lind to Bryan, December 19, Lind Papers.

Having decided on a course of amateur diplomacy, the Wilson administration launched the Lind mission with singular ineptness. Lind had no preparation or briefing before his mission. Secretly, Bryan summoned him to Washington on July 28 "for consultation about an important matter"—the very day Henry Lane Wilson, who had been recalled for "consultations," conferred with the President in Washington. Lind had no inkling that his summons concerned Mexico until he arrived in the capital.[8] He received no written instructions beyond the President's proposal; his only directions were to secure Huerta's concurrence.[9] Lind's knowledge of Mexico, aside from a discussion with Wilson and Bryan, came from William Bayard Hale, who met him at Veracruz.[10] The President failed to consult the chargé and the embassy staff in preparing his proposal. Neither the Mexican government nor the embassy received any advance notice of Lind's mission, learning of it from Bryan's press statement of August 4 announcing acceptance of Ambassador Wilson's resignation and Lind's departure for Mexico.[11] Bryan informed the embassy of Lind's imminent arrival the day after the staff read the news in the papers. There were no advance arrangements for Lind's trip, and only when he arrived in New Orleans did he discover that no liner departures for Mexico were scheduled for several days. Bryan then arranged transport for him aboard a warship.[12]

Throughout this initial phase, Wilson's failure to notify the Mexican government of the full particulars created an atmosphere of fear. Bryan's message to the embassy on August 5 merely stated the Lind was on a "peace mission," and the Secretary refused to provide details when O'Shaughnessy requested them.[13] The Mexican government quite naturally viewed Lind's arrival as the precursor of armed intervention. Acting Minister of Foreign Affairs Garza Aldape informed the chargé on August 6, "If Mr. Lind . . . does not properly establish his official character, or if he is not the bearer of the recognition of this

[8] Bryan to Lind, July 28 and 29, 1913, Lind Papers.

[9] Bryan to W.Wilson, July 31, 1913, Bryan-Wilson Correspondence, I, 106.

[10] Lind told the Fall committee that he had never heard of Hale until he met him in Veracruz, as neither the President nor the Secretary of State told him about the other agent, *Investigation of Mexican Affairs*, testimony of John Lind, April 27, 1920, pp. 2323–2324.

[11] New York *Times*, August 5, 1913; O'Shaughnessy to Bryan, August 5/8241; and Bryan to O'Shaughnessy, August 6/8241.

[12] Bryan to Lind, August 5, 1913, Lind Papers.

[13] Bryan to O'Shaughnessy, August 5, 1913/8661; O'Shaughnessy to Bryan, August 5/8241; and Bryan to O'Shaughnessy, August 6/8241.

government by yours, his sojourn in this Republic will not be pleasing";
and Huerta told a reporter that he would "absolutely ignore" Lind
unless these conditions were fulfilled.[14]

John Lind entered an atmosphere of uncertainty when he sailed into
Veracruz on the morning of August 9 aboard the battleship *New
Hampshire*. The warship anchored outside the breakwater near the
Louisiana, as the vessels were too large to enter the harbor. Standing
on the deck of the *New Hampshire* as it fired a twenty-one gun salute
to Mexico, Lind got his first glimpse of the nation. Beyond the ancient
fortress of San Juan de Ulua spread the modern harbor of the country's
largest port. The waterfront bore a touch of his old homeland, for the
concrete port installations were faced with Scandinavian granite. Before
disembarking, Lind transferred to the *Louisiana* to confer with William
Bayard Hale, who had come from the capital to meet him. Lind landed
at 5:00 P.M. and encountered his first Mexicans—twenty policemen
detailed to "protect" him. There were no representatives of the Mexican government to greet the special envoy. He remained in the American
consulate overnight and traveled to Mexico City the following day.[15]

Despite an unpretentious title as "adviser to the embassy," Lind was
actually a *de facto* ambassador. He could not formally be invested with
this title since appointment of a new ambassador would constitute
recognition of the Huerta government, but he came with all the plenary
powers of an ambassador and was paid an ambassador's salary. In
fact, Bryan had previously offered Lind the post of minister to Sweden.[16]
Accordingly, the embassy in Mexico City was "completely at Governor
Lind's disposal." The State Department communicated directly with
Lind, and Bryan wrote much of this extensive correspondence in his
own hand. His first message instructed Lind not to "disclose the President's views to anyone," leaving the embassy staff unaware of the
nature of his mission.[17]

On August 8, three days after the initial press reports of the Lind
mission and one day before Lind's arrival in Veracruz, Bryan informed

[14] Garza Aldape to O'Shaughnessy, August 6, 1913, PR Mexico City, 1913,
XXIII, C1. 800; and O'Shaughnessy to Bryan, August 7/8573. For Huerta's statement, *El Imparcial*, August 6, 1913.

[15] *El País*, August 10, 1913.

[16] Bryan to Lind, August 5, 1914, Lind Papers, stating, "You may prepare your
accounts on this basis; the salary of an ambassador is $17,500 a year." W. Wilson to
Lind, June 11, 1913, Lind Papers, for the offer of the post of minister to Sweden.

[17] O'Shaughnessy to Bryan, August 10, 1913/8287; and Bryan to Lind, August
10/8274A.

all nations represented in Mexico that President Wilson would soon unveil a proposal for restoring peace to Mexico:

> The contents of his communication will be made known to you when it is ready. In the meantime it is respectfully suggested that your government consider the propriety of asking its representative in Mexico to confer with Huerta and advise him of its view with regard to the propriety and necessity of giving very serious consideration to any suggestions this government may make and the situation which might arise if these good offices be rejected.[18]

Wilson in this manner asked twenty-one nations to commit themselves to support his proposal before anyone learned its content. Even before this note, newspapers reported that European diplomats regarded the Lind mission "with merriment."[19] When several governments requested details, the Secretary of State replied: "The President's views will be given to the public as soon as any change in policy is made," implying that other governments could read about it in the newspapers. He denied that his previous communication asked endorsement of the policy: "The object of our note was to suggest that foreign governments should advise serious consideration of the policy." This ignored the fact that such advice would imply support.[20]

President Wilson hesitated momentarily after Lind arrived in Mexico, and on August 11, Bryan informed Lind that the President would await his assessment of the Mexican situation before acting.[21] Wilson may have wavered in the face of harsh criticism by Senator William A. Smith, chairman of a Foreign Relations subcommittee investigating Mexico, who charged that an extensive rebel lobby in Washington was influencing administration policy. Wilson had previously informed Vice President Thomas Marshall that he was "very much afraid of even seeming to play into the hands of some of our Republican friends in the Senate who are trying to make the situation impossible."[22] After one day's consideration, Wilson instructed Lind to proceed with his mission.

Huerta was prepared to deal with Lind, for his earlier statements to the contrary were intended for domestic consumption and had achieved their purpose. Huerta's prestige skyrocketed due to his defiance of the

18 Bryan to twenty-one nations, August 8, 1913/8284A.
19 New York *Times*, August 6, 1913.
20 Bryan to American embassy in Berlin, August 12, 1913/8285.
21 Bryan to Lind, August 11, 1913/8278.
22 Wilson to Marshall, August 4, 1913, Wilson Papers, File VI.

United States, and he received numerous messages of support. The Mexican President could easily save face by contending that Lind established his "official character" by presenting a letter stating:

To WHOM IT MAY CONCERN:

This will introduce the Honorable John Lind, who goes to Mexico at my request and as my personal representative, to act as adviser to the American Embassy in The City of Mexico. I bespeak for him the same consideration that would, in other circumstances, be accorded a regularly accredited representative of the Government of the United States.

(signed) WOODROW WILSON
President of the United States[23]

The new Minister of Foreign Relations, Federico Gamboa, received Lind and conducted the negotiations for the Huerta government. Gamboa was a round-faced, suave-looking career diplomat who returned from the Mexican legation in Belgium to assume charge of the Foreign Ministry. Gamboa and Lind both traveled to Mexico simultaneously, resembling two pawns involved in an odyssey that carried them toward an inevitable rendezvous. Gamboa landed at Veracruz only two days in advance of Lind and took the oath of office on the very day he received the American envoy.

Lind conferred with Gamboa briefly on August 12 and presented Wilson's proposal secretly the very next day. On August 15, Lind cautioned Gamboa that rejection of the plan would probably lead Wilson to lift the arms embargo, grant belligerent rights to the revolutionaries, and even intervene militarily.[24] O'Shaughnessy learned the contents of the dispatch on August 15, the same day Bryan transmitted it to other governments. Lind did not desire negotiations, but preferred presenting the plan in the form of an ultimatum. Bryan, however, refused, as he felt that lengthy consideration would allow foreign governments to apply pressure for eventual compliance.[25]

On August 16, Gamboa replied in a scathing note referring derisively to Lind as "Mr. Confidential Agent" and invoking the legal fallacies of the American proposition. Noting that a state of war did not exist between the United States and Mexico, he expressed surprise that Lind

[23] The Wilson letter is dated August 4, 1913, Lind Papers.
[24] Lind to Bryan, August 12, 1913/8314, and undated (August 15), Lind Papers.
[25] Lind to Bryan, August 13, 1913/8334; Bryan to Wilson, August 14/8334; and Bryan to Lind, August 14/8334.

was on a peace mission. Citing the "strange and unwarranted character" of the proposals, he explained that "Mexico cannot for one moment take into consideration the four conditions which His Excellency Mr. Wilson has been pleased to propose. . . . Bandits, Mr. Confidential Agent, are not admitted to armistice." The foreign minister added that an armistice agreement would be completely impossible, since such a course would "ipso facto recognize their belligerency." As for a pledge of early elections, the Mexican diplomat concluded, "Our laws already provide such guarantees."[26]

The Mexican reply caught Wilson by surprise: he had not considered rejection, despite the numerous indications to this effect. Consequently, Lind's instructions did not cover this eventuality, and only after presenting the note did he request directions for this "unlikely" possibility. There was clearly a lack of planning, and in the face of the Mexican rejection the United States hesitated, searching for another course. Despite the ominous warnings that accompanied the proposal, no action followed. Lind remained in Mexico City to continue negotiations. Bryan was convinced that the Mexican government would reopen the exchanges "as soon as the Mexican people have had time to consider the notes."[27] This was more wishful thinking, as Bryan was completely ignorant of the prevailing Mexican spirit and sentiment. When the Huerta regime published texts of the notes after the negotiations ended, the Mexican populace rallied around Huerta as the defender of the nation against Yankee interference, and the popularity of the government rose to new heights.[28] This was an unexpected twist to Wilson's concept of self-determination.

Other nations failed to exert pressure in favor of the American plan, as Wilson had hoped. Lind had implied that the entire world supported the American proposals, but this was far from the case. Only concerted European pressure might have altered Huerta's reply, but the major powers had recognized his regime and accordingly viewed Wilson's plan coldly. The French noted that the proposal raised "difficulties involving questions of international law."[29] British Foreign Secretary Sir Edward Grey directed his minister in Mexico to advise consideration of the note, but to inform Huerta that "although the general rule is that intervention in such a matter as this must only take place when

26 Gamboa to Lind, August 16, 1913/8614A.
27 Bryan to Lind, August 28, 1913/8593.
28 *El País*, August 29, 1913; and *El Imparcial*, August 28 and 29, 1913.
29 Robert W. Bliss (Paris), to Bryan, August 19, 1913/8463.

both parties have invited it, I have made an exception in deference to the desire expressed by the United States government."[30] Only the smaller European states, which had no interests in Mexico, reacted favorably to the plan. The overwhelming majority of the Latin American states did lend their support, partly in response to Bryan's drive to negotiate conciliation treaties with the hemispheric neighbors. The Secretary had initiated his series of arbitration treaties in August and was soon discussing them with nearly every nation south of the Rio Grande. One South American nation that opposed Wilson's Mexican plan was Ecuador, whose Minister of Foreign Affairs replied that "he had no doubt the proposal was made in all sincerity . . . but that in his opinion it was impractical and had no possibility of success as even if Huerta should accept, which was unimaginable, it would be impossible to obtain the co-operation of the many revolutionary leaders."[31] O'Shaughnessy informed Bryan that even those nations that advised acceptance of the proposal did so in a perfunctory manner, as all European diplomats in Mexico opposed this move.[32]

Negotiations dragged on, and reports of Mexican troop movements toward the American border aroused concern. While Wilson conferred with Bryan and Moore and then caucused with military commanders on August 18, the Washington *Post* headlined that the two nations were on a war footing. The United States military attaché reported that the Lind proposals would "probably cause war."[33] Gamboa offered to resign and travel to Washington unofficially to conduct personal negotiations with Wilson and Bryan, but Lind regarded this as an attempt to delay concessions. Wilson therefore replied that he would receive Gamboa only if he accepted the plan as a basis for discussion and withdrew his previous note.[34] Publication of Lind's notes in the United States increased the storm of protests. The New York *Times* noted that adequate preparation would have prevented presentation of an unacceptable proposal and added that recognition of Huerta would eliminate the crisis. The Washington correspondent of the London *Times* reported: "The logic of Señor Gamboa's reply to Mr. Lind impresses many critics here [Washington] as unanswerable."[35]

[30] Sir Cecil Spring-Rice to Bryan, August 11, 1913, Wilson Papers, File II.

[31] Montgomery Schuyler (Quito), to Bryan, August 16, 1913/8400.

[32] O'Shaughnessy to Bryan, August 21, 1913/8501.

[33] Washington *Post*, August 19, 1913; and Burnside to Garrison, August 25, AG 2059431A.

[34] Lind to Bryan, August 21, 1913/10642; and Bryan to Lind, August 22/10642.

[35] New York *Times*, August 22, 1913; and London *Times*, August 28, 1913.

Unwilling to accept the rejection of its proposals, the Wilson administration awaited a new reply and professed to see concessions in the phraseology of this second Mexican rebuff. Lind resubmitted the President's plan on August 25, stating that if Mexico acquiesced, President Wilson would inform American bankers that he would "look with favor" upon a loan to the Huerta regime. [36] In reiterating the Mexican rejection, Gamboa noted that the Mexican Constitution prevented the provisional President from being a candidate to succeed himself. Wilson, Bryan, and Lind interpreted this statement of the obvious as a concession. Lind prematurely proclaimed his mission a success, believing that "every point contended for in the last note is accepted in fact though not in form." [37] Bryan cabled, "Hearty congratulations," adding: "Huerta's announcement that he will not be a candidate is the only thing necessary to the restoration of peace." A few days later, Bryan congratulated Lind on the "elimination of Huerta." Upon publication of the notes, Bryan informed Wilson, "The Constitutionalists are pleased." [38]

In reality, Huerta was far from eliminated; indeed, Wilson's clumsy efforts had provided Huerta with several opportunities to increase his popularity with the Mexican masses, and the crafty Mexican President seized them all. The loan offer, which Lind had made on his own initiative, completed a series of blunders, for the mention of money in such a delicate situation smacked of bribery and enabled the Huerta government to assume an air of shocked indignation. This stance was added to Huerta's previous claim of saving Mexico from Gringo domination. Thus, President Wilson, much to his own consternation, in seeking to oust Huerta had inadvertently strengthened his adversary's position.

After Gamboa's initial rejection of his proposal, Wilson decided to lay the negotiations before Congress at Bryan's suggestion. The Secretary believed that a congressional endorsement might sway Huerta by demonstrating that the entire country supported the President's plan. [39] Wilson elected to impose a total arms embargo rather than lift the restrictions, because he believed that Gamboa's second note

---

[36] Lind to Gamboa and Lind to Bryan, August 25, 1913/24650.

[37] Gamboa to Lind, August 26, 1913/9069; and Lind to Bryan, August 27, Wilson Papers, File II.

[38] Bryan to Lind, August 27, 1913/8593, and August 31/8635A; and Bryan to Wilson, August 28, Wilson Papers, File II.

[39] Bryan to Wilson, August 10, 1913, Wilson Papers, File II.

indicated acceptance of the American plan. As Wilson prepared his message, John Bassett Moore reiterated his recommendation that recognition of Huerta offered the most effective means of protecting American interests, emphasizing that even Lind admitted that Huerta had pacified a large portion of the country.[40] On August 26, the day before Wilson addressed Congress, Bryan informed him that Senator Bacon, chairman of the Senate Committee on Foreign Relations, "thinks that your message ought to hold out a prospect or a promise of something more than you now propose—that is, he thinks that there should be something in there like this: While we are awaiting developments before deciding upon the course to be pursued in case order is not restored, we shall &c., &c., stating the things that you mention."[41] Thus the idea for the phrase "watchful waiting," which became so famous, came from Senator Bacon and not from the President, and was inserted at the last moment as an afterthought. The statement was intended merely to imply continued vigilance rather than to describe any particular projected policy. Despite the fact that administration officials rarely used the phrase after the President's speech, newspapers snapped it up and assumed that it embodied the administration's attitude toward Mexico. In reality, since Wilson did not wait, but continued to intervene in Mexican internal affairs, "watchful waiting" was completely unrelated to his policy.

On August 27, Wilson addressed Congress, indicating the nature of his proposals to Huerta, announcing the total arms embargo, pledging "watchful waiting," and advising all Americans to leave Mexico. Most of the senators supported his actions, and Bryan congratulated the President for having "raised our international relations upon the highest possible plane." The Secretary believed Wilson's appeal "cannot fail to bring a response from the conscience of the world."[42] Everyone did not agree with this assessment, however. The London *Times* observed that the address failed to cast any "new light" on the Mexican problem. Noting Wilson's statement, "If Mexico can suggest any better way in which the United States can show its friendship we are more than willing to consider the suggestion," the *Times* commented: "Not only

[40] Moore, Memorandum, August 22, 1913/10499.

[41] Bryan to Wilson, August 26, 1913, Bryan-Wilson Correspondence, I, 177.

[42] Wilson's address was sent to all governments represented in Mexico, August 27, 1913/8614A; New York *Times*, August 28, 1913; and Bryan to Wilson, August 27, Bryan Papers.

Mexico, but all foreign residents in Mexico and every government whose nationals possess interests in the country, have already pointed out the 'better way' . . . . It is a simple and, we believe, an effective way, and it consists in America's following the example already set by other Powers and recognizing General Huerta." [43] Americans who began to leave Mexico, as the President had advised, found themselves left to their own devices. In response to numerous complaints, Bryan announced that Wilson had merely intended to advise all Americans to depart as soon as it was convenient, rather than calling for an immediate general exodus. Huerta professed to be pleased with the arms embargo, noting that Wilson's efforts had rendered it impossible for the government to purchase arms in the United States for some time. [44]

John Lind had fulfilled his original mission by delivering the President's proposals, but Wilson instructed him to remain in Veracruz to report developments. Lind had left the capital after delivering the proposals to Gamboa the second time, hoping that his departure would frighten the Mexican government into making concessions. He planned to pause in Veracruz a few days before returning to the United States, in case Gamboa requested a resumption of negotiations, but Wilson's new directive altered the special envoy's plans. [45] The Lind mission therefore was extended from a brief errand into a seven-month sojourn, and Lind became the administration's chief adviser in Mexico, despite his desire to return home. Throughout the torrid Veracruz summer he longed for the cool Minnesota lakes.

Wilson's stance dismayed Lind, for the special envoy was a man of straightforward action, unaccustomed to diplomacy. On August 28, he sent Bryan a long analysis of the Mexican problem: "You will appreciate that I have had comparatively little time to become acquainted with the full scope of his [the President's] plans. I am sure he has a plan. It is absolutely essential that there should be one." In the same letter, Lind informed the Secretary that he had "seen enough of the conditions" in Mexico and "learned enough of the Latin character," even though the extent of his contact with Mexican problems was as brief as the period he had had to become familiar with Wilson's plans. Stating that Mexicans recognized only power and authority, he

43 London *Times*, August 28, 1913.
44 New York *Times*, August 27, 1913.
45 Lind to Bryan, August 20, 1913, and Bryan to Lind, August 25, 1913, Lind Papers.

compared Mexican politics to the "Irish of our cities in the matter of the distribution of offices." Recognizing that the President's proposal was impractical, Lind advocated employing American power to support the revolutionaries.[46] This was but the first of a long series of missives in which Lind urged this course. He advocated terminating the arms embargo on the ground that Huerta could purchase arms in Europe and demanded action even if it meant armed intervention. His impatience increased in proportion to the length of his stay in Mexico. At Lind's suggestion, Hale returned to Washington to explain his proposals, for the two "special agents" had become mutual admirers.[47]

Lind continued to report from Veracruz. He resided in the Hotel Terminal until his wife returned to the United States on November 1. The Terminal was near the waterfront, and Lind could catch the Gulf breezes that provided the only relief on the torrid summer days. He had occasion to tour the city despite his time-consuming duties of "observing" Mexico and "watching" events. Veracruz was a city of contrasts, with modern buildings standing beside those erected by the viceroys. Every afternoon Lind walked the narrow cobblestone streets—a tall, light-haired figure wearing a gray felt hat and gray suit, contrasting vividly with the short, dark Mexicans in their sombreros. Certainly, anyone who wished to "aid" Lind's observations by staging a demonstration for his benefit could easily find him. On November 1, Lind moved to the American consulate, occupying a small, dark room that opened onto a courtyard at the rear of the building.

Lind's pro-Carranza feelings made his quarters a rendezvous for revolutionaries. During his first days in Mexico, he had refused to receive ordinary citizens on the ground that he was "wholly ignorant of Mexican political issues."[48] With the rejection of the President's proposals, however, his role changed to that of an observer, and numerous refugees, both Mexican and American, flocked to his room to recite their experiences. American acquaintances who sent regular reports provided a substantial portion of his information. Two such confidants were Loring Olmstead and George Hackley, both pro-Carranza. Olmstead managed the British Club in Mexico City and

[46] Lind to Bryan, August 28, 1913/10487.

[47] Lind to Bryan, August 28, 1913, Lind Papers. The two "special agents" sent glowing accounts of each other, Hale to Bryan, August 20, Wilson Papers, File II; and Lind to Bryan, August 28/10487.

[48] Lind to O'Shaughnessy, August 13, 1913, PR Mexico City, 1913, XXIII, Cl. 800.

reported on British activities. Louis D'Antin, first clerk and legal counsel of the embassy, secretly reported developments in the capital and related actions of the chargé, whom he despised. Sloan W. Emery, manager of an experimental hacienda owned by the University of Minnesota, and J. J. Slade, Jr., a businessman, both Huertistas, also sent Lind their views.[49] As the overwhelming majority of Americans residing in Mexico favored Huerta, the American colony disliked Lind for his pro-Carranza outlook. Sidney Conger, an evangelical minister, summed up the feeling of American residents: "When I first met Mr. Lind I thought he was after the facts. Later on I sort of got the impression that the facts were after him and that he was not anxious to meet them." Lind reciprocated these ill feelings, regarding the colony as a "thankless lot."[50]

Huerta was thoroughly aggravated by Lind's presence and attempted to circumvent him by sending his own "personal and confidential agent" to Washington on September 1. Lind considered this a ruse to gain time, despite O'Shaughnessy's conviction that Huerta sincerely desired an agreement.[51] After Manuel Zamacona, Huerta's agent, had already traveled to Havana, Bryan informed the Mexican government that Wilson would not receive him and preferred to conduct negotiations through Lind. When Zamacona proceeded to Washington, Bryan declared his willingness to receive the Mexican diplomat only to discuss actions to implement Wilson's proposals.[52] The British considered it "very unreasonable of Mr. Bryan to refuse to receive Señor Zamacona, the more so after Mexico's reception of Mr. Lind," and considered this an indication of American adamance.[53] Huerta, on his part, had little desire to negotiate through Lind and flew into a rage at every mention of the envoy's name.[54]

[49] Lind to Bryan, December 17, 1913/10239; and George M. Stephenson, *John Lind of Minnesota* (Minneapolis: University of Minnesota Press, 1935), pp. 230–232.

[50] *Investigation of Mexican Affairs*, Testimony of Sidney Conger, February 27, 1920, p. 1743; and Lind to Bryan, November 17, 1913/9784.

[51] O'Shaughnessy to Bryan, September 1, 1913/8648; and Lind to Bryan, September 4/8671.

[52] Bryan to Lind, September 8, 1913/24260a; and Bryan to Lind, September 15, Lind Papers.

[53] Foreign Office Minute by Gerald Spicer, October 6, 1913, FO 371/1677.

[54] For reports of Huerta's feelings toward Lind, Edith O'Shaughnessy, *A Diplomat's Wife in Mexico* (New York: Harper and Brothers, 1916), p. 54; and Sir Lionel Carden (British minister in Mexico), to Sir Edward Grey, November 16, 1913, FO 204/419.

The Catholic party nominated Minister of Foreign Relations Federico Gamboa for President as the October elections approached, and he appeared to have an excellent chance, for the Catholic party was the best organized in the country. Huerta proved reluctant to recall Félix Díaz to allow him to resume his candidacy but ultimately permitted his return a few days before the election. Díaz' popularity had declined during his absence, while Gamboa had gained new prestige from his diplomatic exchanges with Lind. Huerta's announcement that he would refrain from endorsing any candidate seemed to enhance Gamboa's prospects. Despite repeated declarations that it would refuse to accept the results of any elections in which the revolutionists did not participate, the Wilson administration praised the nomination of Gamboa and appeared to be preparing to recognize him.[55]

The liberals in Congress threatened to postpone the vote to forestall Gamboa's election, for they preferred Huerta to a Catholic party man. Huerta seized this opportunity, announcing that he would veto any bill interfering with the elections. He also stated on September 16 that in accord with the Constitution he would not be a candidate.[56] Meanwhile, he encouraged other candidates to enter the race, for if no one received a majority he would continue in office.

Tension between the Executive and Congress increased. The Chamber of Deputies, composed largely of Maderistas, was anti-Huerta, and O'Shaughnessy reported that Huerta prevented opposition only by threatening to dissolve Congress. A Cabinet reshuffle in October completed the ouster of the Felicista ministers, and Huerta named Manuel Garza Aldape Minister of Gobernación. Garza Aldape also replaced Urrutia as Huerta's closest confidant and constant companion and therefore became the most influential man in the Cabinet. He advocated a "hard line" toward Congress. When Huerta designated Eduardo

[55] Bryan wrote to Wilson, "I know of no objection that can be raised to Gamboa personally and we have, therefore, only to await the election," Bryan to Wilson, September 25, 1913, Bryan-Wilson Correspondence, I, 238. Hale informed the Carrancista agent in Washington, "If the election appears legal, the President will morally sustain" Gamboa, M. Pérez Romero to Carranza, October 3, AREM, L.E. 861, leg. 2 (121–R–4), f 29.

[56] O'Shaughnessy to Bryan, October 3, 1913/9067; and *Diario Oficial*, CXXVIII, 14, 141–152, September 16, 1913, for Huerta's address. Bryan and Lind both hailed Huerta's speech as an indication that Huerta would not be a candidate and would surrender office to the election winner, Bryan to Wilson, September 17, Bryan-Wilson Correspondence, I, 207–208; and Bryan to Lind, September 18, Lind Papers.

Tamariz, a member of the Catholic party, as Minister of Public Instruction in September, the liberals in the Chamber raised a storm of protest. The liberals feared that a Catholic party man heading the Ministry of Public Instruction would give advantages to the parochial schools, and they refused to grant consent for Tamariz to leave Congress to enter the Cabinet. Huerta was furious and offered to appoint Tamariz minister anyway if he resigned from the Chamber, for then its consent would not be necessary.[57] Tamariz decided to remain in the Chamber, but relations between the Executive and Congress were severely strained. Several other clashes over appointments occurred.[58] The Chamber also demanded the release of deputies arrested on charges of aiding the rebels. While some of the deputies were unquestionably working against the government, the arrests violated their legislative immunity.

The conflict sharpened when Senator Belisario Domínguez of Chiapas attempted to deliver an impassioned speech attacking Huerta in the Senate on September 23. Although the senator was prevented from reading the address, it was placed in the minutes. Domínguez advocated Huerta's removal, characterizing him as a man with a disordered mind and an assassin. Criticizing nearly every policy of the Huerta government, Domínguez virtually invited assassination in a desperate attempt to arouse his colleagues against Huerta. He succeeded all too well. The senator disappeared a few days later, and the discovery of his body caused Congress to oppose Huerta openly.[59] There was no need to prove that Domínguez was assassinated on government orders, for this was obvious. The Chamber of Deputies immediately launched an investigation and demanded that Minister of Gobernación Garza Aldape appear to answer questions. A petition circulated demanding Huerta's resignation on charges of murdering Domínguez.[60]

---

[57] *La Nación*, September 19, 20, and 21, 1913; and O'Shaughnessy to Bryan, September 18, 812.002/38.

[58] Among other things, the Senate had refused to agree to the appointment of Emilio Rabasa as rector of the National University, *El Imparcial*, October 3, while the Chamber also refused to halt a trial of José Limantour, despite a Supreme Court ruling that this violated the jurisdiction of federal courts, *Mexican Herald*, September 27, 1913.

[59] Ramón Prida, *De la dictadura a la anarquía* (El Paso, Texas: Imprenta de El Paso del Norte, 1914), pp. 600–609.

[60] O'Shaughnessy to Bryan, October 10, 1913/9166; and *Mexican Herald*, October 10, 1913.

The majority of the Cabinet supported Garza Aldape's conclusion that dissolving Congress was the only solution.[61] On October 10, the day Garza Aldape was scheduled to appear before Congress, the deputies found two hundred secret police in the public gallery. Blanquet's crack Twenty-Ninth Battalion moved to a barracks near the congressional building, and troops lined the streets in the vicinity. Garza Aldape appeared and asked the legislators to reconsider their action, but the Chamber adjourned without discussing his request. Garza Aldape then read a list of one hundred and ten deputies, who were promptly placed under arrest. Upon receiving the news, the Senate, which was not affected by Huerta's decree dissolving the Chamber, adjourned. The government brought charges against seventy-four of the arrested deputies and released the rest within a week. Huerta attempted to justify his actions on the ground that the deputies had invaded Executive functions.[62] While there was considerable truth to this, it hardly justified a dictatorship. Huerta assumed power to rule by decree and ordered the election of a new Congress at the October 26 presidential election.

President Wilson declared that the United States could not recognize the results of an election conducted under these circumstances and warned against violence to the imprisoned deputies. Yet the coup had considerable support in Mexico, and there were no demonstrations opposing it. Indeed, while the arrests were being made, Huerta was dining alone at a restaurant a short distance away, without fear of any outbreaks.[63] The United States protested, calling the coup "bad faith towards the United States," a strange interpretation, since it implied the existence of some sort of agreement.[64] The Wilson administration was the only government alarmed by the coup. The British regarded it as an inevitable step, and this view was shared by European diplomats

[61] Nemesio García Naranjo, *Memorias de Nemesio García Naranjo* (8 vols.; Monterrey: Ediciones de *El Porvenir*, 1956–1962), VII, 172–173; and Querido Moheno, *Mi actuación política después de la Decena Trágica* (Mexico: Ediciones Botas, 1939), pp. 44–48.

[62] Huerta's decree dissolving Congress is *Diario Oficial,* CXXVIII, 36, 452–453, October 11, 1913. Accounts of the coup appear in *Mexican Herald* and *El País,* both October 10 and 11, 1913. Huerta's speech to the new Congress justifying his action is in O'Shaughnessy to Bryan, November 19, 812.032/16.

[63] Sir Lionel Carden (British minister in Mexico), to Grey, October 15, 1913, FO 204/419, reported the absence of demonstrations and Huerta's activity during the coup.

[64] Bryan to Lind, October 12, 1913/10645C.

in Mexico. The British minister informed his government: "The consensus of opinion among heads of missions present appeared to be that the President's action was justified in the circumstances, and more than one expressed surprise that it had not been taken before." Sir Arthur Nicolson of the British Foreign Office viewed the coup as "The Mexican 18th Brumaire." [65] Noting American protests that Huerta's action rendered a fair election impossible, the London *Times* cited previous United States support for the regime of Porfirio Díaz, despite its obviously fraudulent elections, and commented: "We cannot help thinking that they [the Americans] will be well advised not to ponder that matter too deeply."[66]

American attempts to oust Huerta had clearly proven fruitless. If anything, Huerta had strengthened his control of the government. Clearly, new efforts would be necessary if he was to be forced out.

[65] Carden's assessment and the reaction of other diplomats is in Carden to Grey, October 12, 1913, FO 414/235, while Nicolson's Minute is dated November 5, FO 371/1678.

[66] London *Times*, October 14, 1913.

VII

New Efforts and New Complications

The Wilson administration pondered possible means of reacting to Huerta's coup, but the proximity of the Mexican election precluded action before the balloting. Consequently, the initial protest against the *golpe* was followed by a pause while all attention focused on the election. The situation was becoming increasingly complex, for in addition to solidifying Huerta's position, the coup also accented the differences between the European and American stands in Mexico.

Huerta continued his electoral preparations, and as the date approached, American consuls reported that state governors and *jefes políticos* received instructions to select "reliable" inspectors for the polls to ensure Huerta's victory in their districts. Officially, the General was not a candidate, but circulars exhorting the people to vote for him appeared mysteriously throughout the country.[1] Inevitably, there were also rumors that Huerta would resign, for these seemed to circulate continuously. When queried, the Mexican President angrily told reporters: "When I resign it will be to seek a resting place six feet in the soil." He added: "When you hear that Huerta is dead, when you see my body in its coffin, when the priests come in to say Mass over me, then you may tell your newspaper that Huerta has resigned."[2] These statements mirrored Huerta's intention to retain power in spite of the forthcoming elections, although their significance was overlooked. When Félix Díaz returned to Mexico on October 23, Blanquet's secretary met

[1] Reports of instructions to *jefes políticos* in the provinces to secure a vote favorable to Huerta came from Consuls Wilbur Gracey (Progreso), October 13, 1913/9186, Will Davis (Guadalajara), undated (received October 22), /9328, and William Canada (Veracruz), October 24/9405; while Lind reported similar information on October 21/9302, October 23/9343, and October 26/9406. A copy of the orders to the *jefes políticos* can be found in the Lind Papers, and it appears to be authentic.

[2] New York *Times* and New York *World*, October 19, 1913.

Photo by the U.S. Army Signal Corps, courtesy of the National Archives

Francisco I. Madero (seated third from left) with a group of Revolutionary leaders that includes, in the front row, Venustiano Carranza (left) and José Maytorena (fifth from left); and in the second row, Francisco Villa (left), Gustavo Madero (second from left), and Francisco Madero, Sr. (third from left).

Formal portrait of General Victoriano Huerta, president of Mexico, 1913–1914, in medal-bedecked dress uniform.

Secretary of State William Jennings Bryan

President Woodrow Wilson

Photo by Harris and Ewing

Henry Lane Wilson, United States ambassador to Mexico

Photo by Harris and Ewing

Nelson J. O'Shaughnessy, United States chargé in Mexico, 1914

Courtesy of the Minnesota Historical Society

John Lind, governor of Minnesota and Wilson's "personal representative" in Mexico

Photo from the collection of the U.S. War Department General Staff, courtesy of the National Archives

Victoriano Huerta (left), in civilian clothes, in 1914

The Clifton House Hotel in Niagara Falls, Ontario, site of the mediation conference.

The ABC mediators (from left): Romulo S. Naón, Argentine minister in Washington; Dominico da Gama, Brazilian ambassador to the United States; and Eduardo Suárez Mujica, Chilean minister in Washington.

(*Above*) The Huerta delegation to the mediation conference (from left): Emilio Rabasa, chairman of the delegation, Rafael Elguero, and Augustine Rodriguez.

(*Below*) The United States delegation to the mediation
conference: Justice Joseph E. Lamar (top) and Frederick W.
Lehman.

Venustiano Carranza, first chief of the Constitutionalist Army

Francisco Carbajal, Huerta's successor as president of Mexico in July, 1914

Courtesy of the State Historical Society of Wisconsin

General Francisco (Pancho) Villa with his wife in January, 1914

him at Veracruz and ordered him to sail to Havana.[3] Díaz refused, for this would prevent his candidacy. The Secret Police arrested his staff and surrounded his residence, reducing him to a virtual prisoner. He moved to the Hotel Alemán, which was only twenty feet from the rear window of the American consulate, escorted by Lind and Consul William Canada, who arranged to meet him "accidently" to prevent his detention.[4] Lind backed Díaz for President, despite indications that Wilson and Bryan, who regarded Díaz favorably, now supported Gamboa.[5]

Lind predicted that Huerta would announce his candidacy, but he underestimated the subtlety of the Mexican President.[6] Huerta assembled the diplomatic corps on October 23 and read a statement that "he had reason to fear that some of his friends would propose him as a candidate," that any votes for him would be "null and void," and that if he received a majority he would annul the election.[7] Huerta's assurance calmed American fears. In Bryan's view, "This would seem to dispose of Huerta's candidacy."[8] The Americans failed to perceive that the General's statement received little publicity in Mexico. A single declaration would hardly deter his supporters in view of the continuing domestic campaign on his behalf. Every vote Huerta received increased the probability that no legal candidate would obtain a majority. His statement was merely a clever ploy to impress the Americans. The old warrior planned to use the election to secure a legal pretext to retain power. His scheme emerged in reports that the army would go to the polls—and naturally the soldiers would vote for General Huerta. While the Americans eagerly accepted Huerta's disclaimer, the British Foreign Office never doubted that the election would be controlled.[9]

Apathy reigned on election day, October 26. American consuls reported that at nearly deserted polls only soldiers, government officials, and scattered elements of the general population were casting ballots.[10]

[3] New York *Times*, October 23, 1913.

[4] New York *Times*, October 24, 1913.

[5] Lind even arranged a code with the manager of the Díaz campaign to enable secret communication, Lind to Bryan, October 12, 1913, Lind Papers.

[6] Lind to Bryan, October 20, 1913/9285.

[7] O'Shaughnessy to Bryan, October 23, 1913/9344.

[8] Bryan to Lind, October 24, 1913/9344.

[9] Sir Francis Stronge to Grey, July 18, 1913, FO 414/235; and Foreign Office Minute, dated October 11, FO 371/1677.

[10] Reports of light voting and Huerta victories came from O'Shaughnessy, October 26, 1913/9407, and October 27/9419; and Consuls Clement Edwards (Acapulco),

Some booths in the Federal District failed to register a single vote. A system of open voting that required each citizen to sign his name to a printed ballot supplied by the party of his choice, in full view of the election inspectors, intimidated opponents of the regime. In addition, the great majority of the populace was indifferent to the election. Military officers cast the ballots of their entire commands. Reports indicated a Huerta landslide. Nevertheless, returns still filed in the Ministry of Gobernación records show a surprising number of opposition votes. These returns indicate that Díaz carried the state of Oaxaca, while Gamboa triumphed in Jalisco, although Huerta swept the rest of the country by an overwhelming margin.[11] But the number of votes counted in many states appears excessive. Invariably, there were representatives of only one party present at each polling place, and that party scored an overwhelming triumph. The only possible conclusion is that all candidates submitted their own sets of returns. Naturally, the government controlled the elections through the governors and *jefes políticos.*

The new Congress was pro-Huerta, with the Chamber composed almost entirely of Huertistas and Catholic party members. The President's son and personal staff were elected to the Chamber of Deputies, while the new Speaker was Eduardo Tamariz, whom the previous Chamber had rejected as Minister of Public Instruction. Since state legislatures elected the senators, additional maneuvering was necessary to assure control of the upper House. Huerta's nominees in the state of Jalisco were endorsed by a "unanimous" vote only after the state governor summoned troops and threatened to imprison the entire legislature.[12] The new Congress was entirely submissive, approving all government proposals; therefore, while Huerta theoretically relinquished his dictatorial powers when Congress convened, he remained a dictator in fact. Whenever the legislature adjourned, it voted Huerta "extraordinary powers" until its next session.

October 21/9430, and November 6/9990; Claude Guyant (Ensenada), October 27/9409; Alfonso Lespinesse (Frontera), October 27/9410, and October 28/9777; Gaston Schmatz (Aguascalientes), October 30/9477; Wilbert Bonney (San Luis Potosí), October 27/9420; John Silliman (Saltillo), October 28, PR Mexico City, 1913, XXVI, Cl. 800; William Blocker (Ciudad Porfirio Díaz), October 27/9421; Wilbur Gracey (Progreso), November 5/9781; and Will Davis (Guadalajara), October 27, in Will Davis, *Experiences and Observations of an American Consular Officer during the Recent Mexican Revolution* (Los Angeles: Wayside Press, 1920), p. 248.

[11] Election returns are in Gobernación, Elections, 1913.

[12] Will Davis (Guadalajara), to Bryan, November 15, 1913/9993.

The blatant election control evoked considerable protest, but the government silenced the criticism. When *El País* charged that it was "evident and obvious" that the government controlled the election, the *Diario Oficial* criticized the paper for "attacking" Guatemala, warning that this displeased the "Executive of the Union."[13] *La Nación*, the Catholic party organ, claimed victory daily and repeatedly denounced government pressure. It launched a series of editorials condemning dictatorship, the election control, and many Huerta policies, until the Minister of Gobernación ordered the paper closed on December 22, 1913.[14] Immediately after the election, Félix Díaz crawled across the roof of his hotel to the American consulate in Veracruz and sought asylum. A few days later he was placed aboard a United States warship in the harbor.[15]

Having rejected the election before it occurred, Wilson instructed O'Shaughnessy to reiterate the demand for Huerta's resignation and warn him that if he refused to retire the President would "insist upon the terms of an ultimatum, the rejection of which would render it necessary for him to propose very serious practical measures to the Congress of the United States."[16] To Wilson's consternation, the press reported delivery of the note when Bryan refused to comment on rumors of it. Accordingly, Bryan transmitted the dispatch to foreign governments, describing it as an "ultimatum." Newspapers, having reported many United States demands on Huerta, characterized this one as a "final ultimatum."[17] Wilson directed Lind to return to Mexico City to receive the Mexican reply to this latest demand. Lind insisted that Huerta dismiss the new Congress before resigning, while Huerta retorted that such an action was impossible as it would leave no one to whom he could present his resignation.[18] The Mexican government

[13] New York *Times*, November 2, 1913; and *Diario Oficial*, CXXIX, 5, 41, November 6, 1913.

[14] *La Nación*, October 27 through November 10, 1913, with a daily headline claiming victory and charging government pressure, and editorials attacking the government policies, appeared on December 2, 3, 5, 7, and 10, 1913. For the closing of *La Nación*, see *Mexican Herald*, December 23, 1913.

[15] William Canada (Veracruz), to Bryan, October 27, 1913/9418; and Lind to Bryan, October 28/9440.

[16] Bryan to O'Shaughnessy, November 1, 1913/11443a.

[17] Press reports of the note appeared in New York *World*, November 2, 1913, and New York *Times*, November 4, 1913; the head of the Associated Press explained Bryan's "no comment" to Colonel House, House Diary, November 5, 1913. The New York *World* used the phrase "final ultimatum," November 4, 1913.

[18] Lind to Bryan, November 11, 1913/9675, and November 12/9677.

ignored the American notes. On November 9, Minister of Foreign Relations Querido Moheno informed all diplomatic missions that Congress would convene to declare the presidential election null and void and that Huerta would retain office pending another election. Moheno appealed for support from all "cultured countries," thereby virtually requesting European aid against the American pressure.[19] Lind abruptly terminated the negotiations and returned to Veracruz in a rage without awaiting instructions. He declared that he would resume the exchanges only after the Congress was dissolved, even suggesting that Wilson close the embassy in protest.[20]

In Washington, the Cabinet discussed the advisability of lifting the arms embargo and withdrawing American diplomats. Secretary of the Treasury William G. McAdoo and Attorney General James C. McReynolds favored granting belligerent rights to the Constitutionalists, as Lind had repeatedly urged, while Garrison reversed himself and advocated armed intervention.[21] Wilson even considered declaring war on Mexico and blockading its ports, and several foreign diplomats advised their governments that armed intervention was imminent.[22]

Hale had recommended approaching the Constitutionalists when he returned from Mexico, noting that the mere ouster of Huerta would not terminate the conflict. In the wake of Huerta's rejection of the latest American demand, Wilson finally decided to confer with the revolutionists and dispatched Hale to Nogales in November. Wilson anticipated Constitutionalist endorsement of his "mediation" plan. Hale was instructed to hint that in return for acceptance of Wilson's proposal, the United States was prepared to support the revolutionaries openly if the Huerta government refused to consent to mediation.[23] The Wilson administration was in fact proffering a virtual alliance disguised as mediation, since Huerta, having already rejected one mediation effort,

[19] Querido Moheno to all diplomatic missions, and O'Shaughnessy to Bryan, November 9, 1913/9638; and for the bid for foreign support, London *Times*, November 10, 1913.

[20] Before leaving, Lind requested Bryan to designate another mission to serve as custodian of American interests if the embassy was closed, Lind to Bryan, in November 12, 1913/9677.

[21] E. David Cronon, ed., *The Cabinet Diaries of Josephus Daniels: 1913–1921* (Lincoln, Nebr.: University of Nebraska Press, 1963), p. 83; and House Diary, October 30, 1913.

[22] London *Times*, November 11, 1913.

[23] A copy of Bryan's instructions to Hale appears in the Mexican Records, for Hale carelessly showed his directive to the Constitutionalists, Bryan to Hale (undated), AREM, L.E. 861, leg. 2 (121–R–5), f 67.

could be expected to react similarly to a new proposal. Hale informed Carranza that the United States government was "contemplating permitting the passage of arms" in the event that Huerta rejected its proposal, but he stated that this would be possible only if Carranza gave prior guarantees that foreign lives and property would be protected.[24] Wilson discovered that he had reckoned without Carranza, for the revolutionary chief rejected mediation, refusing to negotiate with "Huerta or any remnant of his government." The Carrancistas insisted that "this should be Mexico's last revolution," and they were consequently "unwilling to consider any solution short of the complete triumph of their ideas."[25] Inevitably, the request for guarantees for foreigners raised the question of intervention, and the revolutionaries rejected this suggestion, stressing that they could never consent to anything which they considered intervention in Mexican internal affairs. Wilson was "deeply disturbed" that the Constitutionalists "would trust no one but themselves" and concluded that "they do not understand Constitutional process." He declared that he could not support them and disgustedly ordered Hale to terminate the exchanges on November 19.[26]

This episode revealed Wilson's lack of foresight, for only after negotiating with Huerta for three months did he endeavor to sound out the Carrancistas. When their reply proved unsatisfactory he refused to deal with them, failing to perceive that they were the only group in Mexico strong enough to overthrow Huerta without armed intervention by the United States. Hale contributed to this unreality by praising the Constitutionalists as "plain men" whose "speech is remarkable for its Quaker-like conscientiousness and precision," adding that Carranza's "capacity for silent deliberation is remarkable."[27] In view of Wilson's action, one can only speculate as to what course he would have adopted if Huerta had accepted Lind's proposals and if the revolutionists had rejected them. Surely that would have provided Wilson with a rude shock, and Huerta had missed an opportunity, although he could not have risked the domestic consequences of attempting to achieve a diplomatic victory.

Wilson decided that European cooperation could facilitate his efforts to force Huerta to relinquish power, for the coup had emphasized the

---

[24] *Ibid.*   [25] Hale to Bryan, November 16, 1913/9759 and /9769.

[26] Bryan to Hale, November 16, 1913/9759, and November 19/9825. New York *Times*, November 12 and 20, 1913.

[27] Hale to Bryan, November 14, 1913/9737.

divergence of American and European policy in Mexico. The events accompanying the dissolution of Congress had seemed to indicate that European governments were drawing closer to the Huerta regime. This disturbed Wilson in view of the increasing hostility between the Mexican and American governments. The arrival in Mexico City of the new British minister, Sir Lionel Carden, had alarmed Wilson, for the envoy presented his credentials to Huerta the day after the coup. While the timing was mere coincidence, the American President viewed this as a symbol of British support for the Mexican dictator. The reaction of other governments increased the administration's alarm. The German government contended that the coup indicated that Huerta was a "man of determination" and consequently that his retention of power offered the best hope for peace in Mexico.[28] Reversing their stand, the French now backed Wilson, but the Belgian government supported Huerta because of a railway concession to a Belgian syndicate. Imminent arrival of the new Italian minister to Mexico also caused concern. The Italian ambassador in Washington explained that the Foreign Office dispatched the minister in response to the United States government's request that Italy advise Huerta to accept Wilson's proposal. Since Italy had no representative in Mexico, it could not cooperate and therefore sent the minister to assist the United States, which now considered his arrival an unfriendly act.[29]

In an attempt to terminate British and European support for Huerta, Wilson prepared a note virtually demanding withdrawal of recognition. Despite its general terms, the dispatch obviously was aimed at Britain. Following a suggestion by Bryan that he extend the Monroe Doctrine to forbid foreign concessions in Latin America, Wilson charged that recognition violated the Monroe Doctrine. The President condemned "European financiers" who sought "commercial concessions" and who had "supplied the means whereby General Huerta has attempted to force himself upon his country." He cited the "grave consequences" of recognizing Huerta and demanded withdrawal "in behalf of the people of the western hemisphere."[30] John Bassett Moore refused to transmit this dispatch, returning it to Wilson with a stinging memorandum

[28] James Gerard (Berlin), to Bryan, October 17, 1913/9259.

[29] Moore to Wilson, October 28, 1913/11321A; and Thomas N. Page (Rome), to Bryan, October 31/9890. Italy delayed its minister in Havana until December because of American displeasure, Bryan to Wilson, December 11, 1913, Wilson Papers, File II.

[30] Wilson's draft of the note is undated (October 28), 1913, Bryan Papers. For Bryan's suggestion, Bryan to Wilson, October 28, 1913, Bryan Papers.

instructing the President in the facts of international law. Moore noted, "Recognition is an act performed in the ordinary course of diplomatic relations." He added, "There is nothing in the record to show that the governments that recognized the administration at the city of Mexico in May, June, and July last felt that they were doing anything unusual or requiring explanation. . . . Nor had the United States said anything to indicate to them that it entertained a different view." He stressed that the first American statement opposing recognition was the President's speech of August 27 and that Washington continued diplomatic intercourse with the Huerta regime despite nonrecognition. The counselor cited precedents of delayed American recognition of Mexican governments and noted that the Monroe Doctrine had nothing to do with recognition, stressing: "As we have, since the sending of Governor Lind to Mexico, held towards that country an attitude of interposition in its internal affairs, though not as yet in the physical sense, it may not be advisable too strongly to urge those governments to follow our example." [31] Wilson withdrew the note.

While Moore had prevented Wilson from enunciating these ideas through diplomatic channels, the President had asserted the same doctrine on October 27 in a speech at Mobile, Alabama. Colonel House had urged a public renouncement of territorial ambitions in Latin America and a warning to other nations to desist from attempts to acquire such territory.[32] The President added Bryan's thoughts opposing concessions, by which he feared European countries could control Latin American governments just as surely as by territorial annexation. In his Mobile address, Wilson criticized British support of Huerta, referring to foreign (British) interests seeking concessions in Latin America (Mexico), and he condemned governments that based their policy on material interest. House was delighted with Wilson's speech, but the European reaction was stormy. One German paper denounced the address as "imperialistic delirium." [33]

While conducting negotiations with both parties in Mexico, Wilson continued his efforts to isolate Huerta diplomatically. On November 7, Bryan informed all governments represented in Mexico that it was the President's "clear judgment that it was his duty to require Huerta's retirement" and that the United States would "not regard as binding

[31] Moore to Wilson, October 28, 1913/11321a.

[32] Report of a House-Wilson conversation on October 13, 1913, House Diary, October 28, 1913.

[33] Berliner *Neuste-Nachrichten*, as quoted in New York *Times*, November 1, 1913.

upon the people of Mexico anything done by Huerta since the assumption of dictatorial powers."[34] One day later, Page advised Sir Edward Grey that "he might consider Huerta's elimination certain."[35] The German government promptly requested the name of the American candidate for President of Mexico. Bryan responded with an explanatory note declaring that the United States sought only "peace and order" in Latin America by "insistence upon the noninterruption and continuity of the process of self-government." The United States believed that the "peace and development of America is threatened more by usurpations such as occurred in Mexico . . . than by any other one thing." Accordingly, Bryan announced the administration's aim to "isolate the present chief executive in Mexico City and to force him out by . . . cutting him off from domestic credit, either material or moral, and from foreign aid and sympathy." The note added that the United States would forcibly oust Huerta if necessary.[36] This was merely a restatement of the Wilsonian objective that Huerta must go, but Wilson and Bryan felt it "clarified" American policy.

European governments remained firmly opposed to Wilson's moralistic policies, despite his attempts to explain them. Continental diplomats considered a policy based solely on ousting Huerta unrealistic, for they looked to the future. Europe inquired about the identity of Huerta's replacement and would support the General's removal only if convinced that a successor appeared likely to bring peace and stability more rapidly. Wilson's refusal to support any particular individual to succeed Huerta caused European diplomats to suspect that Wilson was merely seeking to prepare the way for American intervention and occupation of Mexico. The Kaiser himself made the German attitude clear to the American military attaché, commenting that the "stand for morality" was "all right," but inquiring: "What about dividends?"[37] The Germans continued to seek investment profits in Mexico, simultaneously attempting to frustrate the British oil interests there. In accordance with this policy, the German minister assured the Huerta government that if it nationalized the railroads and placed the stock

[34] Bryan to various governments, November 7, 1913/9625A.

[35] Page to Bryan, November 8, 1913/10437.

[36] James Gerard (Berlin), to Bryan, November 8, 1913/9620, and Bryan to all American embassies and legations (except Turkey), November 24, 1913/11443b and /11443d.

[37] James Gerard (Berlin), to Bryan, December 20, 1913, Wilson Papers, File II.

on the world market, Germany would gladly provide unlimited funds, and the Kaiser would personally buy some shares.[38]

The Wilsonian pressure also alarmed Latin Americans, and many Latin diplomats began to view Huerta as their champion in resisting Yankee interference. Wilson's continued attempts to oust Huerta, coupled with broad statements such as the Mobile address, caused some Latins to conclude that Wilson meant to subject Latin America to the commercial domination of the United States, rather than protect it from European dominance. Viewed in this light, Wilson was merely employing more subtle methods to continue the policies of Roosevelt and Taft. Yet Wilson regarded his Mobile speech as a gesture of friendship for Latin America, and he anticipated that the Latin reaction would be one of gratitude for his efforts to protect them from European encroachment. The President failed to perceive that Latin Americans feared the intervention of the United States as much as they did that of Europe.

Lind and Bryan continued to press Huerta, temporarily stressing nullification of the congressional elections. Minister of Gobernación Garza Aldape explained to O'Shaughnessy that it was essential that Congress convene to annul the presidential elections, but he offered to have it dissolved after this act. Bryan maintained that even a single session of the Congress would imply that its election was legal.[39] A few days after this conversation with O'Shaughnessy, Garza Aldape resigned, and the chargé attributed this to his willingness to accept the American demands. Lind, who saw a plot in every Mexican action, regarded Garza Aldape's resignation as a maneuver designed to trick the United States into accepting him as Huerta's successor.[40] In fact, Huerta had suspected that Garza Aldape wished to succeed him if he accepted this plan, and he presented the minister with a photograph of himself inscribed: "To my esteemed friend . . . the only Mexican capable of succeeding me in the presidency of the Republic and to whom I give . . . 24 hours to leave the country."[41]

[38] Nemesio García Naranjo, *Memorias de Nemesio García Naranjo* (8 vols.; Monterrey: Ediciones de *El Porvenir*, 1956–1962), VII, 239–241, reporting the German minister's comments to Huerta.

[39] O'Shaughnessy to Bryan, November 13, 1913/9705; and Bryan to O'Shaughnessy, November 14/9705.

[40] O'Shaughnessy to Bryan, November 16, 1913/9757; and Lind to Bryan, November 16/9762.

[41] Miguel Alessio Robles, *Historia política de la Revolución* (Mexico: Ediciones Botas, 1938), p. 110, for the story of the photograph; *La Nación*, November 17,

The Mexican Congress convened on November 20, despite American objections. Acting on Bryan's instruction, the American chargé did not attend the inaugural session, although all other representatives in Mexico did, once again demonstrating that the American President had succeeded only in isolating himself, not Huerta.

The United States increased its financial pressure as the Grand Committee of the Chamber of Deputies declared the October presidential election null and void on December 10. Congress extended Huerta's term until a new election, scheduled for July, 1914.[42] American efforts provoked a financial crisis in Mexico in late 1913 and early 1914. Huerta had previously found it necessary to increase taxes and import duties which, while partially alleviating the financial squeeze, diminished his popularity. With American pressure constricting the flow of foreign funds, Huerta resorted to internal loans and proved quite resourceful in obtaining operating capital. Mexican banks supplied extensive funds, and private individuals also contributed. Numerous groups of businessmen summoned for conferences with the President "volunteered" to subscribe to new internal loans during their discussions with the Chief Executive. On November 6, Huerta declared bank notes legal tender, due to a coin shortage created by the export of silver pesos. A government fund guaranteed the new currency, and since the issuance of notes required federal permission, Huerta employed this to compel the banks to purchase government bonds. A panic resulted, forcing Huerta to decree a bank holiday on December 22 that was extended until March 31. Banking houses operated normally throughout this period but were empowered to refuse large withdrawals. While new foreign loans enabled the government and the national railroad to meet interest payments in December, Huerta was compelled to suspend debt payments on January 13. As pressure increased, the Mexican Minister of Foreign Relations told O'Shaughnessy in desperation, "Intervene, do something, but don't strangle us financially."[43] Huerta even assured O'Shaughnessy that he recognized the merit of Wilson's policy of opposing governments that seized power by force but that an exception would be necessary for Mexico where order was the primary need.[44] Despite the financial squeeze that caused many ob-

---

1913, mentions a photo but not the inscription; while *El País*, November 17, 1913, reports the inscription, but omits the part about leaving the country.

[42] O'Shaughnessy to Bryan, December 10, 1913/10118.

[43] O'Shaughnessy to Bryan, January 21, 1914/10732.

[44] O'Shaughnessy to Bryan, February 22, 1914/10954.

servers to predict the momentary collapse of the Mexican government, Huerta continued to raise ample funds to purchase arms. Indeed, this was one reason for the shortage of silver pesos. Despite his resourcefulness, Huerta was compelled to send his Minister of Hacienda (finance) to Paris to seek loans during December.[45] The protracted financial crisis stimulated renewed rumors of Huerta's resignation, but he again indicated his determination when he told a reporter: "Hell will hold both Woodrow Wilson and myself before I resign."[46] In Mexico, reports indicated that Félix Díaz planned a new coup on the anniversary of his rising against Madero, and Díaz did approach Villa early in February, seeking support. The arrest of numerous Díaz partisans in the capital during January and February squelched the uprising, and Captain Burnside reported that a coup was unlikely to succeed, for Huerta was "about three days ahead of the average Mexican in foreseeing schemes of this character."[47]

Huerta appeared to be on the verge of yielding to American pressure in March, when he sent Minister of Foreign Relations José López Portillo y Rojas to confer with Lind in Veracruz. The Mexican foreign minister appealed for a modification of the American attitude, particularly for an easing of the financial pressure and the termination of arms shipments to the rebels. In return, he offered a guarantee that Huerta would retire immediately after the July election. Portillo y Rojas also stated that while Huerta could not formally agree to an armistice with the rebels, he was prepared to suspend federal operations during the election campaign if the revolutionaries participated in the ballot.[48] The British viewed these as major concessions, concluding that Huerta's offer conceded the substance of the American demands, altering only the method as a means of saving face. Wilson, however, rejected the Mexican proposal outright, insisting on complete submission to his demands.[49]

[45] De la Lama was unsuccessful, for the administration pressured the French government to warn bankers against loans to Mexico, Myron T. Herrick (Paris), to Bryan, December 26, 1913, 812.51/106.

[46] New York *World*, January 8, 1914.

[47] Burnside to AGWAR, January 28, 1914, WD 5761–909.

[48] Lind to Bryan, March 19, 1914/11218; but for the substance of the exchanges, it is necessary to turn to the British records, as they are not reported in the American documents. British Chargé Thomas Hohler talked to all participants and reported the specifics to Grey, Hohler to Grey, March 23 and 24, 1914, FO 204/431, March 25, FO 371/2027, and March 26, FO 371/2026.

[49] Wilson's reply was in response to a British inquiry, Spring-Rice to Grey, March 26, 1914, FO 371/2026, in which Wilson refused to continue the talks.

Since it was obvious that Huerta could not openly bow to foreign pressure, Wilson's intransigent stand precluded further negotiations. While Huerta's proposal did not meet the full American demands and left some loopholes in view of the recent election control, it could have provided the basis for renewed negotiations had Wilson desired a diplomatic settlement. But the American President had determined upon the complete humiliation of his Mexican opponent.

The continued Mexican rebuffs annoyed Lind, and he bombarded Bryan with recommendations urging overt American support for Carranza. Throughout his stay in Veracruz, the special agent sent a continual stream of notes advocating this course. In a lengthy memorandum dated November 15, he concluded that the wealthy, the army, and the church caused all of Mexico's problems, noting:

> We could defeat but we could neither humble nor humiliate them. This can only be done by their own people, their own blood—the people of the North. . . . To make a dog feel that he is really a cur he must be whipped by another dog and preferably by a cur. Consequently let this housecleaning be done by home talent.[50]

Lind urged extensive American aid to enable Villa to undertake this "housecleaning." Although he had never met Villa, Lind characterized the revolutionary general as the "highest type of physical, moral and mental efficiency that the conditions and the environment could reasonably be expected to produce." Lind stressed that United States military intervention was the only alternative to overt support of the Constitutionalists.[51] Although Bryan assured him, "The President's sympathy [is] entirely with Constitutionalists," Lind continued to recommend American recognition of the belligerency of the Carrancistas and the lifting of the arms embargo.[52] He insisted that the revolutionaries needed American arms to counter Huerta's purchases in Europe. Nearly all his dispatches in December, 1913, and January, 1914, urged this course. His reports became so one-sided that he sought to counter rebel atrocities by pairing them with similar acts by the federals, which he characterized as "provocations" that fostered revolutionary "reprisals."[53]

---

[50] Lind to Bryan, November 15, 1913/9760.

[51] Lind to Bryan, December 5, 1913/10077.

[52] Bryan to Lind, December 13, 1913/10152.

[53] Lind to Bryan, January 7, 1914/10462, January 14/10537, and January 26, Lind Papers.

Lind sailed to Pass Christian, Mississippi, to confer with Wilson briefly on January 2, 1914, and reiterated his recommendations. While the Chief Executive informed Bryan that Lind told him "nothing new," he did feel the talks provided a "splendid opportunity to see things . . . nearer at hand."[54] The President had considered ending the arms embargo earlier and had discussed the matter with Colonel House. Both believed that the embargo obliged the Carrancistas to purchase arms at inflated prices. House felt this "hardly seemed fair." The two agreed that "there was no hope for Mexico excepting through the Constitutionalists."[55] Various senators also urged Wilson to lift the arms embargo during January, as the Constitutionalists launched a concerted campaign to persuade the President to take this step. Wilson once again approached the revolutionary envoys in Washington in a renewed attempt to secure guarantees for foreign residents of Mexico, but the effort proved futile.[56] The revolutionaries were acutely aware that the President was inclining toward removing the last legal barriers to arms shipments in an effort to break the stalemate in Mexico.

On February 1, 1914, Wilson lifted the arms embargo, thus terminating the so-called period of watchful waiting. Large shipments of arms and ammunition immediately crossed the border, for both combatants had anticipated the President's order and had stockpiled munitions at shipping points. The Huerta government succeeded in shipping ordnance by sea from Mobile, while the Carrancistas moved carload lots across the frontier all along the border.[57] It was readily apparent that both adversaries possessed ample finances for arms purchases. The United States government materially aided the revolutionary cause by immediately releasing munitions previously impounded during the embargo period, thus providing large supplies already in the vicinity of the border for immediate shipment. The War Department even approached the Carrancista envoys in Washington, offering to sell a large quantity of rifles to the revolutionary forces. The rebel chiefs

[54] Wilson to Bryan, January 6, 1914, Bryan Papers.

[55] House Diary, December 23, 1913, and January 21, 1914.

[56] Roberto V. Pesqueira (Carrancista agent in Washington), to Carranza, January 29, 1914, AREM, L.E. 760, leg. 1 (75–R–21), f 121; and Carranza to Pesqueira, January 30, AREM, L.E. 732, leg. 16, f 29.

[57] Mexican records indicate the release of arms previously seized by American agents and also show the huge arms shipments that crossed the border at once, AREM, L.E. 760, leg. 1 (75–R–21), f 158–165, *passim*, indicating the rebel arms shipments; while government shipments from Mobile appear in AREM, L.E. 784, leg. 15 (84–R–15), f 20–50, *passim*.

refused the offer, however, since arms manufacturers offered more rapid delivery on purchases of new weapons.[58] The immediate effect of the President's action in lifting the arms embargo was a considerable escalation of the intensity of the Mexican conflict, for both sides were now better equipped. The action obviously benefited the revolutionaries, since they controlled the entire border area and hence could import munitions more readily than the government.

As the end of the arms embargo failed to alter the situation immediately, Lind advocated more drastic American action. Acting as an "armchair strategist" constantly criticizing the pace of the revolutionary forces, Lind began hatching intervention schemes to accelerate the rebel advance. In January, 1914, he proposed that the United States military attaché plan a rebel attack on the federal gunboats at Tampico. The special agent even badgered the military attaché into writing a report outlining possible methods of aiding the revolutionaries.[59] Lind suggested that the United States navy seize the Mexican Gulf ports to cut revenues and railroad fuel, assuming that these cities would surrender upon the appearance of a small American force. When the Mexican gunboat *Zaragoza* sailed to New Orleans, he proposed that the United States aid the Carrancistas in capturing it on the Mississippi River.[60] He even requested authority to direct American marines to seize Mexico City, believing only two companies necessary. He explained that he had arranged to get these troops to the capital "secretly" —via the main railroad![61] Thus, Lind audaciously suggested an American military coup to overthrow a government that the United States opposed because it came to power by this method. Lind was exasperated with the Mexican situation and frequently requested his own recall. Throughout his stay in Mexico, he complained that he was "a little restless" and annoyed at "doing nothing."[62] Bryan finally agreed to Lind's return, and Lind sailed from Veracruz on April 6, 1914, seven

[58] S. Gil Herrera (code name of Sherbourne G. Hopkins), to Carranza, February 5, 1914, and February 7, AREM, L.E. 760, leg. 1 (75–R–21), f 164 and 170; Gil Herrera to Raul Madero, February 9, f 173, Carranza to Gil Herrera, February 10, f 176, Gil Herrera to Carranza, February 11, f 180, and Carranza to Gil Herrera, February 13, f 185.

[59] Lind to Bryan, January 7, 1914/10462. Burnside's report written to "satisfy Governor Lind," is Burnside to AGWAR, January 31, 5761–914.

[60] Lind to Bryan, February 6, 1914/10818, on the gunboat, and March 23/27482, on the port seizures.

[61] Lind to Bryan, March 8, 1914/11098.

[62] Lind to Bryan, March 23, 1914/27482.

months after he arrived. The special envoy looked haggard and drawn when he arrived in Washington and informed reporters that he was "certainly glad" when directed to return.[63]

Lind was the instrument of Wilson's first action in Mexico, and his recall confirmed the failure of American policy. Despite his efforts, Huerta still remained in power. Indeed, Lind's presence had contributed to the deadlock because of Huerta's intense dislike for the special envoy. The British welcomed Lind's withdrawal, since they regarded his presence as "a great embarrassment to all parties" and felt that it had merely prevented meaningful negotiations.[64] For Lind's rigid prorebel stance was apparent to all. The Foreign Office considered the special envoy's departure "difficult to explain" after his protracted sojourn but concluded, "Mr. Lind has been of no use for some time."[65] Yet although he had been of little use as a negotiator, Lind had been helpful to President Wilson in other respects. The "President's personal representative" had come to Mexico with little knowledge of the country and had returned as the chief Wilsonian adviser on Mexican affairs. He exerted considerable influence on Wilson, for the President read his dispatches daily and based much of his policy on the recommendations they contained. The President considered Lind's letters "most instructive" and felt they furnished him with "much food for thought."[66] After some initial misjudgments, Lind gained a better knowledge of Mexico in time, and his analyses improved. Yet he perceived only one side of the Mexican picture, for he devoted his efforts to proving his preconceived views that Huerta was the incarnation of evil, rather than impartially investigating the facts. He had not come to Mexico to seek the most desirable solution; he had come to seek the most effective way to oust Huerta.

After considerable hesitation, the United States government now perceived that in order to have any hope of forcing Huerta from power it must back his strongest opponents, the "men of the north." It was largely Lind's dispatches that made Bryan and Wilson cognizant of the practical steps needed to implement their idealistic policy. While Lind did not assess the Mexican situation impartially, he did provide advice that furthered Wilson's previously determined policy. For

[63] New York *Times*, April 3 and 14, 1914.

[64] Hohler to Grey, February 25, 1914, FO 204/431; and Foreign Office Minute, April 2, 1914, FO 371/2026.

[65] Foreign Office Minute by Gerald Spicer, March 13, 1914, FO 371/2026.

[66] Wilson to Bryan, October 6, 1913, Bryan-Wilson Correspondence, I, 260.

the American President now sought to install Carranza in power instead of merely ousting Huerta. The struggle remained personal, but the objective had broadened. In view of Carranza's refusal to accept elections, this entailed replacing one dictatorship with another, and thus the altruism was blunted by reality.

Even large-scale arms shipments to the Carrancistas failed to force Huerta from office, and Wilson was becoming impatient. A series of revolutions in both Haiti and the Dominican Republic during February may have contributed to Wilson's uneasiness. He had hoped the ouster of Huerta would serve as an example to prevent revolts in other countries, and therefore he may have concluded that Huerta's continued control of the capital inspired these uprisings. Astute observers detected the change in atmosphere in Washington, and the London *Times*, noting previous "unfulfilled threats and abandoned bluffs," which "prove the hideous inefficiency of the present *laissez-faire* policy," commented that the "meekness even of grapejuice diplomacy must have its limits." [67] Lind advocated armed American intervention, and his last dispatch to O'Shaughnessy concluded with the words, "Huerta will have to be *put out*." [68] The special envoy had urged the seizure of Mexican Gulf ports and believed this could be accomplished with little difficulty. Wilson sought to finish Huerta; here was a way. But he did not wish to take this step without some provocation; he needed a pretext. In addition, before intervening militarily, Wilson would need assurance that the British government would not oppose his action.

[67] London *Times*, April 15, 1914.
[68] Lind to O'Shaughnessy, April 5, 1914, Papers of Charles Evans Hughes.

VIII

The Anglo-American Confrontation

Great Britain was second only to the United States as a source of investment capital for Mexico; and although Mexico contained but a minute portion of England's world-wide investments, it received significant attention from British officials. Competition between British and American investors in Mexico inevitably caused the two governments to view each other's actions with suspicion. Britain was the only nation that could possibly rival the United States in seeking to influence the Mexican government and dominate Mexican markets, and thus the two nations were engaged in a protracted competition in that country.

The policies of the Wilson administration and the government of Prime Minister Herbert H. Asquith contrasted sharply. Whereas Wilson was less favorably disposed to big business than his predecessor, the British government pursued the traditional British policy of endeavoring to protect and extend British interests throughout the world. Long accustomed to dealing with underdeveloped areas, the British had evolved a thoroughly realistic strategy of supporting the strongest personality on the political horizon to secure stability and thus enable British concessionaires and businessmen to flourish. Wilson's policy, entailing as it did an idealistic stand that abandoned traditional diplomatic objectives, produced a clash between the two nations in Mexico.

The British were principally concerned with maintaining the flow of Mexican oil to the Royal Navy, which was in the process of converting to oil-burning vessels. Naturally, the Admiralty wished to ensure an adequate supply of fuel in the event of conflict, and Mexico, with its booming petroleum production and a geographic position which made it difficult for a potential enemy to close the shipping lanes to Britain, was an important source of oil for the British navy.[1] In these circumstances, the government inevitably felt obliged to exert every effort to protect the fuel supply, and this entailed maintaining cordial relations with the Mexican government. In addition, the British oil concessionaire in Mexico, Weetman Pearson, First Viscount Cowdray, was intimately connected with the Asquith government. As a former Liberal member of Parliament whose partner, Lord Murray of Elibank, had served as Liberal party whip, Cowdray was well acquainted with members of the Liberal government. Many Americans mistakenly attributed British support of Huerta solely to Cowdray's connections.

Preoccupied with the European situation and mounting unrest in Ireland, British diplomats found themselves in a dilemma in attempting to reconcile the need to maintain the friendship of the United States with the necessity of obtaining adequate quantities of Mexican oil for the Royal Navy. Acutely aware that American support would be essential in Europe, the British government endeavored to promote a *rapprochement* between the United States and Mexico in order to remain on friendly terms with both nations. Wilson, however, made this impossible and compelled the British to choose between two equally vital needs.

The rigid stands that characterized the diplomacy of Wilson and Bryan dismayed the British. Ambassador Sir Cecil Spring-Rice found that his representations proved futile, and he informed Foreign Secretary Sir Edward Grey that altering Wilson's policy by remonstrations was "quite out of the question," for "there is nothing to do with this hardened saint."[2] The ambassador also complained that Wilson was "practically inaccessible," since an interview between Wilson and the British ambassador would inevitably be construed by the press as a British attempt to influence American policy.[3] Negotiations through the State Department proved difficult because of Secretary of State Bryan, whom British diplomats regarded as a complete incompetent. Bryan's idealistic stands alarmed British envoys. Spring-Rice considered the

[1] Speech by Winston Churchill, First Lord of the Admiralty, in Parliament, July 17, 1913, *The Parliamentary Debates*, 5th series, LV, 3d session of the 30th Parliament, House of Commons, Vol. VI of 1913 session (London: Jus Truscote and Sons, 1913), pp. 1465–1478; and London *Times*, December 1, 1913.

[2] Spring-Rice to Grey, February 7, 1914, Stephen Gwynn, *The Letters and Friendships of Sir Cecil Spring-Rice: A Record* (2 vols.; Boston: Houghton Mifflin Company, 1929), p. 202.

[3] Spring-Rice to Grey, March 2, 1914, *ibid.*, pp. 203–204.

Secretary "an orator" who was utterly impervious to reason.[4] In this situation, the British ambassador despaired of effectively conveying the basis of the British stand to the American government, much less of influencing American policy. Spring-Rice was also frustrated by Bryan's inactivity, reporting: "The State Department, like Villa's house, is very often the grave of visitors. News does not get beyond it."[5] The difficulties of dealing with the State Department necessitated the transfer of meaningful negotiations to London, especially when coupled with the aggressive personality of the American ambassador, Walter Hines Page. The ambassador was a fervent disciple of Wilson's moralistic policies and eagerly set out to convert the British government to what he called the "Wilson Doctrine." Yet Page was also isolated from Washington and complained that the State Department ignored his dispatches. The negotiations were therefore conducted in most difficult circumstances.

British diplomats in Mexico were favorably impressed with Huerta when he assumed office. During the Ten Days Revolt, Sir Francis Stronge had cooperated with Ambassador Wilson and found himself in complete agreement with the ambassador's assessments of the Mexican situation.[6] The British minister considered Huerta "a man of great strength" and "conspicuous ability."[7] Stronge declared: "If anyone can extricate this country from its present difficulties he [Huerta] is just the man to do it." Stronge concluded: "An almost desperate situation seems to have produced a man capable of dominating it."[8] The Foreign Office naturally supported Huerta in the light of these reports.

Huerta shrewdly courted the British minister, seeking a counterpoise to the opposition of the United States. Stronge noted that the Mexican President "made a point of treating the representative of Great Britain with exceptional cordiality and frankness" at all times.[9] The Huerta government even gratuitously furnished coal for the H.M.S. *Shearwater* in an effort to retain British vessels in Mexican waters to offset the presence of American warships.[10] These attentions placed

---

[4] Spring-Rice to Grey, May 19, 1913, FO 414/235.

[5] Spring-Rice to Grey, March 2 and May 25, 1914, Gwynn, *The Letters and Friendships of Sir Cecil Spring-Rice*, pp. 203–204 and 207–209.

[6] Stronge to Grey, March 1, 1913, FO 371/1671; and Stronge to Grey, undated (received March 1), FO 414/235.

[7] Stronge to Grey, April 22 and May 13, 1913, FO 414/235.

[8] Stronge to Grey, August 18, 1913, FO 204/419, and May 13, 1913, FO 414/235.

[9] Stronge to Grey, May 13, 1913, FO 414/235.

[10] Sir Ralph Paget to Stronge, September 19, 1913, FO 204/421.

British diplomats in a delicate position. The Asquith government had not intended its stand to oppose the United States—the decision was based solely on conditions in Mexico and British needs. Huerta's actions caused many Americans to conclude erroneously that the British were merely endeavoring to frustrate American interests in Mexico.

The British experienced considerable difficulty attempting to comprehend the American policy and regarded Wilson's diplomacy as "quite hopeless."[11] They concluded that Wilson's broad proclamations either mirrored a lack of experience with underdeveloped areas or served as a cover for other designs. Wilson's outright demand for Huerta's resignation appeared unrealistic and improper to them, and they found Wilson's support of the revolutionaries incomprehensible. In Stronge's words: "It seems incredible that the United States Government should have read the reports of their consul on the sack of Durango by the revolutionists, and should still consider these people as worthy of serious consideration as a political party."[12] Searching for realistic motives to explain Wilson's stand, Spring-Rice concluded that the President might have yielded to agitation in the southwestern states favoring annexation of northern Mexico and that his policy merely sought to prepare for armed intervention. The British ambassador also noted that Wilson was endeavoring to avoid alienating Senate support for his domestic legislation and observed that recognizing Huerta might forfeit the votes of senators from the southwest.[13] Thus, the British attributed Wilson's stands to the exigencies of domestic politics.

All Europeans found themselves in a similar dilemma in attempting to diagnose Wilson's objectives. Many Continental diplomats considered Wilson's stand a ruse designed to force Europe out of Latin America to enable United States domination of the area. Ambassador Page reported from London that when he informed the German ambassador that the United States did not desire any territory in Latin America, "He looked at me—a mere glimpse of 1/100th of a second—and I saw this flit across his mind: 'You are a consummate liar or an irresponsible idiot.' I'm sure such a proposition is simply incomprehensible to him."[14] European diplomats in Mexico, alarmed by what they considered an American policy of "drift," resolved to exert pressure on Washington

[11] Foreign Office Minute by Paget, April 27, 1914, FO 371/2027.
[12] Stronge to Grey, August 11, 1913, FO 414/235.
[13] Spring-Rice to Grey, July 12 and 21, 1913, FO 414/235.
[14] Page to Wilson, February 22, 1914, Wilson Papers, File II.

to alter this stand. At the suggestion of the Belgian and Italian ministers, the European heads of mission in Mexico assembled at the British legation and drafted identic telegrams to their governments. Stronge's version declared:

> European representatives met informally at this legation to-day to discuss the situation which we consider critical. . . . We believe that present situation is largely the result of reluctance of United States Government to recognize the present administration or to exercise any influence on the course of events in this country. If the present government falls, we fear that complete anarchy, accompanied by every kind of outrage, will ensue.
>
> We earnestly recommend that representations be made at Washington before it is too late.[15]

As a result, nearly all major European governments approached the United States in July, urging recognition.

Announcement of the Lind mission seemed to indicate a change in the American position, and although the special envoy was bearing a mediation proposal that the British realized would prove unacceptable to Huerta, British diplomats attempted to facilitate the negotiations. Mexican declarations indicating a reluctance to receive Lind impelled Stronge to assume the role of intermediary. The British minister convinced Huerta to meet the American emissary "as private citizens" for an "unofficial" exchange of views. Endeavoring to cool the tempers of both antagonists, Stronge met privately with Lind and Huerta, constantly urging a "conciliatory tone."[16] Lind was thoroughly aggravated by Stronge's advice, viewing the British minister as a supporter of Huerta.[17]

Stronge concluded that the Mexican-American dispute centered on Huerta's candidacy in the forthcoming elections. Despite his conviction that Huerta intended to continue in power, the British diplomat attempted to persuade the General to yield to the American remonstrances and renounce the presidency while retaining command of the army. Stronge regarded this as a concession to form, advising the Foreign Office that Huerta was "indispensable for the moment" and that "any Government resulting from the elections could only

---

15 Stronge to Grey, July 5, 1913, FO 414/235.

16 Stronge to Grey, August 12, 18, and 19, 1913, FO 414/235.

17 Lind to Bryan, August 10, 1913, Lind Papers; and Lind to Bryan, August 16, Wilson Papers, File II.

succeed with his active support." [18] Although he would have preferred that Huerta retain the presidency, Stronge concluded that if the General relinquished this office all other questions with the United States could be settled, and Lind apparently endorsed this view. But the British envoy's efforts failed to break the deadlock.

The day after Huerta's coup of October 10, the new British minister, Sir Lionel Carden, presented his credentials to the Mexican President. Lind and Wilson interpreted this as an endorsement of the dictatorship. This conclusion brought the policies of the United States and Britain into direct conflict. Obviously, the United States would find it necessary to terminate British support of Huerta if it was to have any prospect of forcing him from office.

The very appointment of Carden had aroused concern in Washington. A career diplomat experienced in Latin America and fluent in Spanish, Carden had enthusiastically promoted British commercial interests during previous tours in the region. The resulting conflicts with American concessionaires had given him an anti-American reputation, and the United States had twice unsuccessfully protested his actions. [19] Carden was also closely associated with Lord Cowdray and owned land on the Isthmus of Tehuantepec near Cowdray's railroad. Carden's presentation of his credentials especially incensed John Lind, a strong Anglophobe who saw a plot in every British action. Lind contended that British oil interests planned the coup to coincide with the minister's arrival and that only British support enabled Huerta to continue in office. [20]

On his part, Carden was alarmed by the Mexican situation. The minister feared that Wilson's policy aimed at nothing less than the "gradual extension of the Monroe Doctrine up to the point of implying a right of suzerainty over Latin America." Naturally, he considered such an action detrimental to British interests. Like his predecessor, Carden was convinced that Huerta offered the only prospect for stability, and he considered supporting anyone else "absolutely suicidal." [21]

[18] Stronge to Grey, August 22 and 23, 1913, FO 204/419.

[19] Information on past protests includes Knox to William Phillips (London), April 22, 1910, 701.4114/3A; and Page to House, December 27, 1913, Wilson Papers, File II.

[20] Lind to Bryan, October 8, 1913/9127, October 15/9218, October 25/9401, and October 23/9355. On the basis of these notes, Bryan informed Page: "Carden seems to be Huerta's chief reliance in opposing this government's demands," Bryan to Page, November 9, 1913/10437.

[21] Carden to Grey, September 12, 1913, FO 414/235.

In view of his conviction that the continuation of Huerta in power comported with British interests, Carden tried to promote a settlement of the Mexican-American dispute. The British minister sought a face-saving way for Huerta to accede to American demands for his retirement and yet retain control of the country by continuing in command of the army. As the initial step, Carden approached Huerta, urging a conciliatory line regarding the upcoming elections. It was at Carden's suggestion that Huerta issued the statement renouncing his candidacy and pledging that all votes for him would be nullified.[22] Carden regarded this as a significant concession and hoped that the United States government would view it as an indication that Huerta would yield if allowed to do so discreetly.[23] Sir Ralph Paget, Assistant Under Secretary for Foreign Affairs, commented: "Unless the United States government entirely disbelieve all assurances given by Huerta this should appease them."[24]

The Wilson administration, however, adamantly refused to compromise with Huerta, and instead of welcoming the British conciliation attempts, Bryan tried to persuade the Asquith government to alter its stand. The Secretary bluntly informed Spring-Rice that "it was impossible for the President to go back on the policy which he had announced," and he insisted that the British government aid the Americans in forcing Huerta from office. Spring-Rice remained unmoved by Bryan's efforts, noting that Senator Henry Cabot Lodge and State Department Counselor John Bassett Moore advocated support of Huerta.[25] Wilson and Bryan regarded the British conciliation efforts as encouragement to the Mexican President, and Bryan informed the British embassy that the attitude of the Foreign Office was "likely to encourage him [Huerta] in his lawless conduct."[26] This statement astounded the British. Noting that Huerta's coup of October 10 was a "matter of internal politics which does not affect our relations with Mexico," the Foreign Office concluded: "There seems to be some confusion in the minds of the United States as to our attitude." Paget opined: "The United States Government seems to be suffering rather from nerves. They do not seem exactly to know what to do and what

[22] Carden to Grey, October 23, 1913, FO 204/419.
[23] Carden to Grey, October 27, 1913, FO 204/421.
[24] Foreign Office Minute by Paget, October 24, 1913, FO 371/1677.
[25] Spring-Rice to Grey, August 19, 1913, FO 204/421.
[26] Spring-Rice to Grey (transmitting a memorandum by Ernest Scott, first secretary of the British embassy), October 23, 1913, FO 371/1677.

they mean to do themselves but they want us to do it with them."[27] Accordingly, Sir Edward Grey telegraphed the British embassy in Washington bluntly: "I do not understand the Secretary of State's statement that our attitude is likely to encourage Huerta in his lawless conduct." Observing that Britain would await the outcome of the Mexican elections before taking further steps, Grey concluded: "To reserve our decision can hardly be described as encouraging Huerta," and he directed: "This should be explained to [the] Secretary of State."[28] Bryan's complete disregard for Grey's arguments brought the British to their first realization that Wilson's stand was based exclusively on moralism and hence that the Americans were unlikely to propose any "practical suggestion."[29]

American newspapers severely criticized Carden's frequent conferences with Huerta, igniting a public furor that raged during these diplomatic negotiations. The American press charged that Carden was a tool of Lord Cowdray, implying that oil interests were dominating British policy in Mexico. Grey informed Ambassador Page that he "resented these attacks" upon his minister in Mexico, noting that Carden's actions were entirely proper.[30] The American government, however, had already concluded that the presence of Carden in Mexico was inimical to its policy; hence officials continued to give credence to these newspaper reports. Bryan directly accused the British of allowing the Cowdray oil firm to influence their policy in Mexico and even implied that the British were acting exclusively at the behest of Cowdray. Grey shrewdly replied that he had also heard rumors that United States policy in Mexico was dictated by Standard Oil but that he had not given the slightest credence to these reports.[31]

In London, Page had launched a virtual crusade to convert the British government and secure the recall of Carden. He constantly espoused the President's policy, even discussing it with the King. Page was firmly convinced of the superiority of Wilson's moralistic

[27] Foreign Office Minute by Gerald Spicer, October 24, 1913, FO 371/1677; and Foreign Office Minute by Paget, October 24, FO 371/1677.

[28] Grey to Spring-Rice, October 27, 1913, FO 371/1677.

[29] Foreign Office Minute by E. H. J. Leslie, October 29, 1913, FO 371/1677; and Spring-Rice to Grey, October 29, FO 204/421.

[30] New York *Times* and New York *World*, both October 24 and 25, 1913. Grey to Carden and Spring-Rice, October 28, 1913, FO 204/421, reporting a conversation with Page.

[31] Spring-Rice to Grey, October 29, 1913, FO 204/421; and Grey to Spring-Rice, November 11, 1913, FO 204/421.

policy and reported, "These things are not in the European ruling vocabulary."[32] In the ambassador's view, Wilson was rescuing Latin America from European domination, for "in a few years these states would have been bound up hand and foot and the Monroe Doctrine would have been as dead as Hector."[33] Page considered the British "dense" about the "obligations of democracy" and naively told Wilson, "I never expected to have the holy joy of putting the British government through an elementary course in the meaning of democracy."[34] He informed Sir Edward Grey that the United States would intervene militarily to "make 'em vote and live by their decisions" and that if this failed to produce the desired results, "We'll go in and make them vote again." He indicated a willingness to shoot a few Latins to convert them to democracy, if this proved necessary. Sir Edward laughed heartily at this remark, undoubtedly wondering how the dead men could vote.[35]

The European powers were increasingly exasperated in the face of the American position, for all agreed that stability was the most urgent need in Mexico and that Huerta provided the greatest prospect for domestic tranquility. Exchanges among the powers were stimulated by Bryan's request for a withdrawal of recognition of the Mexican government in protest against the coup. The Spanish government suggested joint representations by the European powers, urging Washington to support Huerta. Although the British Foreign Office had concluded that "everybody except the United States Government is agreed that General Huerta is the only hope for Mexico," British diplomats considered it "highly improbable that the United States Government will listen to reason."[36] Grey informed the Spanish ambassador that

feeling was running very high in the United States, that the press there had worked up an apprehension that European Powers meant. to interfere in Mexico in a way contrary to what was called the Monroe Doctrine, and that . . . in the present state of feeling any concerted action by the European Powers in Washington . . . would

[32] Page to Wilson, October 25, 1913, Burton J. Hendrick, *The Life and Letters of Walter H. Page* (3 vols.; Garden City, N.Y.: Doubleday, Page and Company, 1922–1925), I, 184–185.
[33] Page to House, December 23, 1913, Wilson Papers, File II.
[34] Page to Wilson, November 22, 1913, Hendrick, *Life and Letters of Walter H. Page*, I, 185.
[35] Undated Memorandum by Page (apparently November, 1913), *ibid.*, I, 188.
[36] Foreign Office Minute by Leslie, October 20, 1913, FO 371/1677.

be very much resented and would produce an effect contrary to that desired.[37]

The Foreign Secretary informed other governments that he was convinced the Wilson administration was "quite irreconcilable as regards Huerta" and hence that joint action would be "worse than futile."[38] Grey therefore prevented a joint *démarche* by the European powers and Japan. The European governments did, however, agree to follow the lead of the French and reply to Bryan's notes by stating that withdrawing recognition would constitute intervention in internal Mexican matters.

In an effort to obtain greater insight into Wilson's views and the prospects for altering them, Grey dispatched his private secretary, Sir William Tyrrell, to Washington in November, 1913. Accompanied by Ernest Scott, first secretary of the British embassy, Tyrrell conferred with House and Wilson, informing them that Grey had directed Carden to avoid interfering with American policy. Tyrrell found himself confronting the Wilson-Bryan rigidity. The British envoy reported that Bryan was "very suspicious" of Carden and noted: "Nothing Mr. Scott or I could say seemed to make any impression on the Secretary of State."[39] Bryan reiterated earlier allegations that British policy was based on oil and dictated by Lord Cowdray. Tyrrell commented: "That's just what the Standard Oil people told me in New York. Mr. Secretary you are talking just like a Standard Oil man. You are pursuing the policy which they have decided on. Without knowing it you are promoting the interests of Standard Oil."[40] Bryan, however, rejected these arguments, adamantly refusing to alter his stand.

Tyrrell concluded that Wilson was "committed to getting rid of the Mexican President or any nominee of his" and found that the American President was unable to suggest any alternatives to Huerta. Wilson's policy remained essentially negative, and his only objective was to "teach the Latin American Republics to elect good men." Tyrrell was convinced that Wilson was willing to resort to military intervention to

[37] Foreign Office Minute by Grey, October 29, 1913, FO 414/235, reporting a conversation with the Spanish ambassador in London on October 27; and further answers by Grey to Carden, October 30, FO 371/1677, and Grey to Sir E. Goschen (Berlin), October 27, FO 204/421.

[38] Foreign Office Minute by Grey, October 29, 1913, FO 414/235.

[39] Tyrrell to Grey, November 8, 1913, FO 371/1678.

[40] House to Page, November 14, 1913, House Papers.

oust Huerta and that he desired to justify this action by citing European support of Huerta.[41] In Tyrrell's view, Wilson's contention that ousting Huerta would bring stability and constitutional government to all of Central America by example implied a "*de facto* American protectorate" over the region. The British envoy felt that although Wilson "did not seem to realize" this implication, "others" in the government did and regarded this as the ultimate aim of American policy in Mexico. While Tyrrell found this prospect alarming, he realistically concluded that Britain had "neither the intention nor the power to oppose this policy" and hence that the British must "live with" the American domination of the region.[42] The exchange of views made possible by Tyrrell's visit gave American and British diplomats a clearer view of each other's objectives. Colonel House concluded that Tyrrell's assurances had allayed the President's suspicions of British motives, while Page considered Tyrrell "a changed man" after his return.[43] But although these exchanges had cleared the atmosphere, they failed to reconcile the positions of the two governments.

Wilson and Bryan continued their attempts to compel the Foreign Office to alter Britain's neutral stand and openly oppose Huerta. The Americans desired the British and other European powers to formally notify Huerta that they would not oppose American policy in Mexico, for Wilson and Bryan believed that such a declaration would force Huerta to retire. Wilson also reiterated his proposal that Britain withdraw recognition of Huerta. The Foreign Office considered this proposal "without precedent" and noted that international practice did not sanction withdrawal of recognition for matters of internal politics. Accordingly, British diplomats concluded: "Mr. Bryan's views seem most impractical and unreasonable."[44]

Subtly linking the canal-tolls controversy to Mexico, Wilson applied pressure on the British. As the leading maritime nation, Britain naturally objected to the provision exempting American merchant vessels engaged in coastal trade from tolls in the soon-to-open Panama Canal. Although Wilson privately assured the British ambassador that he

[41] Tyrrell to Grey, November 8, 1913, FO 371/1678.

[42] Tyrrell to Grey, November 14, 1913, FO 371/1678.

[43] Page to House, undated (November, 1913), Charles Seymour, ed., *The Intimate Papers of Colonel House* (3 vols.; Boston and New York: Houghton Mifflin Company, 1926), p. 198.

[44] Foreign Office Minutes, all dated November 10, 1913, by Leslie, Langley, and Nicolson, FO 371/1678.

favored repeal of this law, he delayed action to avoid injecting a divisive issue during congressional debates on key domestic legislation.[45] Wilson remained silent on the canal tolls until March, 1914, and hence held the measure in abeyance throughout the period of controversy over Mexico, employing it as a lever to alter the British stand. The President refrained from directly linking the two issues, but he and Page implied a relationship by stressing that public opinion would be the crucial factor in the congressional vote on the Panama tolls and noting that press reports of a conflict over Mexico were arousing sentiment against England.[46]

These American statements literally compelled the British to choose between Huerta and the United States, for the Wilson administration made it clear that the British could not retain the friendship of both governments. This presented the British government with a cruel dilemma in view of the deteriorating situation in Europe. The British fleet depended heavily on Mexican oil, and the ability to obtain it would be a crucial factor in the event of conflict. On the other hand, the British would also need American support and trade.

In view of the evident determination of the Wilson administration, the British reversed their position in November, 1913, and formally notified Huerta that they could not support him against the United States.[47] Grey apprised Page of this declaration, and Bryan promptly expressed his gratification.[48] Prime Minister Asquith publicly proclaimed the new policy in the course of an address, stressing that it represented only a slight modification by noting that there never had been any possibility of British intervention in Mexico; hence a British-American confrontation in that country was impossible.[49] Lord Cowdray made several visits to the American embassy in London to deny that he was supporting Huerta and to declare that he would refrain from seeking new concessions in Mexico. Because of American objections, Cowdray's partner relinquished newly obtained grants from the government of Colombia and terminated negotiations with

[45] Bryce to Grey, April 24, 1913, FO 414/235.

[46] Page to Bryan, October 21, 1913, SD 811f.812/428, and December 9, 1913, SD 701.4112/10; Page to House, December, 27, 1913, Wilson Papers, File II; and George Macaulay Trevelyan, *Grey of Fallodon: The Life and Letters of Sir Edward Grey, afterwards Viscount Grey of Fallodon* (Boston: Houghton Mifflin Company, 1937), pp. 207–208. The tolls exemption was repealed June 15, 1914.

[47] Grey to Carden, November 10, 1913, FO 204/421.

[48] Spring-Rice to Grey, November 13, 1913, FO 371/1678.

[49] London *Times*, November 11, 1913.

Ecuador. Thus, the man the Wilson administration regarded as the prime mover behind British policy in Mexico completely bowed to American wishes in matters of new concessions.

While the British had agreed to support American policy in Mexico, the Foreign Office renewed its efforts to serve as a channel of communication. In this manner, the British hoped to prevent chaos in Mexico by securing an orderly transfer of government when Huerta left office. Carden resumed negotiations with Huerta, informing him that the British regarded his retirement as essential and that his only chance lay in consenting to this course and negotiating with the United States for a face-saving way of relinquishing office. The British assumed that the Americans desired only the elimination of Huerta and hence would be willing to make concessions in other respects to obtain the General's retirement. Huerta submitted a proposal that was forwarded to Washington through British diplomatic channels. The Mexican President offered his retirement following new elections, although he intended to retain command of the army.[50] While Wilson and Bryan had indicated a desire to negotiate with Huerta, they considered this plan entirely unacceptable. The Americans viewed the proposal as a ploy to gain time and at first simply ignored it. Embarrassed by the American silence, the British formally requested a response. Wilson informed the British ambassador that he considered Huerta's proposals "so absurd that he does not deem them worthy of any reply." Grey consequently informed Carden: "His Majesty's Government can do no more in the matter."[51] Wilson's action caused the Foreign Office to conclude that the Americans had "no intention of negotiating with Huerta in spite of what they have said about wishing to provide a dignified retreat" and: "The United States cherish very sinister designs toward Mexico and desire that a condition of complete anarchy should supervene."[52]

The decision to dispatch the West Indies cruiser squadron to Mexican waters to protect British property caused new tension. Bryan objected to the presence of these warships in Veracruz, where an American flotilla was anchored, and so the ships proceeded to other Mexican

[50] Carden to Grey, November 21, 1913, FO 414/235; and Grey to British embassies in Rome, Berlin, Tokyo, Madrid, and Paris, reporting that Huerta made proposals to the United States through Carden, November 24, FO 204/421.

[51] Grey to Spring-Rice, December 1, Spring-Rice to Grey, December 2, and Grey to Carden, December 3, 1913, FO 414/235.

[52] Foreign Office Minutes by Spicer, December 1 and 3, 1913, FO 371/1678.

ports. The British commander, Rear Admiral Sir Christopher Cradock, outranked the commander of the larger American squadron, Rear Admiral Frank Fletcher; and as senior officer, Cradock would command any joint military action. Lind viewed this as another British plot, but the situation merely reflected American promotion policy. Fletcher was the third-ranking officer in the American navy, while Cradock was a "junior" admiral in the British navy. The United States insisted that Cradock waive his right of precedence. Despite the objections of the Admiralty, the Foreign Office ordered Cradock to leave the scene of any action to enable Fletcher to assume control.[53] This move was specifically designed to placate the Americans. Wilson and Bryan resented the fact that Cradock visited Mexico City and dined with Huerta shortly after his arrival on the Mexican coast. Cradock openly praised Huerta and condemned Wilson's policy. The Mexican press and government hailed his squadron as a counterpoise to American naval units, thus adding to the American reaction.[54]

Despite Britain's reluctant compliance with American policy, the Wilson administration continued to regard the presence of Sir Lionel Carden in Mexico as a symbol of British opposition. Lind and O'Shaughnessy constantly reported that Carden tried to frustrate American policy, but they were unable to furnish conclusive evidence despite Bryan's frequent requests.[55] The Secretary instructed Page to demand Carden's recall, but the ambassador declined to lodge a formal protest, citing the failure of a previous attempt.[56] Page had launched a subtle campaign, drawing Carden's name into every discussion of the Panama tolls question, informing Sir Edward that Carden had alienated many senators. The ambassador refrained from citing particulars but stressed that Americans considered Carden anti-American, and that regardless of the veracity of this view, the widespread conviction to this effect would hinder Wilson's efforts to arrange the canal tolls in a manner satisfactory to Britain.[57] At length, Page learned that Carden would be recalled, but his telegram advising the State Department "leaked"

---

[53] For the American protests, Lind to Bryan, November 27, 1913/9931, Bryan to Lind, December 3/10152, Bryan to Page, December 13/10169A, and December 15/10237B; and for the British reactions, Grey to Carden, December 17, FO 414/235.

[54] *El País*, December 3, 1913; and *El Imparcial*, December 2, 1913.

[55] Bryan to O'Shaughnessy, December 16, 1913/10206; Bryan to Lind, December 16/10185; and Lind to Bryan, December 17/10239.

[56] Bryan to Page, December 9, 1913, 701.4112/10; and Page to House, December 27, Wilson Papers, File II.

[57] Page to House, December 27, 1913, Wilson Papers, File II.

and appeared in the papers the same day.[58] Naturally, the British government immediately denied the report and announced that Carden would return to London only for consultations.

Carden remained in London until April 8, and after his return to Mexico, the British government announced his transfer to Brazil. Inevitably, there were questions in Parliament about yielding to American pressure, but Grey contended that the envoy was originally sent to Mexico only for one year during the period of crisis and was now being transferred to a more prestigious post.[59] The Wilson administration considered this a tremendous victory.

The British endeavored to comply with American wishes in Mexico but found this difficult in view of the absence of a positive American policy. Grey concluded that Wilson was now compelled to force Huerta from power, because his pronouncements had "created a situation in which the personal credit of the President and Secretary of State was involved." In this sense, Huerta's retirement had become a "point of honor for the United States." [60] But while the British avoided involvement in domestic Mexican matters, they were hard pressed to determine exactly what the Wilson administration desired. Sir Arthur Nicolson, the permanent Under Secretary, concluded that the British could do little until Wilson produced "some definite and positive line of policy" and added: "It is difficult to understand what the United States Government do want." [61]

In February, 1914, a new crisis developed when Francisco Villa executed William S. Benton, a British citizen. Villa claimed Benton had attempted to assassinate him and was convicted by a court-martial, but all indications pointed to outright murder. The death aroused great excitement in Britain, for the government frequently dispatched troops to protect its nationals in similar cases. Grey agreed to permit the United States to make representations to Villa, and the British government faced a storm of protest when Villa refused to allow an

[58] Page to House, January 8, 1914, SD 701.4112/13, for the "leak"; and New York *World* and Washington *Post*, January 6, 1914; and New York *Times*, January 7, 1914.

[59] Spring-Rice to Wilson, quoting Grey's statement in Parliament, March 20, 1914, Wilson Papers, File II. Huerta fell from power before Carden left Mexico, and when the revolutionaries entered Mexico City, Carranza ordered Carden out of the country within twenty-four hours.

[60] Grey to Carden, January 28, 1914, FO 204/434.

[61] Foreign Office Minutes by Nicolson, January 31 and February 4, 1914, FO 371/2025.

investigation. The British press charged that since the United States had armed the Mexican revolutionaries it bore the ultimate responsibility for Benton's death.[62] Sir Edward's statement in Parliament implied that he would demand the trial of Villa if the Constitutionalists proved victorious, although he refrained from enunciating this explicitly in deference to Bryan's request.[63]

Page observed that the incident revived the "universal feeling" in England that the "Constitutionalists are mere bandits."[64] Grey warned the ambassador that to support Villa would be a "horrible anti-climax" to the American idealism. Page noted: "If half the crimes that are charged to Villa by correspondents and everybody here who has been to Mexico are true, to hope for his assassination is a pious exercise."[65] Wilson replied: "There has been less disorder and danger to life where the Constitutionalists have gained control than there has been where Huerta is in control."[66] This statement seemed incredible to Europeans in view of Villa's mistreatment of foreigners. British newspapers continued to focus on the fact that if Benton's murder reflected his progovernment sympathies, the lives of all foreigners in Mexico were in jeopardy. The London *Times* commented: "Even the [Wilson] administration seems at last to be waking up to the fact that the Constitutionalist leaders need something besides wings to become political angels."[67] But Wilson continued to disregard Constitutionalist atrocities. When O'Shaughnessy reported that he feared "anarchy and the commission of indiscriminate atrocities" in the event of a revolutionary triumph, Wilson, in a rare outburst, wrote "Rats W. W." on the dispatch.[68] The furor in Britain merely revealed that the government could exert little influence in Mexico in the face of

[62] Page to Bryan, February 24, 1914/10964; and Grey to Spring-Rice, February 26, FO 204/434. For the British press reaction, London *Times*, February 23 and 27, 1914, and New York *Times*, February 24 and March 4, 1914, quoting British papers. Regarding the resulting questions in Parliament, London *Times*, February 24, 26, and 27, 1914, and numerous questions referred to the Foreign Office for answer, FO 371/2025, *passim*.

[63] For exchanges regarding Grey's statement, Grey to Spring-Rice, February 28, 1914, FO 204/434, Page to Bryan, February 28, SD 321.41/153, Bryan to Page, March 1, 321.41/153; and for Grey's statement, Page to Bryan, March 4, 321.41/206.

[64] Page to Bryan, March 4, 1914, SD 321.41/169.

[65] Page to Wilson, May 1, 1914, Wilson Papers, File II.

[66] Wilson to Page, June 1, 1914, Hendrick, *Life and Letters of Walter H. Page*, I, 228–230.

[67] London *Times*, April 13, 1914.

[68] O'Shaughnessy to Bryan, April 28, 1914, Wilson Papers, File II.

American opposition. The British were compelled to confine their actions to remonstrations to the United States to exert whatever influence they could on Villa and Carranza.

Thus the British, while thoroughly abhorring the Wilsonian position in Mexico, realized that they were powerless to oppose it and reluctantly complied with American wishes. Although they regarded Wilson's policy as hopeless, they were forced to abandon efforts to alter it after several futile attempts at mediation revealed the stubborn determination of the American President. The Wilson administration had accordingly removed another obstacle to its policy and advanced its objective of isolating Huerta from foreign support. When coupled with other Wilsonian measures, this further cleared the way for firm action in Mexico.

Wilson's patience was wearing thin; but the knowledge that he was free to act without interference from Britain now increased his propensity to take drastic steps to terminate the Mexican imbroglio. Carden had warned the Foreign Office: "The relations of the United States and Mexico . . . have reached a phase not unlike that which immediately preceded the Spanish-American war, in which an untoward incident, even of relatively small importance, might bring about an outbreak of hostilities at a day's notice." [69] This observation proved very perceptive.

[69] Carden to Grey, September 12, 1913, FO 414/235.

IX

Direct Action and Confused Intervention

On the morning of April 9, 1914, a whaleboat pushed off from the U.S.S. *Dolphin*, flagship of Rear Admiral Henry T. Mayo, commander of the American squadron at Tampico. Mexico's second-ranking port, Tampico was a small city that owed its economic and strategic significance to the surrounding oil fields. Located on the Pánuco River, ten miles from the Gulf, the city was besieged by the Constitutionalists. Despite a momentary lull in the fighting, the combat would inevitably resume whenever the revolutionists elected to renew their attack. A tense air prevailed along the federal defense perimeter. The whaleboat flew the American flag fore and aft as a precaution, for it turned from the river into the canal that skirted the edge of the city—the first American vessel to enter this defense zone since the siege began. The dinghy proceeded to a wharf near the warehouse of Max Tyron, where the men began loading cans of gasoline. Frequent courier boat runs between the *Dolphin* and the *Connecticut*, which was unable to enter the shallow river because of its deep draft, had exhausted the Americans' fuel supply. Lieutenant Commander Ralph T. Earle, captain of the *Dolphin*, had accepted Tyron's offer to replenish the stock. Normal sources of supply were not available because the rebels controlled the refinery areas on the outskirts of the city. The wharf was less than a hundred yards from Iturbide Bridge and the defense perimeter. The federals anticipated the main assault at this point, and sentries scanned all approaches.

Shortly after the whaleboat docked, a squad of Tamaulipas State Guard troops arrived. The Mexican officer gestured to the two men stowing the gasoline cans aboard the whaleboat to join their companions on the wharf, for the Americans spoke no Spanish. When the sailors hesitated, the Mexicans leveled their rifles at them and Ensign Charles C. Copp, the whaleboat commander, then directed the men to leave the boat. Tyron, who spoke Spanish, protested, but the Mexican officer replied that he had orders to arrest anyone in the area without a pass and therefore must consult his superiors. The Americans were taken a short distance up the street to the headquarters of Colonel Ramon H. Hinojosa, the sector commander. Hinojosa informed Copp through an interpreter that the Americans had entered a sector that was under military jurisdiction and hence closed to all unauthorized personnel. Hinojosa ordered the Americans returned to complete their loading but detained at the dock until he obtained permission for their release from the commander of Tampico, General Ignacio Morelos Zaragoza.[1]

Upon learning of the arrest from Tyron, Mayo ordered Commander Earle to protest to Morelos Zaragoza. Consul Clarence Miller accompanied Earle to the federal commander's headquarters. Morelos Zaragoza was "dumfounded" when Earle explained the incident. The federal commander readily apologized, adding that the men involved were state troops and were "evidently ignorant of the first laws of war."[2] He immediately ordered the release of the Americans, and the detained men were allowed to return to their ship within an hour of their arrest. Those involved in the incident considered it minor. The officer of the watch recorded it in the ship's log as an afterthought. It seemed no more important than an incident of the previous night when federal troops detained a marine courier at Iturbide Bridge, near the same point. In that instance, Admiral Mayo accepted the apologies of the federal commander, explaining that the courier had become lost while traveling from the Consulate to the *Dolphin*, although the gunboat's anchorage was in the opposite direction.[3] It is possible that the courier sought to cross federal lines with a message for the Constitutionalists, a factor which would explain Mayo's lack of protest.

With the release of the whaleboat's crew, the incident seemed closed—to everyone except Admiral Mayo. To him, the overriding

---

[1] Clarence Miller (Tampico), "Political Conditions at Tampico," May 21, 1914, PR Tampico, 800/1089; and statements by Ensign Charles C. Copp and Max Tyron to Lieutenant Commander Ralph T. Earle, all April 9, 1914, RG 45/659.

[2] Statements of Copp and Tyron; and Miller, "Political Conditions."

[3] Ignacio Morelos Zaragoza to Mayo, and Mayo to Morelos Zaragoza, April 8, 1914, RG 45/659.

consideration was that American sailors were removed at gunpoint from an American ship. The Admiral regarded a vessel flying the American flag as sovereign territory of the United States and therefore construed the affair as an insult to the flag. He also erroneously concluded that marching the men down a city street had publicized the arrest. Mayo did not consider it necessary to consult Washington, for he regarded the matter as a local one. He failed to inform Rear Admiral Frank Fletcher in Veracruz until after he took action. Mayo lacked direct wireless contact with the United States, and even Fletcher's ships could reach Key West only at night and for short periods.[4]

The Admiral dispatched Commander William A. Moffett to deliver a strong protest to Morelos Zaragoza. Mayo's note declared that removing men from a boat flying the American flag was a "hostile act not to be excused," adding that "responsibility for hostile acts cannot be avoided by a plea of ignorance." He sought reparation rather than investigation, demanding a "formal disavowal" and "apology" conveyed by suitable officers of Morelos Zaragoza's staff and punishment of the officer involved. Referring to the "publicity" of the event, he also stipulated that Morelos Zaragoza would be required to "hoist the American flag in a prominent position on shore and salute it with twenty-one guns," promising that the salute "will be duly returned by this ship." He allowed the federal commander twenty-four hours to comply.[5] The Mexican General promptly replied that such steps would require the permission of higher authorities, and Mayo extended the deadline another twenty-four hours.[6] Morelos Zaragoza had considered the incident insignificant and reported it to the Ministry of War only after Mayo's protest. Throughout the controversy, Morelos Zaragoza disputed Mayo's contention that the arrest constituted an insult to the American flag. In his initial report, the Mexican commander denied that the whaleboat flew the American flag, a stand which he consistently maintained throughout the controversy.[7] Naturally, the Mexican Foreign Office accepted his report.

[4] Robert E. Quirk, *An Affair of Honor: Woodrow Wilson and the Occupation of Veracruz* (Lexington, Ky.: University of Kentucky Press, 1962), pp. 18–19 and 24–25. The British Foreign Office had concluded earlier that Mayo "seems a most injudicious person," based on the reports of Admiral Cradock, Foreign Office Minute, January 1, 1914, FO 371/2025.

[5] Mayo to Morelos Zaragoza, April 9, 1914, RG 45/659.

[6] Quirk, *An Affair of Honor*, pp. 25–26.

[7] Morelos Zaragoza to Blanquet, April 10 and 18, 1914, AREM, L.E. 796, leg. 17 (90–R–17), f 34–35 and 105.

Consul Miller considered Mayo's demands excessive. He had understood that Earle's acceptance of Morelos Zaragoza's explanation closed the incident and regarded this apology as sufficient. Yet Miller could not oppose the Admiral and found himself even unable to protest, for Mayo's radio constituted the consul's only contact with Washington. At Tampico, the navy had superseded the State Department.[8]

Mayo's message to Fletcher at 5:00 P.M. contained only the barest outline, and since he neglected a full report for several days, President Wilson remained unaware of the precise details of the affair. Wilson received the news during a weekend at White Sulphur Springs, West Virginia.[9] There were many things on his mind: his wife's illness, the impending marriage of his daughter Eleanor to Secretary of the Treasury William G. McAdoo, the mining strike in Colorado, and the selection of the members of the newly created Federal Reserve Board—a matter Wilson considered of vital importance. Bryan informed him: "I do not see that Mayo could have done otherwise."[10] The matter did not disturb Wilson, for with scanty information the President had little cause for concern. He never mentioned the incident to McAdoo, who was with him, for as usual Wilson did not seek advice. Wilson concurred with Bryan's conclusion that "Mayo could not have done otherwise." The President directed O'Shaughnessy to press Mayo's demands "with the utmost earnestness, firmness and frankness," stressing the "extreme seriousness" of the incident and emphasizing that "unless the guilty persons are promptly punished consequences of [the] gravest sort might ensue." Wilson thus took the matter partly out of Mayo's hands. He informed Bryan that Lansing would "supply you with the precedents," *i.e.*, precedents to rationalize the course Wilson had already selected.[11] The Chief Executive was not interested in precedents that might suggest an alternate course.

O'Shaughnessy received his first news of the incident from Mexican Subsecretary of Foreign Relations Roberto Esteva Ruiz. The chargé was completely unaware of the demands that Esteva Ruiz requested be withdrawn.[12] O'Shaughnessy hastened to confer with Huerta, accompanied by the Mexican Subsecretary. While Esteva Ruiz was in charge

[8] Miller, "Political Conditions."

[9] Quirk, *An Affair of Honor*, pp. 28–29 and 32.

[10] Bryan to Wilson, April 10, 1914/11633a.

[11] Wilson to Bryan, April 10, 1914/11483.

[12] Roberto Esteva Ruiz to O'Shaughnessy, April 10, 1914/11659.

of the Foreign Office in the absence of the minister, he had never met Huerta, and the American chargé found it necessary to introduce the two Mexican officials.[13] O'Shaughnessy obtained a statement from Huerta and then released the news to reporters. The chargé identified the sailors as "marines" and inadvertently stated that the men were "paraded" through the streets, implying a deliberate attempt to publicize the incident.[14]

Mayo's demands astounded the chargé. Huerta promised an investigation, and Esteva Ruiz had already reported the arrest of Colonel Hinojosa. Both depicted the incident as a minor misunderstanding. In response to a query from the San Francisco *Examiner*, Huerta dismissed the affair with the comment: "The Tampico incident is of no particular importance."[15] O'Shaughnessy could "not quite understand such an ultimatum being issued without superior authority, in view of the tense situation now existing."[16] Secretary of the Navy Daniels concurred. Although Mayo was one of his favorites, he felt that the Admiral had exceeded his authority. Daniels, however, "found that in the State and Navy Departments I was almost alone in feeling that Mayo, when apologies were promptly offered, should have accepted them."[17] Colonel House reached the same conclusion and convinced the President to instruct Mayo to consult Washington in any future situations.[18] Wilson, however, had already resolved to seize this instance as a new opportunity to press Huerta.

Bryan desired a compromise, fearing that a firm stand would result in open conflict, yet he took no action to promote an agreement. The Secretary of State failed to send instructions to O'Shaughnessy and Mayo.[19] O'Shaughnessy's telegram cheered Bryan; and noting that Huerta's attitude appeared conciliatory, the Secretary assured reporters that the "greater includes the less" and opined that Mayo would undoubtedly accept the apology and rescind his demand for a salute.[20] Bryan never indicated his view to Mayo. The same day that Bryan issued his statement, the Admiral moved the cruiser *Des Moines*

[13] Quirk, *An Affair of Honor*, pp. 38–40.

[14] New York *Times* and New York *World*, April 11, 1914.

[15] San Francisco *Examiner*, April 16, 1914.

[16] O'Shaughnessy to Bryan, April 10, 1914/11484.

[17] Josephus Daniels, *The Wilson Era: Years of Peace: 1910–1917* (Chapel Hill, N.C.: University of North Carolina Press, 1944), pp. 188 and 191.

[18] House Diary, April 15, 1914.

[19] Quirk, *An Affair of Honor*, pp. 42–43.

[20] New York *Times* and New York *World*, April 12, 1914.

close to shore, her decks cleared for action. Bryan advised Wilson: "Mr. Lansing thinks that the fact that our marines were violating martial law in landing without notice or asking permission is a fact that ought to be taken into consideration." The Secretary of State cautioned: "If that is true we cannot demand as much as we could have demanded if we were clearly within our rights," but the President remained adamant. Wilson insisted, "The salute will be fired," on his return to Washington.[21] He was not concerned with the details of the incident. He directed O'Shaughnessy to renew the demand for full compliance with Admiral Mayo's conditions and then set out for the golf course.

Esteva Ruiz formally notified the embassy that the Mexican government could not accede to Mayo's demands, contending that a salute would offend Mexican national dignity.[22] Thus both nations cited national dignity as the basis for their stands. This factor was far more important for Mexico—small nations, especially those in Latin America, always being more sensitive about their sovereignty. Huerta perceived that an appeal to national dignity might revive his sagging prestige. Once again, the United States had "come to his rescue" by supplying an opportunity to assume his pose as defender of the nation. He was prepared to risk armed intervention by the United States, for the Americans had already resorted to everything short of this to oppose him. A limited intervention might rally the revolutionists to his standard and unite the country behind him. If it was a remote possibility, it nonetheless constituted his only hope.

On April 14, Wilson conferred with John Lind, who had advocated direct action and urged the seizure of Mexican Gulf ports for some time. British observers attributed the strong American stand exclusively to Lind's influence. Spring-Rice reported that Lind was using "very violent language."[23] Like the President, Lind ignored the consequences of seizing ports, for both were firmly convinced that the Mexican people would welcome American troops as liberators from Huerta's cruel domination. One hour after his talk with Lind, Wilson convened the Cabinet for a briefing on the Mexican crisis. The next day he explained his policy to members of the congressional committees on foreign relations. The President did not request advice at either session.

[21] Bryan to Wilson, April 13, 1914, Wilson Papers, File II; New York *World*, April 14, 1914, for Wilson's statement.
[22] O'Shaughnessy to Bryan, April 12, 1914/11486.
[23] Spring-Rice to Grey, April 16, 1914, FO 371/2027.

After the Cabinet meeting, Wilson ordered the Atlantic Fleet to proceed to Mexico, although he had refrained from informing the Cabinet of his intention.[24] The Counselor of the State Department assured him that he had sufficient constitutional authority to employ the military to enforce demands. Lansing had also found a precedent in the shelling of Greytown (San Juan del Norte), Nicaragua, in 1854 in retaliation for an insult to the United States consul there.[25]

Wilson issued a press statement on April 15, charging the Mexican government with "studied contempt" toward the United States and citing two more insignificant "incidents." Wilson asserted that an American sailor had been "arrested and put into jail," when in reality neither had occurred.[26] On April 10, a Mexican soldier accosted a seaman from the U.S.S. *Minnesota*, apparently mistaking him for a marine deserter. A police officer escorted both men to the local precinct, where an interpreter clarified the matter in minutes. The incident did not even appear in the ship's log, and Admiral Fletcher found "no cause for complaint," but the consul had incorrectly reported the sailor's arrest.[27] The President was obviously unaware of Fletcher's report and ignorant of newspaper accounts of the "incident." The second "incident" stemmed from the telegraph censorship imposed by Huerta in the wake of the Tampico crisis. The censor inadvertently detained a message from Bryan to O'Shaughnessy but released it upon the chargé's request. Although the delay was a mere fifty-five minutes, Wilson chose to interpret the misunderstanding as interference with official United States government dispatches.[28] His statement indicated that the crisis would continue even if Mexico saluted the flag at Tampico. Commenting on the President's pronouncement, the London *Times* noted that Huerta had always been "meticulously correct" in his exchanges with the United States and concluded: "Mr. Wilson is utterly misinformed when he depicts Señor Huerta as determined to insult the United States."[29] Sir Ralph Paget of the Foreign Office summed up the British attitude with the observation: "The United

[24] Quirk, *An Affair of Honor*, pp. 50–51.

[25] Robert Lansing, Memorandum, April 14, 1914/11510½. All available navy ships in West Coast ports were also dispatched to Mexican waters, San Francisco *Examiner*, April 16, 1914.

[26] New York *Times*, April 16, 1914.

[27] Canada to Bryan, April 12, 1914/11478; and Fletcher to Daniels, April 16/11559.

[28] O'Shaughnessy to Bryan and Bryan to O'Shaughnessy, April 12, 1914, SD 119.23/a and 119.23/1.

[29] London *Times*, April 17 and 18, 1914.

States are making a good deal out of very minor grievances."[30] Reporters noted that Wilson appeared angry at his press conference of April 15.[31] When Colonel House arrived in Washington on April 14, Dr. Grayson informed him that the President was upset "because of the acuteness of the Mexican crisis" and also "felt Eleanor's marriage keenly." House "went to bed tired and uneasy about Mexico."[32]

While Americans, responding emotionally, generally endorsed Wilson's stand, the reaction abroad was quite the reverse. Congress and the domestic press overwhelmingly endorsed the President's actions. In Argentina, Brazil, and Chile, the press agreed that the Tampico incident was of minor significance and that the American demands were completely unwarranted.[33] German papers ridiculed the American position. The London *Chronicle* noted wryly that the arrest of a few marines affected American policy more than the numerous atrocities perpetrated during a full year of civil war.[34] Citing the mistreatment of foreigners by the Constitutionalists, the London *Times* commented pointedly that Wilson's firm stand over the Tampico incident was "curiously inconsistent with the way in which he turned the other cheek after the one had received General Villa's rebuffs."[35] The *Evening Post* concluded: "President Wilson's policy is not quite intelligible to observers outside the United States."[36]

While O'Shaughnessy attempted to secure an agreement on the original grievance, the administration in Washington seemed to be extending the crisis. Huerta stressed that Mexican dignity would not allow the firing of the salute; and O'Shaughnessy reported, "The old Indian was more eloquent than I have ever seen him."[37] The chargé used his friendship with Huerta to the utmost and finally secured a "concession" at a conference before a diplomatic reception in Chapultepec Castle on April 15, when the Mexican President agreed to a simultaneous salute.[38] The British considered this an "admirable" idea that

[30] Foreign Office Minute by Sir Ralph Paget, April 17, 1914, FO 371/2027.

[31] New York *Times*, April 16, 1914.

[32] House Diary, April 14, 1914.

[33] *El Mercurio*, April 21 and 25, 1914, quoting *La Prensa*, *La Razón*, and the *Journo do Brazil*.

[34] New York *Times*, April 16, 1914, referring to German press comment; and New York *World*, April 17, 1914, quoting the *Chronicle*.

[35] London *Times*, April 27, 1914.

[36] New York *World*, April 17, 1914, quoting the *Evening Post*.

[37] O'Shaughnessy to Bryan, April 14, 1914/11514.

[38] O'Shaughnessy to Bryan, April 15, 1914/11522.

"speaks well for Mr. O'Shaughnessy's tact."[39] Wilson, however, immediately rejected this plan, since it omitted the public apology he demanded. The issue remained Huerta's desire to save face and Wilson's determination to humiliate his opponent. Rejection of a simultaneous salute caused considerable comment in Europe. The London *Times* concluded that the entire affair was "rather a quibble." The *Times* regarded it as "unthinkable" that a dispute regarding the technicalities of firing the salute should prevent agreement.[40] When O'Shaughnessy reported that Huerta refused to yield further, Bryan rushed this message to Wilson. The President left his golf course, meeting Bryan for a roadside discussion. Afterward, Wilson returned to the White House and composed a new ultimatum warning that if Huerta did not fire the salute by 6:00 P.M. the next day, he would lay the matter before Congress "with a view to taking such action as may be necessary to enforce the respect due to the nation's flag."[41]

Foreign Secretary José López Portillo y Rojas reiterated Mexico's fear that the United States would not return the salute and requested O'Shaughnessy to sign a protocol guaranteeing it. The chargé agreed.[42] The Mexican proposal was based on a suggestion by the British chargé, who acted in view of American pledges assuring that the salute would be answered.[43] That evening, Portillo y Rojas returned to the embassy with a document that exonerated the Mexicans of all guilt and implied recognition of the Huerta government. O'Shaughnessy obviously could not sign it, and when he reported the matter, Bryan instructed him to reject any protocol.[44] Mexican fears were well founded, for although United States ships had frequently fired salutes to Mexico since Huerta assumed office, a reluctance had recently developed. When the gunboat *Zaragoza* visited New Orleans, the United States forts failed to return its salute. Although Bryan admitted that precedent required the return of the salute and Daniels had previously instructed Mayo to do so, navy regulations forbade firing salutes to unrecognized governments.

But by this time, the salute was of little importance. Wilson had

[39] Foreign Office Minute by E. H. J. Leslie, April 16, 1914, FO 371/2027.

[40] London *Times*, April 18, 1914.

[41] Quirk, *An Affair of Honor*, pp. 63–65; and Bryan to O'Shaughnessy, April 18, 1914/11540.

[42] O'Shaughnessy to Bryan, April 18, 1914/11555.

[43] Hohler to Grey, April 16, 1914, FO 204/431.

[44] O'Shaughnessy to Bryan, April 18, 1914/11555; and Bryan to O'Shaughnessy, April 19/11555.

mobilized American forces and aroused American public opinion, and it was too late to alter his course. The initial erroneous reports that the United States had agreed to the Mexican proposal for a simultaneous salute prompted the San Francisco *Examiner* to comment: "The magnificent American fleet apparently has been assembled for the ridiculous purpose of saluting the Mexican flag. . . ."[45] The President himself professed to be alarmed by press advocacy of military action, which contributed to the growing popular feeling.[46] Yet all Wilson's actions during the crisis, eagerly grasping at every possible "affront" to increase the tension, indicated that he intended to use this incident as a pretext for armed intervention.

It was obvious that the United States would take military action in Mexico, and Tampico seemed the logical point. Mayo had prepared plans for the seizure of the city, although the navy Board preferred declaring a belligerent blockade of Mexico and did not recommend the occupation of ports "as an initial measure."[47] Lansing advised Wilson against declaring war on Mexico or securing any resolution from Congress that could be so construed, for that "would seem to be substantially a recognition of the Huerta government."[48] Wilson wished above all to avoid recognition of Huerta, even if the recognition came in the act of removing him by force.

The situation changed abruptly on April 19. Consul William Canada constantly observed the landing of arms shipments at Veracruz as part of the American surveillance of Huerta's sources of supply. On April 18, Canada reported that the Ward liner *Mexico* delivered one thousand cases of ammunition and that the German liner *Ypiranga* would arrive shortly with two hundred machine guns and fifteen million cartridges.[49] Wilson feared this shipment would enable Huerta to prolong his rule and might even be employed against American troops. He determined to intercept these munitions, and in so doing, forgot the Tampico incident. At 2:00 P.M. on April 20, Daniels ordered Mayo to withdraw his ships from the river and send all but the *Dolphin* to Veracruz. Admiral Badger was directed to proceed to Veracruz with the Atlantic Fleet at full speed, for he had been cruising toward

[45] San Francisco *Examiner*, April 17, 1914.

[46] Wilson's observation was reported in the Indianapolis *News*, April 20, 1914.

[47] Quirk, *An Affair of Honor*, pp. 68–69; and Daniels to Bryan, April 18, 1914 /18617.

[48] Lansing to Bryan, April 19, 1914, 711.12/30½.

[49] Canada to Bryan, April 18, 1914/11547.

Tampico slowly to keep the flotilla intact. Badger could not possibly arrive at Veracruz in time to intercept the arms shipment, but the squadron at Tampico could.[50] The order, which contained no explanation, shocked Mayo, and he requested a confirmation. Mayo and his officers were "downcast and despondent" when they notified Miller of the new directive. Miller could not understand the obvious abandonment of the Americans in Tampico. Mayo's orders were confirmed in the morning, and he informed Miller,"I am helpless."[51] The delay had removed all possibility of his ships arriving at Veracruz in time to aid the landing. Fletcher requested only the *San Francisco* and the *Chester*, but Mayo dared not return the gunboat to the river for fear that the Mexicans would interpret this as a landing attempt.

President Wilson addressed Congress on April 20, requesting a resolution authorizing the use of the armed forces, even though this was unnecessary. He stressed that he would take action against Huerta, not against the Mexican people, but he gave no indication of what steps he contemplated. In addition to a salute to the flag, Wilson demanded a "new spirit" that would preclude the recurrence of similar "incidents." Declaring his intention to "enforce respect for our government," he received a standing ovation. The House promptly passed Wilson's resolution, but Senate Republicans proposed a stronger substitute that stressed the protection of American lives and property, something Wilson had neglected to mention. The resulting debate caused a delay, and thus Wilson failed to secure congressional approval in advance, for the Senate passed the resolution after American troops had landed at Veracruz.[52]

When Canada reported that the *Ypiranga* would arrive in the morning, Wilson ordered the seizure of the customs house at Veracruz.[53] The United States military attaché noted: "This, of course, was a typical civilian order. The taking of one building in the center of a fair-sized city without taking the remainder of the town, is naturally somewhat of a problem, if the native population does not entirely resemble a flock of goats."[54] At Veracruz, Admiral Fletcher acted with dispatch despite the limited size of his force. There were only three vessels

[50] Quirk, *An Affair of Honor*, pp. 70–73.

[51] Miller, "Political Conditions."

[52] Quirk, *An Affair of Honor*, pp. 73–77.

[53] Canada to Bryan, April 20, 1914/11564; and Daniels to Fletcher, April 21, Daniels Papers, Miscellaneous File.

[54] Burnside to AGWAR, May 6, 1914, WD 5761–974.

under his command, and since the battleships *Utah* and *Florida* were too large to enter the harbor, only the gunboat *Prairie* was inside the breakwater. The landing party, composed of marines and bluejackets, contained merely 787 men. Yet the day was ominously dark, and Fletcher feared a storm, which would prevent the launching of boats from the battleships outside the harbor. Therefore, he decided to strike with the forces at hand instead of delaying in the hope that Admiral Badger might arrive in time. He directed Consul Canada to notify Military Governor General Gustavo Maass, as the first boats left the warships, that the Americans would seize only the port area.[55]

The Americans encountered no initial resistance as they clambered ashore, but they were soon engaged by Mexican troops and therefore were compelled to occupy the entire city. Maass sent a small detachment to offer token resistance and distributed arms to the citizens of Veracruz and prisoners in the military jail. He could field only one thousand troops, for his garrison was thinned to supply reinforcements for Tampico. The Minister of War's order to evacuate the city arrived after the engagement had begun. Mexican resistance was haphazard, and the Americans suffered only light casualties despite poor tactics that moved men in groups.[56] Throughout the night, ships trickled in from Tampico and the Atlantic Fleet, and at dawn about three thousand men were ashore. At 11:00 A.M., the city was in American hands.

The *Ypiranga* arrived at 1:30 P.M. on April 21, at the height of the fighting, and was temporarily detained. An officer from the *Utah* boarded her and informed the captain that he would not be permitted to land his cargo or leave the port. Bills of lading aboard the vessel indicated that the arms were purchased in New York and shipped to Germany as a ruse. The administration made strenuous efforts to trace the source of the load and the agent who purchased it. It also attempted to intercept other shipments en route to ports controlled by Huerta's forces. The State Department requested the Ward line to divert the *Monterrey*, which had cleared New York with arms for Huerta, and deposit its cargo at Havana.[57] Upon receipt of the news that Fletcher had detained the *Ypiranga*, Bryan apologized to German Ambassador Count Johann von Bernstorff. Since no state of war existed, the United

---

[55] Quirk, *An Affair of Honor*, pp. 85–103.

[56] Gustavo Maass to Blanquet, April 22, 1914, AHDN XI/481.5/315, Caja 148.

[57] Long to Bryan, April 21, 1914, 812.113/3450; and Bryan to Long, April 21, 812.113/3451.

States had no right to detain the ship.[58] The *Ypiranga* left Veracruz and landed its arms at Puerto Mexico on May 27. Thus Huerta received the munitions despite the seizure of Veracruz. Subsequent shipments to Puerto Mexico stimulated rumors that the United States would occupy this port. But while the original aim of seizing Veracruz was to prevent the landing of the *Ypiranga*'s cargo, Wilson lost sight of this objective once the occupation was effected, just as he had forgotten the Tampico incident.

Wilson had ordered the landing in the conviction that Mexicans would welcome the Americans, and news of the bloodshed shocked him. Senator Lodge found him greatly agitated, and he appeared "pale, parchmenty," and "positively shaken" when he received reporters. He confided to Grayson: "The thought haunts me that it was I who ordered those young men to their deaths."[59] Members of his administration shared this view. Secretary Daniels read the first dispatches "with ill-concealed agitation," while Bryan rushed to the White House excitedly with the initial reports.[60] Speaking at funeral services for the sailors and marines killed at Veracruz, Wilson revealed his disillusion by stating: "We have gone down to Mexico to serve mankind if we can find a way."[61]

News of the invasion caused a sensation in Mexico, for thanks to Huerta's censorship, Mexicans learned of the incident at Tampico only one day in advance of the landing. Initial details appeared in the *Diario Oficial* and Mexican papers on April 20, and in these reports, Portillo y Rojas denied that the whaleboat flew the American flag. The government charged that Mayo proposed to seize and neutralize the port of Tampico and dubbed this a second Tampico incident.[62] News of the American landing at Veracruz brought a flood of patriotic sentiment, and Mexicans rallied around Huerta to defend their country. Large numbers of workers volunteered for military training to resist the Yankee invaders. Anti-American demonstrations erupted throughout Mexico. In Monterrey, a mob led by a federal officer attacked the American consulate general and tore down, trampled, and burned the American flags. Consul General Philip Hanna was imprisoned,

---

[58] Quirk, *An Affair of Honor*, pp. 98–99.

[59] Henry Cabot Lodge, *The Senate and the League of Nations* (New York: Charles Scribner's Sons, 1925), p. 18; and Admiral Cary Travers Grayson, *Woodrow Wilson: An Intimate Memoir* (New York: Holt, Rinehart and Winston, 1960), p. 30.

[60] New York *World*, April 22, 1914.

[61] New York *Times*, May 12, 1914.

[62] *Diario Oficial*, CXXXI, 43, 415–419, April 20, 1914.

although Constitutionalists released him next day when the federals evacuated the city. Vice Consul John Silliman was arrested at Saltillo on April 28 and detained until May 12, when he was deported. The State Department feared for other consuls, although eventually they all emerged unharmed. Demonstrations in Tampico endangered Americans in that city. Admiral Mayo could not risk re-entering the river, for that would seem to signal the start of landing operations. The British cruiser *Hermione* and the German cruiser *Dresden*, which were on the river, took the Americans aboard. The Americans thought they were being removed temporarily to allow a landing but were shipped to the United States. They were unprepared for this and did not desire to leave their homes in Tampico. As a result, they were extremely bitter about their treatment. In the midst of these problems, Bryan caused a panic in the State Department when he inadvertently sat on the push buttons on his desk while talking to a reporter. Messengers and aides rushed into his office from all directions in a state of great agitation.[63]

Upon receiving news of the landing at Veracruz, Huerta immediately severed diplomatic relations with the United States, handing O'Shaughnessy his passports on April 22.[64] Huerta's son escorted the chargé to Veracruz to guarantee his safety. O'Shaughnessy left American affairs in charge of the British legation, an act which displeased Wilson due to the previous clash between the two nations over Mexican policy. Bryan directed the chargé to place the Brazilian legation in control of American affairs, for Brazil, like the United States, had not recognized Huerta.[65] O'Shaughnessy replied that Brazilian Minister Cardozo de Oliveira had indicated that he would leave the country if O'Shaughnessy received his passports. The Brazilian minister was scarcely on speaking terms with Mexican officials, who resented Brazil's support of the United States stand.[66] Bryan, however, arranged to transfer custody of American interests to the Brazilian legation.[67]

Foreign reaction to the United States landing reversed previous stands. Throughout Latin America, the press condemned the action as

[63] New York *Times*, April 28, 1914.

[64] Portillo y Rojas to O'Shaughnessy, April 22, 1914, *Diario Oficial*, CXXXI, 47, 451; and O'Shaughnessy to Bryan, April 22, 123Os4/122.

[65] O'Shaughnessy to Carden, April 23, 1914, 703.4112/4; O'Shaughnessy to Bryan, April 26, 703.4112/4; and Bryan to O'Shaughnessy, April 24, 703.3212/17b.

[66] O'Shaughnessy to Bryan, April 22, 1914, PR Mexico City, 1914, XIV, Cl. 800.

[67] Lansing to Dominico da Gama (Brazilian ambassador in Washington), April 28, 1914, 703.3212/44.

intervention. In Chile, *El Mercurio* observed editorially that the United States had committed a grave error, for there was no possibility that occupation of the port could in itself oust Huerta. The paper noted that the Wilson administration was unlikely to make the "superhuman sacrifice of recognizing its error." *El Mercurio* felt that Wilson had not given proper consideration to the situation before acting and agreed with *La Prensa* that the President's address to Congress explaining his position appeared to be a justification "improvised on a summer night."[68] Student demonstrators rioted before the United States legation in Montevideo, while Paraguayan labor union leaders proclaimed a boycott of United States products. The British press supported the initial landing, viewing it as the intervention that it had long advocated. The Foreign Office found the limited American objectives as incomprehensible as the entire controversy over the Tampico incident. When Bryan informed Spring-Rice that the United States "had no intention of making war or advancing into the interior," Sir Arthur Nicolson, the permanent Under Secretary, commented: "Of course the United States are in fact at war with Mexico. Mr. Bryan talks nonsense."[69] Wilson's contention that his actions were directed only against Huerta, and not the Mexican people, caused Paget to observe: "President Wilson has certainly a peculiar way of doing things."[70]

Huerta issued a decree of amnesty on the day of the landing to allow all Mexicans to unite to "defend the national territory," but despite isolated instances of revolutionaries joining the federals to oppose the Americans, the principal leaders remained aloof.[71] Huerta decreed a new military decoration, The Order of the Second North American Invasion. In the north, Mexican troops evacuated frontier cities in anticipation of a full-scale invasion by the United States. General Álvaro Obregón considered combining forces with Huerta's troops to repel the Yankee invasion, but Carranza rejected this course. Zapata announced that he would aid Huerta against the Gringos but soon changed his mind. Infuriated by revolutionary refusal to suspend the civil war in the face of the American intervention, the Huertista Congress enacted long-contemplated statutes depriving Morelos of statehood

[68] *El Mercurio*, April 25, 26, and 27, 1914.

[69] Foreign Office Minute by Nicolson, April 22, 1914, FO 371/2027.

[70] Foreign Office Minute by Paget, April 23, 1914, FO 371/2027.

[71] Huerta's decree is dated April 21, 1914, Gobernación, Asuntos Varios, 1913–1914. For indications of the negotiations between rebel leaders and the government, AREM, L.E. 797, leg. 16 (90–R–33), *passim*; William Blocker to Bryan, April 23, 1914/11648; and George Carothers to Bryan, April 22/11618.

and dividing Chihuahua into two territories to punish these states for harboring the Revolution.[72]

In the United States, there was fear that the revolutionaries and federals would jointly attack border cities. The resulting panic along the frontier enraged General Bliss, who wrote General Scott:

> Every time a Mexican gets "tanked up" with mescal and informs the by-standers in forcible but rude and impolite language what he proposes to do to the Gringos when the proper time comes, everybody in the community thinks that Huerta is just around the corner. They make no attempt to employ additional policemen or to swear in deputy sheriffs or to stop the lucrative sale of arms and ammunition or do anything to help themselves. . . . A one-eyed, one-legged, rheumatic, octogenarian Mexican with a wooden gun, would make them throw up their hands. Every old woman in South Texas who has lost a hair pin, claims that a detachment of Mexican troops came over and robbed her. The situation thus far, is one that calls for horse whips, cold douches or whatever remedies are resorted to in lunatic asylums.[73]

Carranza wired Wilson "inviting" him to "suspend the hostile acts already initiated."[74] This was another surprise to Wilson, who had expected the Constitutionalists to welcome American aid. Wilson sent assurances to Carranza, explaining that his action was directed solely at Huerta. The revolutionary leader rejected these explanations, contending that whatever the justification, the seizure of a port constituted a violation of Mexican sovereignty that injured the entire Mexican body politic.[75] Villa supported the American action and broke with Carranza, although the wily rebel chieftain was only seeking to curry favor in Washington in the hope of obtaining supplies and backing against Carranza.[76] In view of Carranza's attitude, the administration reimposed the arms embargo on April 27.[77]

[72] *El País*, May 14, 1914.

[73] General Tasker H. Bliss to General Hugh Scott, April 27, 1914, Scott Papers.

[74] George Carothers to Bryan, April 22, 1914/11618, relaying Carranza's message.

[75] For the exchanges between Wilson and Carranza, Carranza to Carothers, April 22, 1914, AREM, 44–17–187, f 2–4; Carothers to Bryan, April 22/11618; S. Gil Herrera to Carranza, April 23, AREM, L.E. 861, leg. 2 (121–R–5), f 80; and undated Memorandum by the revolutionary Ministry of Foreign Relations, Isidro Fabela, ed., *Documentos históricos de la Revolución Mexicana* (12 vols. to date; Mexico: Fondo de Cultura Económica and Editorial Jus, 1960–1967) II, 44–46.

[76] Carothers to Bryan, April 9, 1914/11461.

[77] Adjutant General to Bliss, April 27, 1914, AG 2150626.

Wilson had ordered the seizure of Veracruz with no idea of advancing further inland. The landing had failed to oust Huerta, although it rendered his position more precarious. Once again, the President proposed to wait for this new action to take full effect by depriving Huerta of supplies. He needed an excuse to halt the fighting but retain possession of Veracruz. Accordingly, when mediation was proposed, he jumped at the chance to hold negotiations with a government he did not recognize.

X

The Niagara Falls Conference

On April 25, 1914, the representatives of Argentina, Brazil, and Chile in Washington offered to mediate the United States-Mexican dispute. The Wilson administration accepted immediately, for the American President was unnerved by the fighting at Veracruz and desired an excuse to confine military operations to that city.[1] Indeed, British dispatches indicate that the Wilson administration undoubtedly suggested mediation to the ABC powers as a means of extricating itself from the Veracruz situation.[2] When the proposal reached Mexico, Huerta indicated that he would prefer British mediation to that of the three South American republics, since the ABC states had refrained from recognizing his government.[3] The British, however, declined to proffer their good offices in view of the obvious American preference for the ABC powers. British Minister Sir Lionel Carden urged Huerta to honor the mediation proposal, and he accepted on April 27. Carden's persuasion was the key factor in Huerta's decision, and Bryan had specifically requested British aid in securing Huerta's assent.[4] The British Foreign Office found this American plea ironical, and Paget observed: "After all the abuse heaped on Sir L. Carden in the United States it is somewhat humorous to see them so ready to avail themselves of his good offices and friendship with Huerta."[5] Carranza accepted the offer "in principle," and his reservation seemed the only ill omen.[6]

[1] Dr. Dominico da Gama, Dr. Romulo S. Naón, and Eduardo Suárez Mújica to Bryan, and Bryan to same, April 25, 1914/11744C.

[2] Spring-Rice to Grey, April 25, 1914, FO 371/2027.

[3] Carden to Grey, April 27, 1914, FO 204/431.

[4] Spring-Rice to Grey, April 25, 1914, FO 371/2027, for Bryan's request for Carden's aid in securing Huerta's acceptance of mediation; and Carden to Grey, April 27, FO 204/431 (two dispatches with same date), for the British minister's efforts.

[5] Foreign Office Minute by Sir Ralph Paget, April 29, 1914, FO 371/2027.

[6] Carranza to mediators, April 29, 1914, Buckley Papers.

The South American press praised both Mexico and the United States for assenting to mediation, viewing this as a new departure in American policy. Latin Americans believed it foreshadowed cooperation between the United States and the ABC countries.[7] Nearly all papers in the United States hailed the mediation, although the Washington *Post* cautioned: "'Trust in God, but keep your powder dry' was Cromwell's sound advice. 'Hope for peace by mediation but keep the troops moving forward' is good counsel at this juncture."[8]

The mediators were Brazilian Ambassador Dr. Dominico da Gama, Argentine Minister Dr. Romulo S. Naón, and Chilean Minister Eduardo Suárez Mújica. Naturally, da Gama, as ambassador, served as chairman. Suárez and da Gama were career diplomats with broad experience, while Naón was an expert on international law. These eminent diplomats, all well regarded by their colleagues, sought an equitable solution to the crisis. The mediators desired a neutral site and selected Niagara Falls, Canada.

The agenda suggested by the ABC delegates confined the deliberations to the international conflict between the United States and Mexico, but the Wilson administration sought to include Mexican internal affairs. An undated communication to the mediators, probably sent on April 30, stated:

> The government of the United States feels itself bound in frankness to make the following confidential communication to the representatives of the Republics of Brazil, Argentina, and Chile. . . . No settlement could have any prospect of permanence or of proving acceptable to public opinion in the United States or to the practical judgement of the Government of the United States which did not include these features: First, the entire elimination of General Huerta; Second, the immediate setting up in Mexico of a single provisional government acceptable to all parties and pledged to proceed at once to the establishment of a permanent government.[9]

Obviously, the United States envisioned a much broader conference than that proposed by the mediators. Lansing stated:

> It must be borne consistently in mind that this is not a mediation between two established governments. . . . It is an attempt to restore

[7] *El Mercurio*, April 26 and 29, 1914, citing various papers in the ABC countries.

[8] Washington *Post*, April 29, 1914. For other newspaper comments, New York *Times*, April 26 and 27, 1914, which surveyed newspaper reaction throughout the country.

[9] Undated, unsigned Memorandum, Wilson Papers, File II.

peace between Mexican factions. . . . In reality, therefore, the mediation is between the factions, and not between the United States and either one of the factions. . . . Since neither faction in Mexico has been recognized, it would be contrary to the present policy of the United States to have an official representative in attendance.[10]

Because the United States desired to include internal affairs, Wilson wished Carranza to participate in the negotiations.

Huerta's selection of a delegation of prominent personages who were not identified with his regime indicated his desire for meaningful negotiations that would yield a settlement with the United States. Huerta named Emilio Rabasa, Agustin Rodríguez, and Luís Elguero as Mexican delegates to the conference. All were distinguished members of the upper class rather than Huertistas; indeed, Huerta was not even acquainted with them personally.[11] Rabasa, an expert on international law known as the "John Bassett Moore of Mexico," served as chairman of the delegation. William F. Buckley, an American lawyer who had an extensive practice in Mexico, acted as counsel to the delegation at the request of Rabasa, who was his consulting attorney in Mexico City. The American military attaché in Mexico City reported: the "Peace commissioners are no Huertistas or politicians but men having the confidence of educated and wealthy classes," while the British minister considered this delegation a "guarantee of good faith" on Huerta's part.[12] In Washington, the administration took the narrow view that everyone who accepted an office from Huerta was a Huertista. To John Lind, the Mexican delegates were "able men in argument, diplomacy, and duplicity."[13] This was a miscalculation, for the delegates were devoted to Mexico rather than to Huerta.

The Mexican President allowed the delegates considerable latitude. He caucused with them for only ten minutes, and the lengthy memorandum of "instructions" prepared by the Ministry of Foreign Relations merely reviewed the Tampico incident and the occupation of Veracruz. Huerta warned that the mediation should be confined to the United States-Mexican crisis and directed his representatives to

[10] Robert Lansing, "Memorandum on the Peace Conference of Mediators and Representatives to attend on behalf of the United States," May 1, 1914/11800½.

[11] Boaz Long to Bryan, May 9, 1914/11955½; and Nemesio García Naranjo, *Memorias de Nemesio García Naranjo* (8 vols.; Monterrey; Ediciones de *El Porvenir*, 1956–1962), VII, 313.

[12] Burnside to AGWAR, May 12, 1914, 5761–952; and Carden to Grey, May 5, FO 204/431.

[13] Lind to Bryan, undated (May, 1914), Wilson Papers, File II.

seek a settlement that provided a simultaneous salute of the flags by both countries and American compensation for the damages at Veracruz.[14] Yet he also instructed them to consult the Minister of Foreign Relations when they deemed it necessary, thereby allowing them to select the occasions for such consultation. Naturally, this suggested that the envoys were free to act on their own. None of the delegates even mentioned Huerta's proposals at the conference. Since Huerta had forced the retirement of his Minister of Foreign Relations, the Subsecretary, Roberto Esteva Ruiz, was in charge of the Foreign Ministry. But Esteva Ruiz had little contact with the delegates, for Minister of Hacienda Adolfo De la Lama assumed control of the negotiations. He discussed the conferees' proposals privately with Huerta and was the only minister involved, for the Cabinet did not convene during the entire conference. De la Lama communicated Huerta's decisions directly to Rabasa, and only routine confirmations were channeled through the Foreign Office. While the delegates needed Huerta's assent before formally signing any agreement, it was the delegation that initiated the proposals, and its members consistently rejected any instructions which they considered unrealistic.

Woodrow Wilson selected Associate Justice of the Supreme Court Joseph E. Lamar and Frederick W. Lehman, former solicitor of the Department of Justice, as the American representatives. At the suggestion of State Department Counselor Robert Lansing, Wilson designated the delegates as "Special Commissioners of the President of the United States near the Mediators." As unofficial representatives, they carried no credentials.[15] This title enabled the President to maintain the fiction that United States attendance at the conference did not constitute recognition of Huerta. Just as the United States had dealt with Huerta through the embassy for more than a year while denying recognition, its delegates would sit across a conference table from his representatives and negotiate with them while pretending that their government did not exist. The American delegates had no plenary powers—indeed, they had almost no powers and acted exclusively *ad referendum.* They conferred with Bryan by long-distance telephone nightly and constantly received detailed instructions by telegram. President Wilson controlled the negotiations personally, typing most of the instructions himself.

[14] Huerta instructions to the Mexican delegation, May 8, 1914; and unsigned, undated Memoradum by the delegation, Rabasa, Correspondencia.

[15] Bryan to Wilson, May 14, 1914/23493b, relaying Lansing's recommendation.

John Lind, serving as adviser to the State Department, provided the recommendations that guided American policy throughout the conference. The former "special agent" informed the President: "In dealing with Huerta it must not be lost sight of for a moment that we are dealing with a Frankenstein devoid of all moral judgement, ruled by appetite and passion, and guided by cunning." Lind advocated outright backing of Carranza and was certain that the "mediation will result in nothing." He feared the mediators would "regard the Mexican government as the principal factor in the Mexican situation," cautioning, "No compromise is possible."[16] Wilson accepted this advice, informing Bryan: "We cannot spare Lind while these mediation negotiations are in progress."[17] Lind also advised against pressing for a cessation of hostilities, contending that this would strengthen Huerta. Wilson heeded these warnings and opposed an armistice, which normally would be a prerequisite for any meaningful negotiations.

Lind played a pivotal role in the conference, for in addition to providing counsel that shaped American policy, he also served as adviser to the Constitutionalists. Thus, he simultaneously guided the policy of two different parties to the mediation. Lind conferred with Carranza's agents in Washington frequently, under the guise of providing liaison between the Constitutionalists and Bryan, but in reality to discuss policy.[18] The confidential agent kept the revolutionists fully informed about Wilson's plans and helped formulate the Constitutionalist position. Lind drafted many of Carranza's statements regarding the negotiations and consistently warned against an armistice.[19] The Constitutionalist agents in Washington considered Lind the Revolution's "most loyal and most important friend among the Americans."[20]

[16] Lind, Memorandum, April 30, 1914, Lind Papers.

[17] Wilson to Bryan, May 19, 1914, Bryan-Wilson Correspondence, II, 198.

[18] The New York *Times* reported frequent meetings between Lind and the Constitutionalist agents in Washington throughout the conference. Lind later told Bryan that he "did volunteer advice" to these agents, Lind to Bryan, July 14, 1914, Lind Papers.

[19] Lind's papers contain drafts he made of statements Carranza later issued, with notations that Lind wrote them, and also copies of the final statements, Lind Papers, undated Memorandum, the draft being the same as Carranza to Bryan, May 4, 1914/23426; and undated Memorandum, Lind Papers, being the same as a Carranza statement released to the press on May 27.

[20] Rafael Zubaran Capmany (Carrancista agent in Washington), to Carranza, June 19, 1914, Isidro Fabela, ed., *Documentos históricos de la Revolución Mexicana* (12 vols. to date; Mexico: Fondo de Cultura Económica and Editorial Jus, 1960–1967), III, 127–128.

It was largely due to Lind's efforts that the American stand at Niagara Falls became almost identical to that of the Carrancistas.

Difficulties began before the conference convened. On May 6, the Huerta government charged that the landing of arms and men at Veracruz violated the agreement to suspend hostilities. Bryan replied that the troops disembarked at a point under the control of the United States and would refrain from initiating any aggressive action.[21] Three days later, Mexico complained that the United States seized Lobos Island and imprisoned the lighthouse keepers. Bryan replied that the Mexicans had abandoned their post, compelling the United States to take charge. He offered to allow the Mexican lighthouse keepers to return, and Huerta assigned a new crew.[22]

On April 30, the mediators requested Carranza to suspend hostilities as a consequence of his acceptance of mediation, but he refused, thereby creating an impasse that threatened the conference at the very outset.[23] Carranza charged that Huerta had provoked the conflict with the United States intentionally, and therefore the revolutionary commander thought it "inconvenient" to suspend hostilities. He contended that the internal conflict was "independent" of the crisis with the United States.[24] The mediators considered Carranza's declaration "incompatible" with their proposal of good offices. Stressing that the discussions must encompass all matters contributing to the crisis, the ABC representatives informed the rebel leader: "If you should not so understand we would be compelled to withdraw as inofficious our invitation."[25] Carranza remained adamant. Since a substantial portion of his "troops" were revolutionary bands outside the organized Constitutionalist army, he would have difficulty holding them together during an armistice. Furthermore, leaders of the various small guerrilla forces might ignore a call for a cease-fire. The government columns, conversely, could have employed the lull in combat to train their recruits and hence improve the effectiveness of their forces. Consequently, Carranza could not agree

[21] Esteva Ruiz to mediators, May 4 and 5, 1914, Fabela, *Documentos históricos*, III, 39 and 46; and Bryan to mediators, May 8/23427.

[22] Esteva Ruiz to mediators, May 9, 1914, Fabela, *Documentos históricos*, III, 85; Bryan to mediators, May 12/23430; and Esteva Ruiz to mediators, May 14, Fabela, *Documentos históricos*, III, 86.

[23] Mediators to Carranza, April 30 and May 2, 1914/12631; and Carranza to mediators, May 3/12631.

[24] Carranza to mediators, May 3, 1914/12631.

[25] Mediators to Carranza, May 3, 1914/12631.

to a suspension of hostilities without weakening his position. Yet the mediators' stand was quite correct, for it would be pointless to hold a conference while the conferees continued fighting. Just as an armistice would hurt Carranza, prolonged combat would weaken Huerta, for the Constitutionalists were advancing.

The conference convened on May 20 in the Clifton House in Niagara Falls, and the mediators moved rapidly to secure a compromise. Before the inaugural session, the mediators informed the Huerta delegates that the only way to avert a complete revolutionary triumph was for Huerta to retire in favor of some neutral person acceptable to all and whom Woodrow Wilson would be willing to recognize. If Huerta refused to resign, the United States would lend its full support to the revolutionaries.[26] When the Huerta delegates reported this to the Minister of Hacienda, he assured them that Huerta would carry out his pledge to seek peace, "cost what it may," and that he would relinquish the presidency if necessary.[27] The ABC negotiators conferred with Lamar and Lehman immediately after the opening ceremonies, proposing that Huerta resign after appointing a man of "standing and character and of Constitutionalist principles" as Minister of Foreign Relations. An immediate cessation of hostilities, with United States agreement to embargo all arms shipments to Mexico, would permit the provisional government to conduct elections. The mediators suggested Pedro Lascuráin, Madero's Minister of Foreign Relations, as provisional President. Lamar and Lehman noted that the mediators seemed quite confident that Huerta would resign, and they assumed the Constitutionalists would win the election.[28] Bryan informed the delegates that the President was "pleased and encouraged by the character of the proposal" but would find it necessary to investigate Lascuráin's attitude before replying. In the meantime, the Secretary instructed the negotiators to present an American plan proposing a junta composed of Lascuráin, a Constitutionalist, and a third man chosen by these two. Bryan noted that this would "get away from the apparent succession to Huerta."[29]

[26] Undated, unsigned Memorandum by the Mexican delegation reporting a meeting May 18, 1914, in Washington, Rabasa, Correspondencia; Rabasa to De la Lama, May 15, Rabasa, Correspondencia.

[27] Nopalimpura (Subsecretary of Hacienda), to Rabasa, May 20, 1914, and Esteva Ruiz to Mexican delegation, May 20, Rabasa, Correspondencia.

[28] Lamar and Lehman to Bryan, May 20, 1914/23435.

[29] Bryan to Lamar and Lehman, May 21, 1914/23435.

On May 23, another plenary session convened to allow Rabasa to state:

President Huerta declares that if his separation from power is an element which can lead to a solution of the pending international questions and to the pacification of Mexico, he is ready to present his resignation because his sole purpose in continuing in power has been to secure peace according to the solemn promise he gave to the nation. But he presents as an indispensable condition for his resignation that it shall result in peace.[30]

Bryan concluded that Huerta's elimination was "clearly inevitable" and that:

The object of our conference now is to find a method by which the inevitable can be accomplished without further bloodshed. By the inevitable we mean not only the elimination of Huerta but the completion of the revolution by the transfer of power from Huerta to those who represent the interests and aspirations of the people whose forces are now in the ascendancy.[31]

At this point, the United States and the mediators switched positions on the structure of the provisional government. The United States, which had proposed a junta, now advocated a single provisional president and insisted that he must be a Constitutionalist.[32] The mediators, who had proposed a single president, now advocated a junta, consisting of a neutral president with four ministers: a Huertista, a Constitutionalist, an individual from Mexico City, and a resident from the north.[33] The United States pressed for a government composed entirely of Constitutionalists, although Bryan stressed that the United States did not advocate a direct transfer of government from Huerta to Carranza.[34] Da Gama commented that he must give "serious consideration" to whether the installation of a Carrancista regime was "within the spirit of the original proposal" of mediation.[35]

The conference was clearly deadlocked. The Washington *Post* opined:

[30] Dodge to Bryan, quoting official minutes of the Second Plenary Session, May 23, 1914/12421. Huerta approved Rabasa's statement, Nopalimpura to Rabasa, May 23, Rabasa, Correspondencia.

[31] Bryan to Lamar and Lehman, May 24, 1914/23452d.

[32] Lamar and Lehman to Bryan, May 25, 1914/23444.

[33] Lamar and Lehman to Bryan, May 26, 1914/12631.

[34] Bryan to Lamar and Lehman, May 26, 1914/12631.

[35] Lamar and Lehman to Bryan, May 26, 1914/12631.

If the situation at Niagara grows much worse, it will be up to the representatives of the Balkan States or some other disinterested and illustrious diplomatic agency to offer to mediate for the mediators. The A.B.C. negotiators are at loggerheads with the United States government regarding Carranza, and Carranza has just defied the United States. Huerta, as usual, defies them all. In this juncture, why should not Abyssinia, Servia, and Senegambia—the A.S.S. powers—tender their good offices? Send out the SOS for the A.S.S.[36]

Wilson, one could imagine, failed to see the humor of this and doggedly pursued his goal of teaching Mexico how to select a president. The President was "seriously disappointed" by the mediators' proposal of a junta encompassing all elements of the Mexican power structure. He stated that such a course would be unacceptable to the Constitutionalists and hence impossible, for they were the "victorious party." Bryan explained, "It would, in our judgment, be futile to set up a provisional agency which would be neutral." The Secretary considered the Mexican delegates "*científicos*" seeking to preserve their privileges from Carranza's reforms.[37] On his part, Huerta began having second thoughts about resigning, noting that the succession of government was not encompassed in the original mediation proposal.[38] Rumors of Huerta's resignation offer had appeared in the press, and Rabasa informed reporters that the General would retire as soon as the country was pacified, noting that this meant political rather than physical pacification. This announcement undermined Huerta's already precarious position in Mexico, while strengthening his diplomatic posture. The New York *World* praised Huerta's "important concessions," noting: "Men of his type do not as a rule surrender their personal pretensions."[39]

From the outset, the United States attempted to convince the mediators to admit Carrancista delegates to the conference without an armistice. On the second day, Lamar and Lehman proposed that the mediators extend a new invitation to Carranza, with no mention of a cease-fire. The mediators refused, stating that since Carranza had rejected the initial invitation, another "would not be consistent with the honor of the nations represented by the mediators nor with the dignity and prestige of the mediation."[40] They contended that negotiations would

36 Washington *Post*, June 3, 1914.

37 Bryan to Lamar and Lehman, May 27, 1914/23445.

38 Esteva Ruiz to Mexican delegation, May 27 and 29, 1914, Rabasa, Correspondencia.

39 New York *World*, May 29, 1914.

40 Lamar and Lehman to Bryan, May 22, 1914/23437.

be impossible while the revolutionaries continued to strengthen their position on the battlefield, especially after Huerta had weakened himself by pledging to relinquish his office. The mediators pointed out that the United States could easily impose a cease-fire by halting arms shipments to the Carrancistas, but Wilson would not consider this.[41] Lamar and Lehman reported that the mediators appeared "disappointed" over the failure to secure a cessation of hostilities.[42]

The Constitutionalists reiterated their opposition to an armistice and announced that they would send delegates only to discuss the United States-Mexican dispute. They indicated their intention to reject any provisional government, because Carranza considered it essential that he rule as head of a military regime to assure him adequate power to initiate reforms.[43] The first chief sent the mediators a letter to this effect only after he released it to the press, causing the ABC representatives to refuse to accept it. Only a concerted effort by Lamar and Lehman convinced Naón to receive Carranza's messenger alone.[44]

Wilson instructed the American delegation to inform the mediators that "no progress can be made toward a peaceful settlement . . . without considering the opinions and wishes of the Constitutionalists. If they are not to speak for themselves the burden of conferring with them is thrown upon us."[45] He was "seriously disturbed by the attitude of the mediators with regard to admitting representatives of the Constitutionalists to the conference."[46] When the mediators continued to insist on an armistice, Bryan informed Lamar and Lehman, "The President is not willing to stand for such a demand."[47] Wilson and Bryan contended that the ABC negotiators' insistence on a cease-fire indicated a prejudice against the Constitutionalists.[48] The American officials were oblivious of the fact that their own threat to speak for the Carrancistas exhibited an equal bias in favor of the revolutionaries. The mediators' views and those of the Wilson administration were exactly opposite. To Wilson's way of thinking, the problem of peace in

[41] Lamar and Lehman to Bryan, May 23, 1914/23439.
[42] Lamar and Lehman to Bryan, May 25, 1914/23444.
[43] New York *World*, May 29, 1914.
[44] Lamar and Lehman to Bryan, May 29, 1914, 23450; and Rabasa Diary, May 29, Rabasa, Correspondencia.
[45] Bryan to Lamar and Lehman, May 29, 1914/23452g.
[46] Bryan to Lamar and Lehman, May 31, 1914/23451.
[47] Bryan to Lamar and Lehman, June 2, 1914/23453a.
[48] Bryan to Lamar and Lehman, June 3, 1914/12631.

Mexico was a question of securing acceptance of the Constitutionalist "triumph." He rejected the idea that the Constitutionalists should yield anything, insisting that Huerta make all the concessions.[49] When the Chilean government supported its minister's insistence upon an armistice, Bryan retorted that the United States government felt the mediators should act as individuals, without consulting their governments.[50]

At length, the mediators were compelled to accede to the American proposal and dispatched a new invitation to Carranza, which made no mention of an armistice.[51] The revolutionary leader received the mediators' note coldly and proved reluctant to designate delegates. Carranza contended that the selection of a provisional president was an internal matter that was not a proper subject for discussion by the conference and continued to insist that only he could be the provisional president.[52] Wilson and Bryan found the first chief's intransigence incomprehensible. The Wilson administration hoped to end the combat in order to prevent further bloodshed and to save face by demonstrating to Europe that their diplomatic stance in favor of the revolutionaries could bring peace to Mexico. Having used pressure to convince the mediators to abandon their call for a cease-fire and invite Carranza to the conference, Wilson and Bryan now found it necessary to press the Constitutionalists to participate. While assuring the Carrancista envoys in Washington that the United States would support their interests and do everything possible to bring about a settlement favorable to the revolutionary faction, Bryan warned that a peaceful settlement through mediation was essential. The Secretary emphasized that the revolutionaries could achieve their objectives peacefully at the mediation conference, with the support of the United States. In the face of this pressure, Carranza reluctantly designated Rafael Zubaran Capmany and Luis Cabrera as delegates, but again the first chief stressed that they would be authorized to discuss only the international conflict.[53] The mediators would not formally admit the Carranza delegation to the conference but proposed to have them parley with the other negotiators privately.

[49] *Ibid.*

[50] Lamar and Lehman to Bryan, June 4, 1914/12631; and Bryan to Lamar and Lehman, June 4/12631.

[51] Dodge to Bryan, June 13, 1914/12240, and Zubaran to Carranza, June 8, Fabela, *Documentos históricos*, III, 114–116.

[52] Dodge to Bryan, June 15, 1914/12270.

[53] Zubaran to Carranza, June 8, 1914, Fabela, *Documentos históricos*, III, 114–116.

As if to keep things confused, the Constitutionalist representatives never went to Niagara Falls. Instead, they traveled to Buffalo, New York, and paused only to confer with the American delegates before departing. Lamar and Lehman expected the Constitutionalists to provide a list of acceptable presidential candidates. They received a rude shock when Zubaran and Cabrera informed them that the Plan of Guadalupe required that Carranza become president, thus precluding consideration of other candidates. The Carrancistas even refused to guarantee an election. They added that Carranza would reject the results of the mediation under any circumstances, even if the agreements favored his party. This stand infuriated the American delegates, who felt the Constitutionalists had "repudiated" and "deceived" them. Lamar and Lehman reported: "We are suddenly informed that Carranza too has all along opposed what we were seeking to accomplish in his behalf and would not accept it if we secured it. The way to save the situation is promptly to break with Carranza, proceed with the mediation, and let the future determine what is best to be done."[54] Bryan warned Zubaran that if Carranza persisted in rejecting negotiations, the United States would "look for another Constitutionalist" leader.[55] President Wilson's conviction that a Constitutionalist triumph was necessary prevented the adoption of this attitude. During the early days of his administration, Wilson would gladly have seized this opportunity to remove Huerta, with no concern about his successor, but now he insisted that Carranza must become president. If the revolutionaries would not attend the conference, then the United States delegation would speak for them. Bryan was pleased to have this "excuse" to do so.[56] Wilson was so firmly convinced that only the Constitutionalists would bring democracy to Mexico that he saw nothing unusual about spreading democracy by installing a government that refused to pledge to hold elections.

As the conferees continued to explore plans for the creation of a provisional government, Wilson raised new objections. John Lind reminded him that if a provisional president assumed office by being named Huerta's minister of foreign relations, this might imply recognition of the Huerta government.[57] Wilson immediately informed the

[54] Lamar and Lehman to Bryan, June 18, 1914/23478.

[55] Zubaran to Carranza, June 19, 1914, Fabela, *Documentos históricos*, III, 127–128.

[56] Bryan to Wilson, undated, Wilson Papers, File II.

[57] Lind to Bryan, May 29, 1914, Bryan Papers.

American delegation that this method of installing the provisional president would prove unacceptable, since it would imply Huerta's right to transfer an office the United States contended he held illegally. Wilson proposed that Huerta resign and Lascuráin succeed him "as if by right." [58] That such a plan was unconstitutional did not bother Wilson. Under the Mexican Constitution, only the ranking minister could succeed to the presidency. The mediators secured a compromise providing that the United States would recognize the provisional government the day it assumed office, avoiding mention of the method of its ascension to power. [59] Once again the patience and good sense of the mediators had prevented the collapse of the conference.

The mediators found it impossible to secure agreement on the structure of the provisional government. While the Mexicans accepted the mediators' proposal for a neutral president with ministers representing both of the conflicting parties, the American delegates demanded a Constitutionalist provisional president. Huerta had agreed to appoint any neutral designated by the conferees as foreign minister before resigning, enabling him to accede to the presidency under the Constitution, but the General could hardly be expected to transfer his powers to a member of the revolutionary party. [60] When Buckley noted that the United States had previously agreed to a neutral president, Bryan replied, "When you can't keep a promise you can't keep it, and that is all there is to it." [61] The United States also proposed a three-man electoral commission and insisted that two of its members be Constitutionalists. [62] The Mexican negotiators rejected this plan.

The mediators considered a neutral president essential and threatened to terminate the conference if the United States persisted in its stand. [63] The Mexican delegation was also prepared to walk out in protest. [64]

[58] Bryan to Lamar and Lehman, May 29, 1914/23446.

[59] Lamar and Lehman to Bryan, June 11, 1914/12631.

[60] Mexican delegation to mediators, June 8, 1914; and Rabasa Diary, June 8, 1914, Rabasa, Correspondencia.

[61] United States Senate, Committee on Foreign Relations, *Investigation of Mexican Affairs*, 66th Cong., 2d sess. (2 vols.; Washington: U.S. Government Printing Office, 1921), Testimony of William F. Buckley, December 6, 1919, pp. 794–795.

[62] Dodge to Bryan, June 16, 1914/12288.

[63] Lehman, Memorandum of a conversation with Elguero, June 9, 1914/12631; Rabasa Diary, June 9, and Rabasa to De la Lama, June 16, 1914, Rabasa, Correspondencia.

[64] Esteva Ruiz to Mexican delegation, June 14, 1914, Rabasa, Correspondencia.

Despite these reactions, Woodrow Wilson remained adamant, and Bryan informed Lamar and Lehman:

> The President is so convinced of the fairness and reasonableness of the plan he has proposed, namely, agreement upon a Constitutionalist for provisional president and upon an electoral commission containing two Constitutionalists and one of the opposition, that he does not feel at liberty to advise modifications.[65]

The endless negotiations caused one newspaper to comment that the conference had thus far proved only that "Niagara Falls faster than Huerta does." [66] In an attempt to break the deadlock, Naón traveled to Washington to confer with Bryan and Wilson, threatening to adjourn the conference. The American leaders wished the talks to continue and suggested an additional week of exchanges to allow them to arrange for Constitutionalist representatives to meet with the Huerta delegates.

Discussion continued, with the mediators proposing that the conferees seek agreement on a particular individual for provisional president. The delegates discussed numerous candidates without result. Despite repeated requests, Huerta refused to submit a list of nominees, but when Rabasa offered some suggestions, Huerta accepted only one: Francisco Carbajal y Rojas.[67] Huerta apparently still thought he could select his successor and hence need submit only one name. Yet on June 19, Huerta suddenly appointed Pedro Lascuráin, Madero's Minister of Foreign Relations, to the same post. The mediators viewed this as a concession and regarded Lascuráin as a suitable provisional president. Huerta's action presented the Wilson administration with an embarrassing dilemma, for Wilson had contended that Lascuráin and not Huerta was the legal president. Huerta's resignation at this point would compel the United States to support Lascuráin or disavow its earlier contention. But the Wilson administration had reversed its position many times and did not hesitate to do so again. The United States delegation stated that anyone who accepted an appointment from Huerta was a Huertista and hence unacceptable as provisional president.[68]

While the conferees deliberated, American insistence on supplying

65 Bryan to Lamar and Lehman, June 19, 1914/23482.
66 Brooklyn *Daily Eagle*, June 2, 1914.
67 De la Lama to Rabasa, June 14, 1914, Rabasa, Correspondencia.
68 Lamar and Lehman to Bryan, June 19, 1914/23482.

Carranza with arms despite the embargo introduced new complications. On May 30, the ship *Sunshine* attempted to leave Galveston for Tampico with one million rounds of ammunition. When the customs collector refused clearance, the vessel sailed for Havana and then landed at Tampico "under stress of weather." The day was bright and clear, and Tampico was not on the route to Havana.[69] While the ship was at sea, the administration virtually protected it, as Assistant Secretary of the Navy Franklin D. Roosevelt announced that the United States would use force to prevent any blockade of Tampico.[70] Bryan instructed Lamar and Lehman to inform the Mexican delegates that the United States would "depreciate any interference with trade of the Port of Tampico."[71] When the Mexican delegation protested, Lamar and Lehman blandly informed the mediators that the embargo applied only to the Texas border and did not affect naval shipments.[72] Thus, the administration virtually invited the revolutionaries to continue shipping arms. Mexican consular dispatches indicate that numerous cargoes of munitions for the revolutionaries departed from Gulf ports throughout the negotiations.

On June 3, the Ward vessel *Antilla* sailed from New York for Tampico carrying three million rounds of ammunition and two planes. Newspapers reported the impending departure while the *Antilla* loaded its cargo. This ship became a *cause célèbre*, as the Mexicans immediately protested to the mediators. Bryan informed the press that he was unaware of the shipment until after the vessel sailed—he apparently did not read the newspapers.[73] The United States delegation assured the Mexican delegates that orders prohibiting the shipment of arms to Mexico arrived in New York one hour after the *Antilla* weighed anchor.

[69] Fred C. Pabst (Collector of Customs, Galveston, Texas), to Secretary of Commerce, June 18, 1914, JD 157013A-3; and Clarence Miller (Tampico), to Bryan, June 4/12436. The *Sunshine* was fined by the customs collector on its return to Galveston, and after paying the fine, promptly sailed with another cargo of arms for the revolutionaries, Canuto Bulnes (Mexican consul in Galveston), to Arturo M. Elias (Mexican inspector of consulates, San Antonio), June 26 and 28, AREM, L.E. 813, leg. 1 (99–R–3), f 285 and 287–288.

[70] New York *Times*, May 21, 1914, quoting Roosevelt. Lind to Wilson, May 16/23433, suggested the naval action to support the delivery; and Wilson approved, Wilson to Bryan, May 18/23433.

[71] Bryan to Lamar and Lehman, May 26, 1914/23444.

[72] Lamar and Lehman to mediators, May 30, 1914/12631.

[73] Reports of the cargo-loading appeared in New York *Times*, June 2 and 3, 1914; and Bryan's press statement denying knowledge of it is in New York *Times*, June 4, 1914.

Yet within the next three days three more vessels loaded with munitions cleared the port of New York.[74] The administration contended that it was powerless once the vessel left port, refusing to ask the line to halt delivery, as it had at the time of the Veracruz seizure. Citing American efforts to intercept the *Ypiranga* at Veracruz, the Washington *Post* noted, "What is sauce for the goose is good sauce for the gander," and called for the United States navy to halt the vessel. But the New York *Times* reported that Wilson was "known" to feel that the *Antilla* cargo would compensate for the arms the *Ypiranga* delivered to the Huertistas at Puerto Mexico.[75]

Having declared that the cargo of arms left New York without its knowledge, the administration threatened to employ force to support its landing in Tampico. In view of the United States declaration that it could not intercept the arms shipment, Huerta announced a blockade of Tampico. The United States refused to recognize the blockade, and American naval units at Tampico received orders to "use force" to "prevent interference with commerce."[76] When the Mexican gunboats *Zaragoza* and *Bravo* left Puerto Mexico for Tampico to establish the blockade, the United States cruisers *Tacoma* and *Sacramento* shadowed them. Huerta was compelled to bow to superior force, and thus only American naval power allowed the landing of a cargo of arms for the revolutionaries.

After a Cabinet discussion, all port authorities in the southern United States received orders to detain arms shipments, but the administration continued to facilitate the departure of munitions.[77] During the conference six ships were "forced" into Tampico by "bad weather," and by some coincidence all carried arms.[78] Lind informed

---

[74] Bryan's instructions to reply that embargo orders arrived right after the sailing are in Bryan to Lamar and Lehman, June 11, 1914/24716. Reports of other ships leaving New York with arms appear in New York *World*, June 5, 1914, and New York *Times*, June 6, 1914.

[75] Washington *Post*, June 6, 1914; and New York *Times*, June 7, 1914.

[76] United States refusal to recognize the blockade is Bryan to de Oliveira, June 7, 1914/12198. Admiral Badger ordered his ships to use force, Badger to Daniels, June 4, 1914/12155, while Daniels sent orders to prevent interference, Daniels to Badger, June 7/12198; Admiral Mayo informed the Huerta government he would not permit a blockade, Clarence Miller (Tampico), to Bryan, June 8/12436.

[77] Secretary of the Treasury to Bryan, quoting instructions to customs collectors, June 12, 1914, JD 157013–837–8.

[78] Reports of arms deliveries "under stress of weather" came from William Canada (Veracruz), July 23, 1914, 812.113/3468, and July 31, 812.113/3491; and Clarence Miller (Tampico), July 20, 812.113/3492.

Sherbourne G. Hopkins, Carrancista agent in Washington, that if the revolutionists found it "impracticable" to ship arms directly to Tampico, they should transport them to Havana and then secure new papers for Tampico. He assured Hopkins there would be no interference with such activities. Lind told Buckley that there would be no more *Antilla* affairs, because the revolutionists would ship munitions via Havana.[79] The Secretary of War had already informed Hopkins that the United States would allow departures for Tampico from East Coast ports, and shipments continued to flow from Philadelphia, New York, and Baltimore. Wilson directed United States attorneys to release arrested arms smugglers.[80]

As the talks continued, the Mexican delegation pressed for agreement on an evacuation date for Veracruz. The American representatives refused to discuss the subject, even though it was the original reason for the mediation.[81] The mediators informed the Mexican delegation that they believed the United States would have an implicit obligation to withdraw from Veracruz, even in the absence of any stipulations in the protocol.[82] The Mexicans realized the futility of insisting but had difficulty convincing Huerta.

The protocols emerging from the conference settled little. They provided that the composition of the provisional government would be decided in negotiations between the two Mexican factions, thus side-stepping the thorniest issue. There was no specification of how the provisional government would assume office—only the stipulation that the United States would recognize it. The United States agreed not to claim an indemnity or "any other international satisfaction," thus dropping the demand for a salute to the flag. The provisional government of Mexico would pledge to proclaim an armistice upon taking office. With this agreement on June 24, the negotiations were terminated.[83]

[79] Hopkins reported Lind's statement, Hopkins to Carranza, May 8, 1914, later printed in New York *Herald*, June 30, 1914; while Buckley reported the conversation with Lind in *Investigation of Mexican Affairs*, Testimony of William F. Buckley, December 6, 1919, p. 793.

[80] Hopkins told Carranza of Garrison's statement, S. Gil Herrera (code name of Sherbourne G. Hopkins), to Carranza, May 18, 1914, quoted in Washington *Post*, July 4, 1914; while Wilson directed the release of smugglers, Wilson to Bryan, July 7, Bryan-Wilson Correspondence, II, 247.

[81] Lamar and Lehman to Bryan, June 23, 1914/23486; and Lamar to Bryan, June 26/23489.

[82] Rabasa Diary, June 23, 1914.

[83] Dodge to Bryan, June 24, 1914/12421.

Signing the protocols proved to be more than just a formality, for Wilson objected to a reference to the Huerta negotiators as the "Delegation of the United States of Mexico" and raised the old bugaboo of indirect recognition.[84] Dr. Naón was "greatly offended," and the mediators again threatened to adjourn the conference.[85] When Lamar and Lehman informed the President that "signing the minutes is not the adoption but the attestation of what has already been adopted," Wilson authorized the signing. Bryan nonetheless instructed the delegates to attach a statement that "nothing contained herein is to be construed as a recognition of General Huerta."[86]

The delegates signed the protocols on July 1, three days after the ominous assassination of Francis Ferdinand at Sarajevo. The formal closing session of the conference was held July 3. Despite the innocuous protocols, da Gama stated, "We do feel that so far we have averted war."[87] The mediators thus considered the conference a success so far as their principal objective was concerned. Many Latin Americans erroneously concluded that the mediation had arranged the subsequent withdrawal of United States troops from Veracruz. Chileans and Argentines even hailed this as a new departure in inter-American relations, ushering in a period in which the major Latin American nations could affect American policy.[88] The troop withdrawal, however, had nothing whatever to do with the conference. Arrangements for the evacuation began in September, 1914—several months after Huerta fell from power. The evacuation, therefore, occurred only after the occupation had achieved the desired effect. It reflected the changing situation in Mexico, rather than any American cooperation with the Latin nations, a point soon underlined by interventions in the Caribbean and the Pershing expedition into Mexico. As Wilson had suggested, the mediators invited Carranza to send representatives to meet with the Huerta delegation after the conference closed, but Carranza refused. He stated that the Plan of Guadalupe required that he become provisional

---

[84] Lamar and Lehman to Bryan, June 29, 1914/23490.

[85] Lamar and Lehman to Bryan, June 30, 1914/23491.

[86] Bryan to Lamar and Lehman, June 30, 1914/12631; and Lamar and Lehman to Bryan, June 30, 1914/23491.

[87] Dodge to Bryan, July 3, 1914/12441.

[88] For Chilean press reaction, see Frederick B. Pike, *Chile and the United States: 1880–1962* (South Bend, Indiana: University of Notre Dame Press, 1963), pp. 148–149; and for Argentine comments, see Carlos A. Becu, *El "A.B.C." y su concepto político y jurídico* (Buenos Aires: Librería "La Facultad" de Juan Roldán, 1915), pp. 27–29 and 39–40.

president, and that he could not alter the plan without the consent of all signatories.[89] The Huerta delegation waited in vain.

Thus the mediation settled little, for the protocols avoided the main issues. Yet the conference did provide a forum for verbal exchange while each side awaited the outcome of the struggle on the battlefields. It proved impossible for Wilson to use the mediation to oust Huerta. He clung to power, although his regime was obviously tottering.

[89] Mediators to Rafael Zubaran, July 21, 1914, and Zubaran to mediators, June 27, Buckley Papers; and Leon Canova to Bryan, July 6/12429.

XI

Huerta's Fall and Last Hurrah

On July 8, Huerta's family sailed from Veracruz for Puerto Mexico. Since this was not a normal port of call for Gulf cruises, it was evident that Huerta intended to join them there. The Mexican President installed a new Cabinet, with the president of the Supreme Court, Francisco Carbajal y Rojas, as Minister of Foreign Relations. Although Carbajal had served as president of the Supreme Court under Madero, the Constitutionalists promptly declared him unacceptable as provisional president.

Huerta presented his resignation to Congress on July 15. He attributed his fall to the "manifest and decided protection which a great power of this continent has afforded to the rebels."[1] After his address, Huerta paid a farewell visit to his favorite café. People crowded around to cheer him and shake his hand. Tears filled his eyes as he turned and announced: "This will be my last toast in my favorite resort, and I drink to the new President of Mexico."[2] Huerta and General Blanquet left the capital for Puerto Mexico on the evening of July 15. The British cruiser *Bristol* dropped anchor in Puerto Mexico, with orders to offer asylum. Just before the train arrived, the German cruiser *Dresden* entered the harbor at top speed and also offered asylum. After lingering in the city for several days, Huerta sailed aboard the *Dresden* on July 20.[3] News of Huerta's resignation caused premature jubilation in Washington. When the dispatch arrived, during a birthday party for Secretary Lane, McAdoo and Bryan "embraced and danced about like a pair of boys." Colonel House telegraphed Wilson congratulations on his "triumph," while newspapers reported that the President was

[1] New York *Times*, July 16, 1914.
[2] *Ibid.*
[3] Admiral Badger to Daniels, July 15, 1914/12518, and July 20/12579.

"jubilant."[4] This enthusiasm proved short-lived. Huerta's departure failed to terminate the Mexican crisis, for Carbajal was reluctant to surrender the government to Carranza without guarantees for the safety of the residents of Mexico City. Carranza refused to extend any guarantees, and fighting continued until Carbajal followed Huerta into exile. Even the ascent of Carranza to power did not prove to be the panacea that the administration had hoped.

Huerta was overthrown, but the old soldier did not fade away. As he boarded the *Dresden*, he told reporters: "When I assumed the presidency I said publicly that I would restore peace, cost what it might. I have paid—it has cost me the presidency. . . . I am going to Europe, and there I will stay until my country needs my sword sufficiently to call upon me."[5] Few observers attached any significance to his implied promise to return, for many ousted presidents had made similar gestures.

Even as Huerta sailed into exile, rumors of a new Huertista rising began to circulate. The General traveled to London, apparently seeking aid in the country that had once tacitly supported his retention of power. The British position had modified, however, in the face of Wilson's adamant stand. With the European situation darkening, Britain could scarcely afford adventures in Latin America, and support from the United States was even more crucial than Mexican oil. Realism continued to constitute the basis of British policy. His Majesty's government viewed Huerta benevolently because it perceived that as President he could provide stability more effectively and rapidly than the revolutionaries. Employing the same realism, it was obvious that once removed from office Huerta's prospects of regaining power were slim, especially in the face of opposition from the United States. Huerta sailed to Santander, Spain, and then traveled to Barcelona. The old General settled in Barcelona, and for a time it appeared that he would spend a tranquil exile there. But he continued to dream of a return to power. In Mexico, Villa and Carranza had openly split, and Huerta thought he perceived an opportunity. After a virtual Villa *coup d'état* in northern Mexico during June, Carranza cut off Villa's supplies. By March, Carranza had been driven to Veracruz after failing to retain

4 William Jennings and Mary Baird Bryan, *The Memoirs of William Jennings Bryan* (Chicago and Philadelphia: John C. Winston Company, 1925), pp. 355–356, based on Mrs. Bryan's diary entry for July 15, 1914; House Diary, July 16; and New York *World*, July 16, 1914.

5 New York *Times*, July 18, 1914.

control of the capital, while General Álvaro Obregón was defeating Villa. The principal revolutionary leaders appeared to be declining. The Wilson administration, disgusted by Carranza's obduracy, looked on Villa with increasing favor, for he seemed more amenable to American views. Bryan advocated supporting Villa and dismissed John Lind from his post as State Department adviser on June 10 because of his pro-Carranza outlook.[6] The continued anarchy in Mexico undoubtedly disturbed Huerta, just as it had during his presidency, and the General felt that he could terminate it. With his great egotism, the old warrior had become convinced that he alone could restore peace and stability in Mexico. Huerta felt his country needed him. Yet it was ambition that provided the primary motivation. Anyone viewing the situation impartially could perceive that there was scant prospect of Huerta's regaining power. Like Woodrow Wilson, however, Huerta saw what he wished to see.

But he was not alone in dreaming of a return to Mexico, for other opponents of the Revolution were also at work. Pascual Orozco, Jr., headed a group of former officers and officials who assembled in Texas and began laying plans for a return to their country. As early as December, 1914, they began infiltrating men and arms into northern Mexico, dispatching Generals José Inés Salazar and Emilio Campa to begin harassing the Constitutionalists with guerrilla tactics. Orozco and his followers intended to exploit the revolutionary split through guerrilla activity while assembling arms and men to launch a full-scale invasion in an attempt to regain power. The plan called for Orozco to serve as military commander of the eventual counterrevolution, but the participants recognized the need for a strong leader to assume the presidency. While Orozco's popularity in Chihuahua would assure large numbers of recruits during the initial phase, a leader with broader support in other parts of the republic was essential. With this in mind, the group dispatched Enrique Creel, former governor of Chihuahua, to Spain to enlist Huerta's support.[7] This appeal reinforced Huerta's ambitions, for Creel provided precisely the type of advice that the old General desired. Huerta had already begun to plan his own revolt and needed little encouragement to unite his movement with that of Orozco.

[6] New York *Times*, June 10 and 26, 1914.

[7] Michael C. Meyer, *Mexican Rebel: Pascual Orozco and the Mexican Revolution, 1910–1915* (Lincoln, Nebr.: University of Nebraska Press, 1967), pp. 115–122; and Michael C. Meyer, "The Mexican-German Conspiracy of 1915," *The Americas*, XXIII, 1 (July, 1966), 78–82.

On April 1, 1915, newspapers announced that Huerta had sailed for New York.[8] This dispatch caused consternation in Washington, although Huerta radioed the New York *Times* that he had "no plans" and contended that his voyage was merely a "pleasure trip."[9] Villa and Carranza were alarmed at the prospect of Huerta's presence in the United States. Mexican consuls, agents of the convention government, and a coterie of Villista officers all petitioned the State Department to deny Huerta permission to enter the United States.[10] Huerta landed in New York at 6:00 P.M. on April 12 and received an enthusiastic reception. He descended the gangplank wearing a blue suit, brown fedora hat, and black satin necktie with a diamond tiepin. In the words of the New York *Times*, he was "still the same picturesque old warrior."[11] Accompanied by José C. Delgado, his former private secretary, and Abraham Ratner, an arms purchaser for his regime, he waded through a crowd of cheering friends and admirers. As he disembarked, a messenger handed him a package that resembled a bomb, causing momentary alarm, but police discovered that the contents were harmless. It took Huerta almost half an hour to pass through the welcoming crowd. He refused to issue a statement but announced a press conference for April 16. To prevent rumors, he cautioned reporters that all authentic interviews would bear his signature.

Huerta's press statements mirrored his ambitions. He painted a terrible picture of Mexico, calling anarchy "too soft a word" to describe conditions there. He predicted that a strong man would appear to save the country but declined to speculate on the new leader's identity. Those who knew him could be positive that he had only one such man in mind—Victoriano Huerta. The General admitted that he hoped to return to Mexico "someday." Defending his administration, he criticized the American policy that opposed him, charging that Wilson was "misled by false statements."[12] Huerta wrote an article for the magazine section of the New York *Times*, warning against intervention in Mexico. He stressed that other Latin American countries had also experienced civil wars and insisted that Mexicans should be allowed to

[8] New York *Times*, April 1, 1915.

[9] New York *Times*, April 10, 1915.

[10] Enrique Llorente to Bryan, April 10, 1915, 812.001 H87/11; Ramón P. Denegri to Wilson, April 10, 812.001 H87/12; and Gaston Schmatz (Aguascalientes), to Bryan, April 10, 812.001 H87/16.

[11] New York *Times*, April 13, 1915.

[12] New York *Times*, April 16, 1915.

determine their own future.[13] The *Times* noted editorially that these two press statements indicated his intention to lead a new uprising and that his article condemning intervention amounted to a virtual warning to the United States against opposing him.[14]

Within a month of his arrival, Huerta received some four hundred Mexican army officers in small groups. Some of his leading supporters were among the visitors to his suite in the Hotel Ansonia. Ratner brushed off press comments on the visits, claiming that all these individuals had merely stopped to pay their respects.[15] Huerta continued to deny any plans for a new revolt, but his activities sparked constant rumors. At the direction of President Wilson and Secretary of State Bryan, Huerta's movements were closely scrutinized by federal agents.[16] On May 5, Huerta leased a mansion in Forest Hills, New York, and announced that he would establish his residence there.[17] When his family arrived on May 13, the former President moved into his house and seemed to settle down. Huerta informed a census taker that he intended to open offices in New York City as a civil engineer.[18] These elaborate preparations were designed only to alleviate suspicion.

Huerta summoned his former Minister of Public Instruction, Nemesio García Naranjo, to New York to request aid in launching the new revolt. Although García Naranjo had purchased presses to begin publishing the *Revista Mexicana*, an antirevolutionary journal, he still refused to join Huerta's movement. He advised Huerta to abandon his plans, cautioning that there was no possibility of success. But Huerta was grimly determined. García Naranjo reports that Huerta abstained from alcohol at dinner, and Ratner informed him the General had ceased drinking entirely while preparing his plans. Although this was undoubtedly an exaggeration, Huerta was obviously devoting all his energies to organizing the new revolt.[19]

In the course of these preparations, Huerta apparently conferred with German intelligence officials, although the paucity of evidence renders it difficult to determine their precise role in his plot. Naturally, Germany wished to sever the British oil supply from Mexico and had made over-

---

[13] New York *Times*, April 25, 1915.

[14] New York *Times*, April 27, 1915.

[15] New York *Times*, May 6, 1915.

[16] Wilson to Bryan, April 27, 1915, Bryan-Wilson Correspondence, IV, 117.

[17] New York *Times*, May 6, 1915.

[18] New York *Times*, June 11, 1915.

[19] Nemesio García Naranjo, *Memorias de Nemesio García Naranjo* (8 vols.; Monterrey: Ediciones de *El Porvenir*, 1956–1962), VIII, 130–136.

tures to Huerta during his term of office. Yet, attempting to accomplish this by supporting a man who had seemingly favored the leading British oil concessionaire appears to have been a dubious policy. Perhaps the Germans believed they could dominate Huerta if their aid enabled the success of his movement. German officials may even have hoped Huerta would declare war on the United States, but the General was far too realistic to take such a step. It is more likely that the German government decided that Huerta's return to power, or attempt to do so, would distract the United States from the European war. Perhaps the German military even desired American intervention, which might curtail arms shipments to the Allies by consuming ammunition.

Captain Franz Rintelen von Kleist, financial adviser to the Admiralty General Staff, was Huerta's principal German contact. Rintelen, a banker with experience in the United States and Latin America, arrived in New York shortly before Huerta. Some writers have contended that Rintelen conferred with Huerta in Barcelona to urge him to revolt and had traveled to the United States principally to aid his rebellion.[20] The German captain, however, came to the United States with orders to purchase arms and prevent Allied purchases, and the Huerta scheme was a secondary activity.[21] Yet there is some evidence to suggest that Rintelen or some other German agent conferred with Huerta in Spain before he sailed for New York.

There are indications that Huerta may have also met the military attachés of the German embassy in Washington, Captain Franz von Papen and Captain Karl Boy-Ed, but there is no conclusive evidence. Agents of Emil Voska, head of the Czech underground in the United States, reportedly wired a room where Huerta conferred with Boy-Ed and eavesdropped on the conversation.[22] The information was then released through the Providence *Journal* to the New York *Times*, as were all of Voska's exposés.[23] Voska reported that the two men met several times, but only his memoirs and the newspaper articles

---

[20] Barbara Tuchman, *The Zimmermann Telegram* (New York: The Viking Press, 1958), pp. 66–67, and John P. Jones and Paul M. Hollister, *The German Secret Service in America* (Boston: Small, Maynard and Company, 1918), pp. 290–293, claim that Rintelen met Huerta in Barcelona, allege several other meetings in New York, and speak of extensive German aid, but they fail to footnote their contentions.

[21] Captain Franz Rintelen von Kleist, *The Dark Invader* (London and New York: The Macmillan Company, 1933), pp. 176–177 and 182–183.

[22] Emil Victor Voska and Will Irwin, *Spy and Counterspy* (New York: Doubleday, Doran and Company, 1940), pp. 28 and 192–197.

[23] New York *Times*, August 4, 1915.

mention this. Despite the fact that the United States Justice Department was watching Huerta closely, its records fail to indicate any contacts with German officials. American intelligence agents were also observing the movements of the German military attachés, but while State Department files contain detailed reports of their travels, there are no references to any meetings with Huerta.[24] Even the conference Voska allegedly overheard does not appear in either the file on Huerta or that on the German diplomats. It seems highly improbable that any rendezvous could have taken place without the knowledge of the agents shadowing one of the parties.

The question of financial aid by the Germans is even more obscure. Those who contend that Huerta received German support mention arms and financial assistance. Rintelen claimed in his memoirs that he conferred with Huerta in New York and subsequently deposited substantial funds in Huerta bank accounts in Havana.[25] Yet in his conversations with García Naranjo, Huerta referred to the "few centavos" available to launch the revolution.[26] Since Huerta trusted García Naranjo implicitly and offered him the post of minister of finance, the General had no reason to mislead him about the finances of the movement. The fact that Huerta died almost penniless suggests that he spent all his personal funds on the revolt, and this certainly seems to conflict with reports of unlimited German finances. Yet the huge quantities of arms secured by the revolutionaries seem to indicate the availability of substantial funds. Arms were difficult to procure in the United States during this period, in view of the shipments to Europe. It is therefore possible that German officials pledged to supply weapons and munitions, perhaps by U-boat landings, as Rintelen contended. Yet nearly all Huertista arms discovered were of American manufacture. This raises the possibility that Rintelen, finding it impossible to ship the arms he purchased to Germany, gave them to Huerta as a means of indirectly aiding the German cause. The alleged financial deposits may reflect the cost of purchasing the arms, which were subsequently transferred to the rebels. Despite the inconclusive evidence, the quantities of arms involved in the plot do give some credence to the existence of financial support. Certainly the German government was

[24] The Justice Department file on Huerta is 90755–U, while the State Department file on the German military attachés is 701.6211.

[25] George J. Rausch, Jr., "The Exile and Death of Victoriano Huerta," *Hispanic American Historical Review*, XLII (May, 1962), 137.

[26] García Naranjo, *Memorias*, VII, 136–138.

paying careful attention to events in Mexico, as indicated by German newspapers and the subsequent Zimmermann telegram.[27] The Germans later offered financial assistance to Villa, and this action suggests that Huerta received similar aid.[28] Whatever the German role, it was clearly one of encouraging a movement already in progress. The plan was initiated and elaborated by Orozco, Huerta, and their supporters. The German presence on the periphery merely provided the wherewithal to carry it out.

Secretary of State Lansing suspected German contacts with Huerta, but the Department never uncovered any convincing evidence. German Ambassador Count Johann von Bernstorff vigorously denied the allegations of the Providence *Journal*.[29] Lansing invited John Rathom, editor of the paper, to confer with him and submit the evidence to the State Department.[30] Rathom did travel to Washington to meet the Secretary. State Department records have no reports of their conversation, indicating that Rathom was unable to offer any convincing data. The Secretary was seeking evidence against the German diplomats and would certainly have grasped at anything concrete. In December, 1915, when the United States formally requested the recall of von Papen and Boy-Ed, Lansing included contacts with Huerta in his enumeration of grievances. The Secretary's memorandum of the conversation with von Bernstorff noted: "The Ambassador seemed much surprised at the latter statement and said that he knew nothing about it." While Lansing replied that he "had very good proofs" and was "convinced that Captain Boy-Ed had seen Huerta several times," his reference to evidence was mere conjecture.[31] In his private memo books, Lansing made several references to German intrigues. These notations, intended only for his own eyes, indicate that he merely suspected such contacts, and he referred to "unofficial and semiofficial reports" of meetings, complaining, "The proof is not conclusive." The Secretary believed that the Germans were aiding all factions in

[27] Meyer, "The Mexican-German Conspiracy of 1915," *The Americas*, XXIII, 1 (July, 1966), 83–85.

[28] Frederich Katz, "Alemánia y Francisco Villa," *Historia Mexicana*, XII, 1 (July, 1962), 88–102.

[29] Von Bernstorff to Lansing (who had replaced Bryan as Secretary of State), August 5, 1915, SD 701.6211/303, and December 6, 701.6211/326.

[30] Lansing to Rathom, November 18, 1915, 701.6211/325.

[31] Lansing memo of conversation with von Bernstorff, December 1, 1915, 701. 6211/325½; and War Department Memorandum indicating denials by von Papen and Boy-Ed, December 6, 701.6211/330½.

Mexico to keep the country in a state of anarchy, and he also suspected German activity in every trouble spot in Latin America.[32] His memoranda books disclose that he detested von Bernstorff and believed him capable of anything. Lansing apparently credited nearly all rumors about the Count.[33] These private notations, revealing as they do Lansing's innermost thoughts, seem to indicate that the Secretary's accusations against Boy-Ed were based mainly on suspicion.

As early as April, intelligence reports from United States army detachments along the Mexican border indicated rumors of an impending Huerta revolt. These reports disclosed that Huerta's arrival in Mexico would spark a considerable rising, as numerous ex-federal soldiers in the forces of both Villa and Carranza could be expected to join him. Villa's recent defeats had discouraged his men, and many might therefore desert him to fight under a new standard—any standard. During May, intelligence officers detected the presence of numerous Huertistas along the border. Virtually the entire Ojinaga garrison, which had fought so valiantly before fleeing to the United States after exhausting its supplies, abruptly appeared in El Paso.[34]

The administration viewed these reports with concern, and on May 13, Assistant Attorney General Charles Warren instructed the United States attorney in El Paso, Judge J. J. Camp: "In case of the arrival of General Huerta in San Antonio, every possible effort should be made by you to obtain any evidence of violation of the neutrality laws of the United States and to prosecute the same."[35] Camp replied:

> Should Huerta come to this district he will be closely watched, and I will resort to every means known to the law to prevent him from setting on foot another revolution in Mexico, and if evidence can not be obtained against him sufficient to institute prosecution for violation of the neutrality laws of the United States, in all probability we can hold him for investigation for deportation.

He noted that deportation would be the most effective solution, for Huerta would inevitably secure release on bail if indicted for a neutrality violation.[36]

[32] Lansing's memoranda are contained in memo books in the Lansing Papers, dated July 11, 1915.

[33] *Ibid.*, October 10, 1915, and May, 1916.

[34] Major J. Ryan (Thirteenth Cavalry), to Headquarters, Southern Department, April 28, 1915, WD AG 2285786; and Garrison to Thomas W. Gregory (Attorney General), May 6, AG 2286454.

[35] Warren to Camp, May 13, 1915, JD 90755–U–2.

[36] Camp to Gregory, May 21, 1915, 90755–U–4.

On June 26, Huerta suddenly boarded a train and left New York, supposedly en route to the San Francisco Fair, but he changed trains at Kansas City and headed for El Paso. Huerta's son and ten Huertista generals left San Antonio for El Paso at 4:00 A.M. on June 27.[37] Huerta alighted from the train at Newman, New Mexico, twenty miles north of El Paso. This small station was situated on the New Mexico border, and since Huerta's car stopped a short distance from the station, he was actually in Texas. General Pascual Orozco embraced him as he stepped from the train. Huerta's two sons-in-law were standing by with a car.[38] Apparently they intended to rush directly to Mexico, hoping to elude federal agents awaiting the train in El Paso.

As Huerta and Orozco embraced, two Justice Department agents approached and requested the generals to accompany them to the Federal building in El Paso. The agents informed the Mexicans that they were not yet under arrest. Orozco was uneasy, but Huerta was "suave" and agreed immediately.[39] Since the generals offered no resistance, it was not necessary to call upon Colonel George H. Morgan and twenty-five cavalrymen concealed nearby. Morgan had taken the detachment and accompanied the agents and two federal marshals to Newman, when agent Zaccary Cobb heard rumors that Huerta would leave the train there. The convoy bearing Huerta was enveloped by cheering crowds of Mexican refugees as it entered El Paso.[40] The onlookers applauded Huerta as he entered the Federal building, where he was placed under arrest and charged with violating the neutrality laws.[41] Later in the day, a telegram ordering the arrest of Huerta arrived from Washington—the Justice Department agent had acted on his own initiative. The State Department appreciated his "prompt, efficient action." Secretary of War Garrison took a different viewpoint, noting that Morgan acted without orders and failed to inform his superiors.[42] Huerta's detention upset the proposed revolt, for *personalismo* required his presence. His arrest thus forced postponement of carefully timed and planned uprisings.

[37] New York *Times*, June 27, 1915.

[38] Cobb to Lansing, June 27, 1915, 812.001 H87/21.

[39] *Ibid.*

[40] Funston to Adjutant General, June 27, 1915, AG 2301314.

[41] Cobb to Lansing, June 27, 1915, 812.001 H87/18; and Justice Department, 90755–U–14.

[42] Osborne to Cobb, June 27, 1915, 812.001 H87/21; and Garrison to General Frederick Funston (Commander, Southern Department), June 28, AG 2301314.

The Justice Department charged Huerta with conspiracy to violate the neutrality laws, despite the paucity of evidence. Rumors abounded that the Juárez garrison would rally to his standard and that some ten thousand men were poised along the border waiting to enter Mexico at his command. Yet there was no conclusive evidence. A warehouse full of arms discovered in El Paso could not be linked to Huerta. Once charges were placed, legal procedure required bail to be set, and Huerta and Orozco promptly posted the bond of $15,000 and $7,500, respectively, through their attorney Tom Lea, mayor of El Paso.[43] Huerta continued to deny any plot, contending that he was still en route to the San Francisco Fair and had merely detoured to visit his daughter in El Paso.[44]

The Justice Department transmitted all correspondence relating to Huerta's detention to the President, who followed the case closely. Warren advised Wilson that Huerta could not legally be prevented from entering Mexico once released on bail.[45] Camp was promptly informed that the "President . . . desires every effort made to prevent entrance of Huerta and Orozco into Mexico." The Justice Department directed Camp to press the conspiracy charges and secure a postponement of the hearing to allow time to seek evidence.[46] Immigration authorities subsequently determined that Huerta had entered the United States properly and could not be deported.[47] Camp reported that the evidence of conspiracy was "meager."[48] The Justice Department placed Huerta under close surveillance. Its agents reported that sentiment in El Paso was strongly pro-Huerta. Crowds outside the General's apartment cheered his every appearance. Huerta informed the press that he would return to Mexico only when peace was restored, but he continued to caucus with numerous generals and Mexican officers in the city.[49]

Indications of the planned revolt continued to mount, alarming the administration. On June 30, Félix Díaz arrived in El Paso, and Generals Blanquet and Mondragón appeared in New York. The Coast Guard seized a shipload of arms, discovering that it had cleared Seattle for

[43] Cobb to Lansing, June 28, 1915, 812.001 H87/22.

[44] New York *Times*, June 28, 1915.

[45] Warren to Wilson, June 28, 1915, JD 90755–U–8.

[46] Unsigned to Camp, June 28, 1915, 90755–U–5.

[47] Solicitor General to Lansing, and Warren to Wilson, July 5, 1915, 812.001 H87/39.

[48] Camp to Gregory, June 29, 1915, JD 90755–U–8.

[49] New York *Times*, June 28 and 30, 1915.

Mexico and then cruised the Pacific for three months, apparently awaiting the Huerta revolt. Reports from Chihuahua indicated that the mountains were "full of armed men." Huerta's hearing was postponed until July 12.[50]

The Department of State requested army aid in preventing Huerta's entry into Mexico, but General Frederick Funston, of the Southern Department, considered this an impossible task. Funston noted that even if Huerta was encountered in the act of crossing the border it would be necessary to detain him to prevent his entry into Mexico. The only possible charge was violation of the neutrality laws, and since Huerta was already under bond on a similar indictment it would be impossible to arrest him again on the same charge. Funston could find no other pretense to justify detaining the former President.[51] It apparently never occurred to the General that Huerta might be detained for "jumping bail" by leaving the country. Funston also noted that Huerta could easily slip across the border undetected and suggested that the only solution was to apprehend him at once, if anyone could invent a pretext.

On July 3, Pascual Orozco succeeded in eluding the six guards who surrounded his residence, and officials immediately re-arrested Huerta. Huerta resisted arrest, threatening to shoot a deputy marshal, and newspapers reported that his aides attempted to seize the marshal's car, apparently for a dash to Mexico. Huerta angrily told the court: "I gave the bond demanded. Then I was guarded like a prisoner who had not given bond."[52] He refused to post the new bond, although he possessed sufficient resources. The United States attorney believed that Huerta was "remaining in jail for political effect with the Mexican people" and might post bail at any moment.[53] On July 4, Huerta told a reporter, "I am enjoying my novel experience of being in jail in liberty-loving America on the very day you celebrate liberty and justice and independence."[54] Meanwhile, additional arms caches were discovered in El Paso and also in cactus plants near Newman. There were reports that several Huertista officers left Havana for New Orleans. Assistant

50 New York *Times*, June 30 and July 1, 1915.

51 Garrison to Funston, July 1, 1915, AG 2301314A; Funston to Adjutant General, July 1, AG 2301314A; and Funston to Garrison, July 1, 812.001 H87/31.

52 New York *Times*, July 4, 1915.

53 R. E. Crawford (assistant United States attorney, El Paso), to Gregory, July 3, 1915, 90755-U-23¼.

54 New York *Times*, July 6, 1915.

Attorney General Charles Warren informed President Wilson that Huerta would undoubtedly post bail on the second charge at his July 12 hearing, and that he would be almost impossible to guard once released due to the numerous Huertistas in El Paso. Warren added that he was certain Huerta could take Juárez without resistance, and that this could only be prevented if he was detained for deportation. The Solicitor General and Secretary of State reported that once Huerta posted bond on the second charge, "criminal process will have been exhausted," while deportation was "unavailable under the statute."[55] Thus it appeared that Huerta would be free to launch his revolt despite the efforts of the United States. Wilson told Tumulty, "It seems to me imperative Huerta should be prevented from entering Mexico, and removed from the border. Hope sincerely some means may be found to do this. Importance of it very great."[56]

At the July 12 hearing, Huerta surprised everyone by refusing to post bond unless authorities pledged to terminate their surveillance after his release. He refused to promise to leave the border, having previously announced, "I will leave this jail only if my departure is unconditional."[57] The Justice Department ordered him detained at Fort Bliss to isolate him from his supporters in El Paso. Authorities placed Huerta in officers quarters at the fort, guarded by marshals. The United States attorney informed the Secretary of State: "This solves the problem."[58] Huerta was now kept in custody, thus effectively preventing the revolt. The actions of the Justice Department were based on suspicions. While these were certainly well founded, the fact remains that the government had no evidence against Huerta on either charge and had no desire to bring him to trial, knowing this would result in his release. Yet it had arrested Huerta without evidence. These actions contrasted sharply with earlier failure to apprehend Carrancista agents openly purchasing arms for the revolution against Huerta. In these cases, the Justice Department ignored abundant evidence.

Once again, Huerta was defeated by the United States. His attempt to launch his revolt from Texas seems ill advised, for certainly he must have anticipated harassment and opposition in the country that forced him from power. His prospects would undoubtedly have been considerably

[55] Warren to Wilson, July 5, 1915, 812.001 H87/39.

[56] Wilson to Tumulty, July 6, 1915, J.D. 90755–U–26.

[57] New York *Times*, July 9, 1915.

[58] Cobb to Lansing, July 9, 1915, 812.001 H87/45; and New York *Times*, July 7, 9, 10, and 14, 1915.

more favorable had he operated from Guatemala or by amphibious landing from Havana. Perhaps he considered the United States the only place where he could unite his supporters and amass sufficient arms. The favorable terrain in northern Mexico and Orozco's following in Chihuahua were also factors that dictated the use of Texas as a base. Had he succeeded in entering Mexico, Huerta's movement would have been formidable, although it seems unlikely that he could have regained the presidency. A substantial portion of Villa's army would probably have gathered around his standard, and these plus the ex-federals would have constituted a formidable force. Since Carranza was now in power, he could not have employed guerrilla tactics against Huerta as before because of the necessity of defending cities and territory. Therefore, Huerta may have attained his dream of commanding a large army against a major force of revolutionaries in one grand battle or series of engagements. Yet he could not succeed against the opposition of the United States.

Huerta remained at Fort Bliss throughout the summer and fall. He directed his family to come to El Paso, announcing his intention to establish residence in that city. On August 30, Texas Rangers shot Orozco after a chase that began when a party of Mexicans raided a ranch in search of supplies.[59] When coupled with Huerta's detention, Orozco's death ended any possibility of a successful revolt. The Huertista officers began to melt away, for the uprising could not be launched without its leader. Huerta became despondent and began drinking heavily, much more so than before. This, plus his confinement, affected his health. By early November, there were appeals for his release on grounds of illness. The United States had recognized Carranza in the interim, and conditions in Mexico, while far from stable, had improved. On November 7, Huerta was sent to his home in El Paso, still under guard. Officers returned him to Fort Bliss on December 10 as his health had improved, but the recovery proved to be only temporary. Two operations early in January failed to arrest Huerta's illness, cirrhosis of the liver. Authorities allowed him to return to his home to die. The guards withdrew, for he was obviously in no condition to escape.

Victoriano Huerta died on January 13, 1916, and was buried in El Paso, next to Orozco. One day before his death, the United States finally obtained an indictment against him, due to a confession from one of his adherents obtained long after his arrest. The charges against his cohorts were dropped in most cases, and those indicted merely

[59] For Orozco's death, see Meyer, *Mexican Rebel*, pp. 131–133.

forfeited bail. The case was then closed.[60] Thus, Huerta died a prisoner of the United States, the country he had fought throughout his presidency.

Huerta was no worse—and certainly no better—than countless Latin American dictators. Like many *caudillos*, he was corrupt and ruthless. He was convinced that he alone possessed the capacity to solve his country's problems, a common failing of the *caudillo* type. He certainly does not deserve the reputation the Mexican Revolutionaries gave him, for they portray him as the devil incarnate. He might have accomplished much for Mexico if given the opportunity, but Woodrow Wilson never allowed him the chance.

The confrontation between Victoriano Huerta and Woodrow Wilson is certainly not one of the noblest episodes of American diplomacy. It is a story of intervention, experimentation, and bungling on the part of the United States. Whatever Huerta's faults or merits, the United States did not have the right to interfere in Mexican internal affairs. That Wilson's intervention was based on altruistic motives, rather than national advantages, does not justify his stand; it still constituted intervention.

[60] Camp to Gregory, January 12, 1916, JD 90755–U–75, and January 22, 1917, 90755–U–99.

Note on Sources

Only volumes containing significant material for this study are included in the Bibliography; those that were most useful are noted in this essay portion; others which provided some information are in the bibliographical listing which follows. Bibliographies, general volumes that provided figures or minor bits of information, and studies consulted for peripheral information or to help place events in a wider context are omitted.

There are numerous studies of Woodrow Wilson and his policies. The most useful are those by Arthur S. Link, who bases his works primarily on Wilson's papers. Link's volumes are broadly sympathetic to Wilson and seek principally to explain his actions. He examines Wilson's presidential policies in *Wilson: The New Freedom* (Princeton, N.J.: Princeton University Press, 1956), and *Woodrow Wilson and the Progressive Era: 1910–1917* (New York: Harper and Brothers, 1954), generally favoring his Mexican policy, although noting its strengths and weaknesses. In *Wilson the Diplomat* (Baltimore: Johns Hopkins University Press, 1957), Link contends that Wilson had no preconceived notions on foreign policy when he entered the White House. This conclusion differs with that of Harley Notter in *The Origins of the Foreign Policy of Woodrow Wilson* (Baltimore: Johns Hopkins University Press, 1937). Notter analyzes Wilson's writings and concludes that he had a complete foreign policy when he assumed office. Both views are worthy of consideration, although Link's have much more weight because of his extensive use of the Wilson Papers. Josephus Daniels, Wilson's Secretary of the Navy, loyally defends the actions of his Chief in *The Wilson Era: Years of Peace: 1910–1917* (Chapel Hill, N.C.: University of North Carolina Press, 1944). *Lecture and Seminar at the University of Chicago in Celebration of the Centennial of Woodrow Wilson: 1856–1956* (Chicago: University of Chicago Press, 1958), is a collection of articles by various Wilson scholars and acquaintances.

Among the many fine works dealing with the Mexican Revolution is Michael C. Meyer, *Mexican Rebel: Pascual Orozco and the Mexican Revolution, 1910–1915* (Lincoln, Nebr.: University of Nebraska Press, 1967), which presents a valuable analysis of one of the key figures in the early revolutionary period, considering Orozco's relation to Madero and Huerta. Stanley R. Ross, *Francisco I. Madero: Apostle of Mexican Democracy* (New York: Columbia University Press, 1955), is a splendid work on Madero and his administration, which generally sympathizes with his policies. Charles C. Cumberland, *Mexican Revolution: Genesis under Madero* (Austin, Texas: University of Texas Press, 1952), presents the Madero viewpoint. Manuel Bonilla, Jr., a Madero minister who subsequently served in the armies of Villa and Angeles, provides an "inside" account of Madero's term in *El régimen Maderista* (Mexico: Talleres Linotipográficos de *El Universal*, 1922). He secured statements from other participants when he was unable to provide a firsthand account of an event.

On the Constitutionalist phase of the Revolution, Carranza's Foreign Minister, Isidro Fabela, wrote *Historia diplomática de la Revolución Mexicana: 1912–1917* (2 vols.; Mexico: Fondo de Cultura Económica, 1958). His volumes provide insights into the diplomatic stands of the Carrancistas and present the Revolutionary viewpoint of the diplomatic crises. Fabela also edited *Documentos históricos de la Revolución Mexicana* (12 vols. to date; Mexico: Fondo de Cultura Económica and Editorial Jus, 1960–1967), which contains extracts from correspondence of Carranza and other revolutionary leaders drawn from Fabela's personal archive and other Mexican depositories. Luís Cabrera, *The Mexican Situation from a Mexican Point of View* (Washington: The Norris-Peters Company, for the Confidential Agency of the Constitutionalist Government, 1913), and Roberto Pesqueira, "The Constitutionalist Party in Mexico: What it is fighting for," *Annals of the American Academy of Political and Social Science*, LIV (July, 1914), 166–174, by Carranza's confidential agents in the United States, were studies circulated by the Constitutionalist agency in Washington and aimed at winning American support. Alfonso Junco, *Carranza y los orígenes de su rebelión* (Mexico: Ediciones Botas, 1935), criticizes Carranza, stressing his support of Porfirio Díaz and calling him a potential rebel against Madero.

There are numerous studies that touch on the Decena Trágica. Ramón Prida, editor of *El Universal* and Speaker of the Chamber of Deputies under Madero, presents many eyewitness accounts in *De la dictadura a la anarquía* (El Paso, Texas: Imprenta de El Paso del Norte, 1914). Prida criticizes Madero but opposes the coup. Ganzalo Espinosa, Joaquín Piña, and Carlos Ortíz justify the revolt in *La Decena Roja, la revolución felicista, caída del gobierno Maderista, elevación al poder del General Victoriano Huerta* (Mexico: Published by the authors, 1913). These newspaper reporters argue that the country was in a state of near anarchy under Madero, forcing the army to oust him to maintain order. They present Huerta as the man of the hour, who acted at the urging of the Senate and the Foreign Minister to end the terrible destruction of the combat. Gregorio Ponce de León, *La paz y sus colaboradores* (Mexico: Imprenta de la Secretaría de Fomento, 1914), which contains many of Huerta's proclamations and statements, and Alfonso López Ituarte, *La Decena Trágica* (Mexico: Published by the author, no date), present sympathetic accounts of Huerta's endeavors. Guillermo Núñez de Pardo, *Revolución de México: la Decena Trágica* (Barcelona: F. Granada y compañía, 1913), justifies the actions of the Díaz-Mondragón rebels and provides detailed descriptions of the fighting. R. Calixto Maldonado, *Los asesinatos de los Señores Madero y Pino Suárez* (Mexico: Published by the author, 1922), contains testimony from the Carranza government's investigation of Madero's death.

On the Huerta period, Joaquín Piña, *Memorias de Victoriano Huerta* (El Paso, Texas, 1914, and Barcelona, 1915: Published by the author), a newspaper reporter who was a close friend of Huerta's and wrote as if these were Huerta's own memoirs. The volume presents Huerta as a determined man with a plan, and its logic is just the type one would expect of him. It seems to represent accurately Huerta's strong egotism. A recent study, William L. Sherman and Richard E. Greenleaf, *Victoriano Huerta: A Reappraisal* (Mexico: Mexico City College Press, 1960), seeks to correct what it calls the false image of Huerta but is based entirely on secondary works and memoirs. In Jesús Martínez Rojas, *El asesinato oficial del Senador Belisario Domínguez: La disolución de las cámaras federales y el Gral. Victoriano Huerta; Memorias de la penitenciaría por un Diputado del XXVI Congreso de la Unión* (Mexico: Imprenta de A. Carranza e hijos, 1914), a deputy from Chiapas who headed the commission that investigated Domínguez' death, describes the coup and presents a detailed account of Domínguez' death, even naming the supposed assassins. Jan Leander DeBekker, *De cómo vino Huerta y cómo se fué: apuntes para la historia de un régimen militar* (Mexico: Librería General, 1914), includes a pro-Huerta narration of the Ten Tragic Days but severely criticizes Huerta's regime. It contains records of the Senate sessions during the revolt.

Excellent accounts of specific portions of Wilson's Mexican policy include Robert E. Quirk, *An Affair of Honor: Woodrow Wilson and the Occupation of Veracruz* (Lexington, Ky.: University of Kentucky Press, 1962), a well-written volume based mainly on primary sources. A yearbook of the Buffalo Historical Society, Frank H. Severance, ed., *Peace Episodes on the Niagara* (Buffalo, N.Y.: Buffalo Historical Society, 1914), contains an article by Severance entitled "The Peace

Conference at Niagara Falls in 1914." Based on newspaper accounts, it includes the published letters, statements, and protocols of the conference.

Studies containing information on Huerta's attempt to regain power in 1915 include Michael C. Meyer, "The Mexican-German Conspiracy of 1915," *The Americas*, XXIII, 1 (July, 1966), 76–89, a careful examination employing German documents and memoirs, contending that the German government financed the revolt; and George J. Rausch, Jr., "The Exile and Death of Victoriano Huerta," *Hispanic American Historical Review*, XLII (May, 1962), 133–151, which reaches the same conclusion, mainly from secondary sources. Studies dealing with the German Secret Service that mention the Huerta movement include John P. Jones and Paul M. Hollister, *The German Secret Service in America* (Boston: Small, Maynard and Company, 1918), and Emanuel Victor Voska and Will Irwin, *Spy and Counterspy* (New York: Doubleday, Doran and Company, 1940). The latter volume, the memoirs of the head of the Czechoslovak underground in the United States, related an incident when Voska's agents "bugged" a room in which German officials met Huerta. He gives few details of the discussion, however, and offers no further evidence. Dr. Vaclav Beneš, an acquaintance of Voska, assured this author of the credibility of Voska's statements on other matters, but efforts to produce a record of the conversation failed. Barbara Tuchman, *The Zimmermann Telegram* (New York: The Viking Press, 1958), also alleges German support of Huerta but offers little evidence. Memoirs of those involved in the controversy also provide some useful information. Capt. Franz Rintelen von Kleist, *The Dark Invader* (London and New York: The Macmillan Company, 1933), a German intelligence chief, says little about his alleged meetings with Huerta, but contends that he made deposits to Huerta bank accounts in Havana.

Contemporary accounts by foreigners present in Mexico during the Revolution include Henry Hamilton Fyfe, *The Real Mexico: A Study on the Spot* (New York: McBride, Nast, and Company, 1914). Fyfe, an English travel-book author and correspondent of the London *Times*, regards Mexicans as politically immature and advocates American intervention to protect foreigners. Another British citizen, Mrs. Rosa E. King, who lived in Cuernavaca, wrote *Tempest over Mexico: A Personal Chronicle* (Boston: Little, Brown and Company, 1935). Mrs. King became acquainted with Huerta when he fought in Morelos against Zapata, and she was also familiar with General Felipe Angeles and Francisco Madero. This well-written book shows the conditions of the peons and the isolation of the foreigners and upper classes. Manuel Márquez Sterling, the Cuban minister to Mexico at the time of the Decena Trágica, relates his experiences during the revolt in

Los últimos días del Presidente Madero: mi gestión diplomática en México (Habana: Imprenta El Siglo XX, 1917). He blames the deaths of Madero and Pino Suárez on Henry Lane Wilson and narrates his own attempts to save the imprisoned leaders.

Accounts by Americans in Mexico include a petition by the American colony, George W. Cook, *et al.*, *Facts Submitted by the American Colony to President Wilson* (Mexico: Printed by the committee, 1913), which defends the actions of Henry Lane Wilson. Major Cassius E. Gillette, one of the leaders of the American colony in its support for the ambassador, stresses the illiteracy in Mexico and contends that the people are not ready for democracy in "Mexico: its People and its Problem," *Annals of the American Academy of Political and Social Science*, LIV (July, 1914), 201–210. *A Square Deal for Mexico* (Philadelphia: Published by the American Colony in Mexico, 1913), a memorial by the American colony in Mexico published under Gillette's name, takes a similar stand, as does Edward I. Bell, *The Political Shame of Mexico* (New York: McBride, Nast, and Company, 1914), by an American who edited the *Daily Mexican* and served as the New York *Herald* correspondent in Mexico. Mrs. Edith O'Shaughnessy, *A Diplomat's Wife in Mexico* (New York: Harper and Brothers, 1916), contains letters from the wife of the American chargé to her mother, refurbished before publication. She later wrote *Intimate Pages of Mexican History* (New York: George H. Doran Company, 1920). Both volumes show her pro-Huerta feelings and dislike of Woodrow Wilson but also contain some astute observations on the people and events of the time. In Will B. Davis, *Experiences and Observations of an American Consular Officer during the recent Mexican Revolution* (Los Angeles: Wayside Press, 1920), the American vice consul in Guadalajara presents both Mexican factions as corrupt and anti-American.

John Lind gave a speech in 1914, later printed as *The Mexican People* (Minneapolis: The Bellman Press, 1915), describing his impressions of the terrain and people. He narrates Mexican history, with many errors, and his observations include several doubtful statements. His remarks indicate his sympathy for the Carrancistas. Msgr. Francis C. Kelly sought to refute Lind's criticism of the church in *A Book of Red and Yellow* (Chicago: The Catholic Church Extension Society of the United States, 1915). Kelly stresses rebel outrages against the clergy, points out Lind's mistakes in his narration of Mexican history, and charges that Lind plagiarized much of his historical account from the *Encyclopaedia Britannica*. While he does reveal Lind's bias, it is evident that Kelly is equally biased in the opposite direction. George M. Stephenson, *John Lind of Minnesota* (Minneapolis: University of Minnesota Press, 1935), a biography based largely on Lind's papers, provides the details of Lind's background.

Henry Lane Wilson gives his version of the events in *Diplomatic Episodes in Mexico, Belgium, and Chile* (Garden City, N.Y.: Doubleday, Page and Company, 1927), and also in articles, "Errors with Reference to Mexico," *Annals of the American Academy of Political and Social Science*, LIV (July, 1914), 148–161, and "How to Restore Peace in Mexico," in George H. Blakeslee, ed., *Mexico and the Caribbean* (New York: G. E. Stechert and Company, 1920). These works indicate Wilson's conviction that Mexicans were not ready to govern themselves and needed a strong dictatorship to keep the country at peace. The first charges against Wilson by Luís Manuel Rojas in March, 1913, appeared in newspapers at that time. Rojas later expanded his statement as *La culpa de Henry Lane Wilson en el gran desastre de México*: (Mexico: Compañía editorial *La Verdad*, 1928). Much of the book deals with Mexico's readiness for democracy, rather than with Wilson. A more exhaustive anti-Wilson tract, Ramón Prida, *La culpa de Lane Wilson, Embajador de los E.U.A. en la tragedia Mexicana de 1913* (Mexico: Ediciones Botas, 1962), quotes and then disagrees with the ambassador's telegrams, seeking to show that he misinformed Washington. In a series of articles, Robert H. Murray, the Mexican correspondent of the New York *World*, attacks Henry Lane Wilson for his role in the Huerta coup. Murray and the ambassador had a personal feud, for Wilson had once thrown the reporter out of the embassy. Murray's "Huerta and the Two Wilsons," *Harpers Weekly*, LXII (March 25 through April 29, 1916), charged that the ambassador was one of the leading plotters against Madero.

Memoirs of Mexicans active during the Huerta period include Querido Moheno, *Mi actuación política después de la Decena Trágica* (Mexico: Ediciones Botas, 1939). Moheno describes some Cabinet discussions and ministers' decisions regarding the October coup. Garza Aldape's leading role in the administration emerges clearly. *Memorias de Nemesio García Naranjo* (8 vols.; Monterrey: Ediciones de *El Porvenir*, 1956–1962), contains the views of Huerta's Minister of Public Education. Volume VII deals with the Huerta period and reveals the internal operation of the government, as well as the views of the author and other members of the Cabinet. Volume I also contains some comments on Huerta, while Volume VI covers the Madero period. Volume VIII contains an account of García Naranjo's conversations with Huerta at the time of his unsuccessful attempt to return to power, which provides valuable information on a period of Huerta's life for which there are few records. Rudolfo Reyes, *De mi vida, memorias políticas* (2 vols.; Madrid: Biblioteca Nueva, 1929–1930), partly written while Reyes was in prison as a result of Huerta's coup, seeks mainly to vindicate his father and himself, blaming Huerta for the deaths of Madero and Pino Suárez. Carranza's private secretary, Alfredo

Braceda, describes the revolt and includes many letters and documents in *México Revolucionario: 1913–1917* (2 vols.; Mexico: Ediciones Botas, 1941).

The New York *Times* is among the better newspapers for foreign-affairs reporting and usually printed several articles on Mexico, often by reporters with different viewpoints. The New York *World*, a staunch backer of the Wilson administration, still showed muckraking tendencies during this period and thus often relegated foreign affairs to a minor role. Whenever the situation grew tense, the *World* would advocate armed intervention and often predicted marine landings in Mexico. Its chief correspondent in Mexico, Robert Murray, was highly critical of Huerta and a bitter enemy of Ambassador Henry Lane Wilson. The Washington *Post*, an antiadministration paper, favored intervention during both Madero's and Huerta's terms, stressing protection of American interests, and supported Henry Lane Wilson editorially. The Brooklyn *Daily Eagle* sent Paul Davis to Mexico in March, 1914, and this reporter was particularly perceptive. His descriptions of people and events often revealed facets overlooked by other observers, but he spent much of his time in besieged Torreón and therefore sent few dispatches. In June and July, 1914, the New York *Herald* reprinted a series of letters purporting to be from the personal papers of Sherbourne G. Hopkins, indicating that Standard Oil and American capitalists had financed the Madero revolution and showing similar connections between American capitalists and Carranza, whom Hopkins represented in Washington. Newspapers from other parts of the country, such as the Los Angeles *Times*, the San Francisco *Examiner*, and the Chicago *Daily Tribune*, served to illustrate public opinion and indicate the general stance of the press throughout the nation.

Mexican newspapers were subject to government pressure and often to censorship, and hence there was no true opposition paper. *El Imparcial* showed occasional independence but backed the Huerta government in its infrequent editorials. On September 29, 1913, *El Imparcial* acquired a new editor, and thereafter it faithfully followed the Huerta line. *El País*, a highly conservative newspaper, praised the Catholic party as the only true party in Mexico, although it did not consistently support its candidates. *El País* constantly criticized the subservience of the other papers of the capital. Its numerous editorials and guest editorials often opposed Huerta's policies, although its news reporting was generally favorable to the regime. *La Nación*, the organ of the Catholic party, bitterly denounced government pressure against the party at election time, attacked Huerta's October coup, and rejected the elections as fraudulent. As a result, the government closed *La Nación* on December 22, 1913. As a Catholic party organ, the paper was more interested in propaganda than news reporting. The *Mexican Herald*, the newspaper of the American community in Mexico, was pro-Huerta and rabidly supported Henry Lane Wilson. This paper contains few editorials of its own, as it usually reprinted editorials from American papers. The *Mexican Herald* continued publishing throughout most of the Ten Days Revolt and thus furnished a valuable account of the struggle. The paper moved to Veracruz after the United States seizure of that city. All the above Mexican papers are part of the collection of the Hemeroteca Nacional.

The London *Times* indicates British reaction to Wilson's policies. Its coverage of internal Mexican events reflected the European view of trends in that country and provides a contrast with the reporting of many American papers. *El Mercurio* of Santiago, Chile, indicates the South American reaction to Wilson's Mexican policy. *El Mercurio* frequently reprinted editorials from Buenos Aires papers, particularly *La Nación, La Prensa,* and *La Razón,* and therefore indicated the Argentine view as well as the Chilean.

The Senate Foreign Relations Committee twice investigated Mexican events during this time. The first, United States Senate Committee on Foreign Relations, *Revolutions in Mexico,* 62d Cong., 2d sess. (Washington: U.S. Government Printing Office, 1913), was under the chairmanship of Senator William Alden Smith. This investigation sought connections between United States capitalists and the Madero revolution. A second series of hearings, concerned with the entire revolutionary period, United States Senate Committee on Foreign Relations, *Investigation of Mexican Affairs,* 66th Cong., 2d. sess. (2 vols.; Washington: U.S. Government Printing Office, 1920), under the chairmanship of Senator Albert Fall, contains testimony by many members of the American colony in Mexico, most of whom opposed Wilson's policy.

State Department papers in the National Archives contain the dispatches and records from the period. The numerical files are all in Record Group 59. The 812.00 file, entitled Records Relating to the Internal Affairs of Mexico, 1910–1929, is the most valuable of these. It contains most of the dispatches from the embassy and the special agents, as well as the corresponding State Department answers and instructions. Some dispatches from other embassies concerning Mexico are also included. There is a 711.12 file entitled Records Regarding Political Relations Between the United States and Mexico, 1910–1929, containing little information, as nearly all the papers for this time are in the 812.00 file. The files that begin with 812. contain other useful information. The reports of Zaccary Cobb to the Department regarding Huerta's arrest in 1915 are in 812.001 H87. Financial data on Mexico is in 812.51, while 812.032 is a file of presidential speeches, including those of Huerta. File 812.113 deals with arms shipments to Mexico, consisting mainly of permits allowing companies to ship arms during the embargo. The 812.2311 file contains information on troop internment. Latin American comments on United States actions are in the 710.11 file, while information on British Minister Sir Lionel Carden and American efforts to secure his recall is in the 701.4112 and 701.4114 files. British claims, including the Benton case, are in the 312.41 file. The 701.6211 file catalogs the activities of the German diplomats in the United States. State Department agents kept close watch on all German diplomats, including the military attachés, and the file contains no indication of contacts with Huerta. In addition to these, many isolated memoranda by Department members dealing with various subjects cited in the text are too minute to repeat here. The personnel file on Henry Lane Wilson, 123.W691, contained useful information on his career.

State Department papers in Record Group 84 contain the post records of the embassy and the consulates. The 800 or class 8 portion of the post records, dealing with political affairs, contained some analyses and papers not transmitted to the State Department, as well as duplicates of dispatches in the 812.00 file. The consular post records also have correspondence between consulates that was not forwarded to the Department. The post records of the embassy, the consulates general at Monterrey and Mexico City, and the consulates at Veracruz, Tampico, Hermosillo, Saltillo, and Piedras Negras (then Ciudad Porfirio Díaz), proved useful. The records of Monterrey were most valuable, containing dispatches from consulates throughout northern Mexico. Records of Saltillo contained reports on American efforts to promote negotiations between Huerta and Carranza. A four-volume compilation of the "Correspondence of Secretary of State Bryan with President Wilson, 1913–1915," available at the Archives, revealed the thoughts of Wilson and Bryan on Mexican matters and showed the interaction between them.

Records of the War Department in Record Group 165 included a biography of Huerta, W.C.P. 7422, by a war correspondent, Edwin Emerson. The Military Intelligence File in the War College Division, 5761, the most valuable of the War Department records, was made available to the author by special permission of Victor Gondos, Jr., Chief of the Army and Air Force Branch of the Archives, for the file is not declassified. It contained the reports of the military attaché, Capt. William Burnside, and thus provided a military view of the Huerta coup, Huerta's earlier campaigns, and the Revolution. In addition, there are numerous single memoranda and documents in Record Group 165 that cannot be mentioned here. Record Group 94, records of the Adjutant General, also contained valuable reports, mainly in large consolidated files, AG2008188 and AG1875135–A. Files AG214991 and AG2284054, the latter dealing with Huerta's arrest in 1915, also contained useful information. The files on Huerta and the activities of the German military attachés in the United States in the Military Intelligence Division, War College Division, and Adjutant General's Office contained no indication of contacts between Huerta and the German attachés.

Records in the Department of Justice, Record Group 60, contained the Department's file on Huerta's arrest and internment, 90755–U, and also files on violations of the embargo, 90755–G to T. There is also a file entitled Correspondence of Mexican Consuls, 170392, although it contains little information. File 157013–A contained information on efforts to trace the *Ypiranga* cargo and also had important data on the voyage of the *Sunshine*. Other arms violations are in 157013–8 to 13. The author also checked Treasury Department records containing daily reports of Secret Service agents along the Texas border head-quartered in San Antonio, Record Group 87, by permission of the Secret Service, United States Treasury Department, United States Secret Service, Daily Reports of Agents, 1875 through 1936, San Antonio.

Official decrees of the Mexican government appeared in the *Diario Oficial*, published by the government. It also includes brief résumés of congressional sessions. At first, the *Diario Oficial* merely printed these government acts, but in October, 1913, the Huerta government placed a new editor in charge, and the *Diario Oficial* then became an organ of the government, publishing lavish praise of Huerta and reprinting editorials from foreign papers that praised Huerta. The congressional debates regarding Huerta's assumption of power appear in Diego Arenas Guzman, *Historia de la Cámara de Diputados de la XXVI Legislatura Federal* (4 vols.; Mexico: Instituto Nacional de Estudios Históricos, 1963). Documenting the internal activities of the Mexican government proved difficult, due to the normal turmoil of a revolution-ary transfer of power. Quite naturally, the victorious revolutionaries were not very careful about preserving the records of their defeated adversary. Therefore, few of the papers of the Huerta government still exist. Gaining access to government records in Mexico is also far more difficult than in the United States, and special permission was required in all instances.

The Archivo Relaciones Exteriores de México, housed in the Minis-terio des Relaciones Exteriores, was naturally a valuable Mexican source. The series entitled Revolución Mexicana durante los Años de 1910 a 1920, Informaciones Diversas de la República y de las Oficinas de México en el Exterior, H/513–1910–20/1, contained most of the relevant information. The documents were scattered throughout the collection, which is not arranged in chronological order. The published guide to the series, Berta Ulloa, *Revolución Mexicana, 1910–1920* (Mexico: Imprenta de la Secretaría des Relaciones Exteriores, 1963), proved helpful in locating relevant files within the series. The collection affords some indication of the reports by Mexican consuls in the United States, although there are few dispatches from the embassy in Washington and no records of the Niagara Falls Conference. The files also contain some correspondence of the Carrancista chancellory. Unfortunately, the majority of the communications exchanged by the Huerta Foreign Ministry with its agents in the United States deal with rebel troop movements and hence provide more information on internal events than on relations with the United States. There are enough communications dealing with diplomatic questions to shed some light on the Mexican reaction to the stands of the Wilson administration. Another series entitled Cuestión diplomática de la Revolución: Desocupación de Veracruz: Año de 1914, III/252(73:72)914, also contained some information on the seizure of the city.

The Archivo Histórico Defensa Nacional contains the records of the Ministry of Defense. File XI, 481.5, deals with the revolutionary era. While there are extensive records dealing with the Huerta period, most of them concern purely military matters, such as promotions and transfers of officers. The papers illustrate internal conditions in Mexico and provide a picture of the general military situation, as well as detailed accounts of battles.

The papers of the Ministry of Gobernación are in the Archivo General de México. These appear incomplete, however, and contain only papers dealing with routine matters. There are no records of arrests or activities in connection with the elections held. There are some incomplete election returns, and these proved interesting. Fragments of the papers of the Ministry of Fomento (development) are also in the Archives, but nothing remains of those of other ministries. In addition, there are some papers of the Secretaría Particular de la Presidencia and correspondence of Francisco Madero. There are no Huerta papers.

British diplomatic documents dealing with Mexico that contain useful information on this period are located in the Public Record Office, London. File 414/235, entitled "Further correspondence respecting the Affairs of North America," is a compilation of communications from several other files. The 204 file contains the post records of the British legation in Mexico City, while the 371 file contains the Foreign Office records from the period relating to Mexico. These British documents show the calculations involved in the British actions, provide an analysis of Mexican events from a non-American viewpoint, and indicate the British government's reaction to Wilson's policies. They also reveal the views of other European governments through records of the exchanges with them.

Useful published collections of private papers include Ray Stannard Baker, *Woodrow Wilson: Life and Letters* (7 vols.; Garden City, N.Y.: Doubleday, Doran and Company, 1931). Vol. IV contained his public statements on Mexico. Charles Seymour, ed., *The Intimate Papers of Colonel House* (3 vols.; Boston and New York: Houghton Mifflin Company, 1926), illustrates the role House played in the Mexican crises and negotiations with Great Britain about Mexican policy. Burton J. Hendrick, *The Life and Letters of Walter H. Page* (3 vols.; Garden City, N.Y.: Doubleday, Page and Company, 1922–1925), contains many of Page's letters. Page frequently wrote to House and Wilson complaining of troubles or exalting his success, and thus his letters are particularly revealing and indicate his zeal for winning British support of Wilson's policy.

The private papers of individuals in the government during this period who had a part in formulating America's Mexican policy provide many insights into these decisions. The largest group of such papers is in the Library of Congress Manuscript Division. The Papers of Woodrow Wilson contain the President's correspondence with other officials, although Wilson generally wrote only brief letters that did not fully reveal his thoughts. His papers contain many memoranda and dictated reports sent directly to him that cannot be found elsewhere. Most of the information is in the President's Personal File. The Josephus Daniels Papers include his diary, with detailed notes of each Cabinet meeting during the first months of the administration. These notes record the stands of various Cabinet members, but Daniels soon found the burdens of office too pressing, and his diary became merely an appointment book kept by his secretary. His Navy Department files contain the reports of the naval commanders. The Papers of William Jennings Bryan contain little for this period, but there are a few notes not in the State Department papers. The Papers of Robert Lansing contain some pertinent letters from this period. Although his diaries do not start during these years, there are some later entries on individuals involved. The Papers of William Howard Taft contain some interesting correspondence with Henry Lane Wilson and other figures. The Papers of Chandler P. Anderson, Counselor of the State Department, have a few relevant letters and also a "diary" for this period, although this merely consists of material gathered for a diary that he never wrote. The Papers of General Hugh Scott and those of General Tasker H. Bliss include some revealing correspondence between the two generals about border conditions. The Bliss Papers also contain copies of his official reports on border conditions. The Papers of Charles Evans Hughes contain some correspondence with Henry Lane Wilson during the 1916 campaign, when Wilson provided his views to serve as ammunition for attacks on the President's Mexican policy.

The Papers of John Lind at the Minnesota Historical Society in Saint Paul contain most of his dispatches from Mexico, including a few not in the State Department papers. The papers show Lind's sources of information in Mexico and contain correspondence with various informants, thus enabling a judgment on their accuracy. His memoranda and letters also reveal what he knew of the Mexican situation and indicate the extent of his influence. The papers also show his connection with the Constitutionalists during the Niagara Falls Conference and after his retirement. The Papers of Colonel Edward M. House at Yale University contain interesting letters from Walter Hines Page. House's Diary gives a daily summary of his activities and shows his role in Mexican affairs. It also provides insights into the people involved, especially President Wilson. The Papers of William Frank Buckley at the University of Texas contain many newspaper clippings, as well as correspondence between Rabasa and Buckley, and some copies of letters between Carranza and his agents in the United States.

A portion of the Papers of Emilio Rabasa, head of the Huerta delegation to the Niagara Falls Conference, are also at the University of Texas. This consists of the archive of the delegation and is a single volume of typewritten letters and memoranda entitled "Copia de la correspondencia telegráfica con la secretaría de hacienda," although it also contains the delegation's correspondence with the Secretary of Foreign Relations and a diary, kept either by the secretary of the delegation or Rabasa. These papers contain the instructions received by the Mexican delegation and all their proposals. They reveal the Mexican delegates' thoughts on the conference, the views of the mediators, and also the role played by the Secretary of Hacienda (treasury), who superseded the acting Secretary of Foreign Relations in matters pertaining to the conference. There are no other private papers of Huerta government officials existing, as the members of his regime were all compelled to flee the country upon the victory of the revolutionaries and could not carry whatever papers they might have had with them.

Interviews partially compensated for the absence of Mexican private papers. Dr. Roberto Esteva Ruiz, who served as Deputy Minister of Foreign Relations and then as acting minister under Huerta, provided some useful information on the Mexican Foreign Office and its operations during this period. He also offered illuminating comments on some of the personalities involved, as well as information on the Mexican side of the diplomatic discussions. The author also interviewed Nemesio García Naranjo, Jr., several times, and since he was too young to have any personal recollection of the Huerta period, all his comments were based on things his father had told him, thus indicating the views of Huerta's Minister of Public Instruction. His father knew Huerta well, and he provided many insights into Huerta's character, as well as information on other figures in the government and the general political climate of the period. René León, an American financier active in Mexico, provided a view of the era as seen through the eyes of a foreigner. He was acquainted with Huerta, Madero, and many of the other key figures during this period.

In addition to the written records, there is always the intangible factor of understanding the people involved and being familiar with the terrain, for these can provide many insights and enable a better interpretation of the written matter. In addition to research trips and visits of short duration, the author spent one year in Mexico, thanks to a fellowship from the Henry L. and Grace Doherty Foundation. This stay provided an opportunity to become well acquainted with the Mexican people, their culture, and customs at first hand, as well as to consult the records in Mexico. The author became familiar with Mexico City and walked the area that was the battleground during the Ten Days Revolt, examining the Ciudadela as well as the Palace and the Alameda. He also visited the state of Morelos, stronghold of Zapata, traveling the route Huerta's force probably took from Cuernavaca to Yautepec to Cuautla, and examined the difficult terrain and steep mountains that enabled Zapata to successfully avoid federal forces despite his proximity to the capital. The author also observed some of the difficult terrain of the north. This experience has certainly added much to the present study, although such intangibles cannot be footnoted.

ADLER, SELIG. "Bryan and Wilsonian Caribbean Policy," *Hispanic American Historical Review*, XX (1940), 198–226.

ALCERRESA, FÉLIX N. *Crónica de los acontecimientos trágicos y políticos que tuvieron lugar en la Ciudad de México del 9 al 29 de febrero de 1913*. Mexico: Imprenta Mixta, 1913.

ALESSIO ROBLES, MIGUEL. *Historia política de la Revolución*. Mexico: Ediciones Botas, 1938.

ALSOP, EM BOWLES (ED.). *The Greatness of Woodrow Wilson: 1856–1956*. New York and Toronto: Rinehart and Company, 1956.

AMAYA, GENERAL JUAN GUALBERTO. *Madero y los auténticos revolucionarios de 1910*. Mexico: Published by the author, 1946.

AMAYA MORÁN, ARTURO. *Examen histórico-jurídico del gobierno de Huerta*. Mexico: Published by the author, 1952.

ANNIN, ROBERT E. *Woodrow Wilson: A Character Study*. New York: Dodd, Mead and Company, 1924.

ARAGÓN, ALFREDO. *El Desarme del ejército federal por la Revolución de 1913.* Paris: Imprimeries Wellhoff et Roche, 1915.

BAILEY, THOMAS A. *Wilson and the Peacemakers.* New York: The Macmillan Company, 1944.

BAKER, GEORGE W., JR. "The Wilson Administration and Nicaragua: 1913-1921," *The Americas,* XXII, 4 (April, 1966), 339-376.

―――. "Woodrow Wilson's Use of the Non-recognition Policy in Costa Rica," *The Americas,* XXII, 1 (July, 1965), 3-21.

BECU, CARLOS A. *El "A.B.C." y su concepto político y jurídico.* Buenos Aires: Librería "La Facultad" de Juan Roldán, 1915.

BEMIS, SAMUEL FLAGG. *The Latin American Policy of the United States.* New York: Harcourt, Brace and Company, 1943.

BERNSTORFF, COUNT JOHANN VON. *My Three Years in America.* New York: Charles Scribner's Sons, 1920.

BLAISDEL, LOWELL L. "Henry Lane Wilson and the Overthrow of Madero," *Southwestern Social Science Quarterly,* XL, 2 (September, 1962), 126-135.

BLANCO MOHENO, ROBERTO. *Crónica de la Revolución Mexicana: de la Decena Trágica a los campos de Celaya.* Mexico: Libros Mexicana, 1957.

BLUM, JOHN M. *Woodrow Wilson and the Politics of Morality.* Boston: Little, Brown and Company, 1956.

BLYTHE, SAMUEL G. "The Record of a Conference with President Woodrow Wilson," *Saturday Evening Post,* CLXXXVI, 47 (May 23, 1914).

BONILLA, POLICARPO. *Wilson Doctrine.* New York: Published by the author, 1914.

BROOKS, EUGENE C. *Woodrow Wilson as President.* New York and Chicago: Row, Peterson and Company, 1916.

BRYAN, WILLIAM JENNINGS AND MARY BAIRD. *The Memoirs of William Jennings Bryan.* Chicago and Philadelphia: John C. Winston Company, 1925.

BUEHRIG, EDWARD H. (ED.). *Wilson's Foreign Policy in Perspective.* Bloomington, Indiana: Indiana University Press, 1957.

BULLITT, WILLIAM C., AND SIGMUND FREUD. *Thomas Woodrow Wilson: A Psychological Study.* Boston: Houghton Mifflin Company, 1967.

BULNES, FRANCISCO. *The Whole Truth about Mexico: President Wilson's Responsibility.* New York: M. Bulnes Book Company, 1916.

BUSEY, JAMES L. "Don Victoriano Huerta y la Prensa Yanqui," *Historia Mexicana,* IV, 4 (April–June, 1955), 582–594.

BUSTAMANTE, LUÍS F. *Bajo el terror Huertista.* San Luis Potosí, Mexico: Published by the author, 1916.

CABRERA, LUIS. *Obras políticas del Lic. Blas Urrea.* Mexico: Imprenta Nacional, 1921.

CALERO, MANUEL. *The Mexican Policy of President Wilson as It Appears to a Mexican.* New York: Press of Smith and Thomson, 1916.

———. *Un decenio de política Mexicana.* New York: Middleditch Company, 1920.

CALLAHAN, JAMES M. *American Foreign Policy in Mexican Relations.* New York: The Macmillan Company, 1932.

CALLCOTT, WILFRED HARDY. *The Caribbean Policy of the United States 1890–1920.* Baltimore: Johns Hopkins University Press, 1942.

CALVERT, PETER A. "Francis Stronge en la Decena Trágica," *Historia Mexicana,* XV, 1 (July–September, 1965), 47–68.

CLENDENEN, CLARENCE C. *The United States and Pancho Villa.* Ithaca, N.Y.: Cornell University Press, 1961.

CLINE, HOWARD F. *The United States and Mexico.* New York: Atheneum Publishers, 1963.

COLETTA, PAOLO E. "Bryan, Anti-imperialism and Missionary Diplomacy," *Nebraska History,* XLIV, 3 (September, 1963), 167–187.

COSÍO VILLEGAS, DANIEL. "Sobre Henry Lane Wilson," in *Memoria del Colegio Nacional.* Mexico: El Colegio de México, 1961.

CREEL, GEORGE. *Rebel at Large: Recollections of Fifty Crowded Years.* New York: G. P. Putnam's Sons, 1947.

CRONON, E. DAVID (ED.). *The Cabinet Diaries of Josephus Daniels: 1913–1921.* Lincoln, Nebr.: University of Nebraska Press, 1963.

CUMBERLAND, CHARLES C. "Huerta y Carranza ante la Ocupación de Veracruz," *Historia Mexicana,* VI, 4 (April–June, 1957), 534–537.

DAVENPORT, E. H., AND SIDNEY RUSSELL COOKE. *The Oil Trusts and Anglo-American Relations.* New York: The Macmillan Company, 1924.

DIDAPP, JUAN P. *Los Estados Unidos y nuestros conflictos internos.* Mexico: Tipográficos de *El Republicano*, 1913.

DOBLADO, MANUEL. *México para los Mexicanos: El Presidente Wilson y su gobierno.* Mexico: Imprenta de Antonio Enríquez, 1913.

FERNÁNDEZ GUEL, ROGELIO. *Episodios de la Revolución Mexicana.* San José, Costa Rica: Imprenta Trejos Hermanos, 1915.

FERNÁNDEZ ROJAS, JOSÉ. *De Porfirio Díaz a Victoriano Huerta*, 2d ed. Guadalajara: Tipo de la Escuela de Artes y Oficios del Estudio, 1913.

FERRELL, ROBERT H. "Woodrow Wilson: Man and Statesman," *Review of Politics*, XVIII, 1 (April, 1956), 131–145.

FIGUEROA DOMENECH, J. *Veinte meses de anarquía.* Mexico: Privately printed, 1913.

FLORES D., JORGE. "Carlos Pereyra y el Embajador Wilson," *Historia Mexicana*, VIII (July–September, 1958), 95–121.

GALLARDO GALVARINO, NIETO. *Panamericanismo.* Santiago, Chile: Imprenta Nacimiento, 1941.

GARRATY, JOHN A. "Woodrow Wilson, a Study in Personality," *South Atlantic Quarterly*, LVI (April, 1957), 176–185.

GARZA TREVIÑO, CIRO DE LA. *Wilson y Huerta, Tampico y Veracruz; ensayo de divulgación histórica.* Mexico: Published by the author, 1933.

GEORGE, ALEXANDER AND JULIET. *Woodrow Wilson and Colonel House: A Personality Study.* New York: John Day Company, 1956.

GERARD, JAMES W. *Face to Face with Kaiserism.* New York: George H. Doran Co., 1918.

GIBBS, GEORGE SWEET, AND EVELYN H. KNOWLTON. *The Resurgent Years: 1911–1927*, II. *The History of Standard Oil.* 2 vols. New York: Harper and Row Company, 1956.

GOLTZ, HORST VON DER. *My Adventures as a German Secret Service Agent.* London: Cassell and Company, 1918.

GONZÁLES BLANCO, EDMUNDO. *Carranza y la Revolución de México.* Madrid: Imprenta Helénica, 1916.

GONZÁLEZ BLANCO, PEDRO. *De Porfirio Díaz a Carranza.* Madrid: Imprenta Helénica, 1916.

GONZÁLEZ GARZA, FEDERICO. *La Revolución Mexicana*. Mexico: A. del Bosque, impresor, 1936.

GONZÁLEZ RAMIREZ, MANUEL. *La Revolución Social de México*. Mexico: Fondo de Cultura Económica, 1960.

GORDON, WENDELL C. *The Expropriation of Foreign-Owned Property in Mexico*. Washington: American Council on Public Affairs, 1941.

GRAYSON, ADMIRAL CARY TRAVERS. *Woodrow Wilson: An Intimate Memoir*. New York: Holt, Rinehart and Winston, 1960.

GREY, SIR EDWARD, FIRST VISCOUNT OF FALLODON. *Twenty-five Years: 1892–1916*. 2 vols. New York: Frederick A. Stokes Company, 1925.

GUZMAN, RAMÓN. *El Intervencionismo de Mr. Wilson en México*. New Orleans: Published by the author, 1915.

GWYNN, STEPHEN. *The Letters and Friendships of Sir Cecil Spring-Rice: A Record*. 2 vols. Boston: Houghton Mifflin Company, 1929.

HACKETT, CHARLES W. "The Mexican Revolution and the United States: 1910–1926," *World Peace Foundation Pamphlets*, IX, 5 (1926).

HALE, WILLIAM BAYARD. *Woodrow Wilson: The Story of his Life*. Garden City, N.Y.: Doubleday, Page and Company, 1911.

HARRISON, JOHN P. "Henry Lane Wilson, el trágica de la decena," *Historia Mexicana*, VI, 3 (January–March, 1957), 374–405.

———. "Un análisis Norteamericano de la Revolución Mexicana en 1913," *Historia Mexicana*, V, 4 (April–June, 1956), 598–618.

HART, ALBERT BUSHNELL. "The Postulates of the Mexican Situation," *Annals of the American Academy of Political and Social Science*, LIV (July, 1914), 136–147.

HIDY, MURIEL E. AND RALPH W. *Pioneering in Big Business: 1882–1911*. Vol. I, *The History of the Standard Oil Company*. 2 vols. New York: Harper and Row Company, 1955–1956.

HINKLEY, TED C. "Wilson, Huerta, and the Twenty-One Gun Salute," *The Historian*, XXII, 2 (February, 1960), 197–206.

HOHLER, SIR THOMAS B. *Diplomatic Petrel*. London: John Murray, 1942.

HOUSTON, DAVID FRANKLIN. *Eight Years with Wilson's Cabinet: 1913–1920*. 2 vols. Garden City, N.Y.: Doubleday, Page and Company, 1926.

JAMES, DANIEL. *Mexico and the Americas.* New York: Frederick A. Praeger, 1963.

KAHLE, LUIS G. "Robert Lansing and the Recognition of Venustiano Carranza," *Hispanic American Historical Review*, XXXVIII, 3 (August, 1958), 353-373.

KATZ, FREDERICH. "Alemánia y Francisco Villa," *Historia Mexicana*, XII, 1 (July-September, 1962), 88-102.

KEMMERER, EDWIN W. *Inflation and Revolution: Mexico's Experience of 1912-1917.* Princeton, N.J.: Princeton University Press, 1940.

LANE, ANNE W., AND LOUISE H. WALL (EDS.). *The Letters of Franklin K. Lane.* Boston: Houghton Mifflin Company, 1922.

LANSING, ROBERT. *War Memoirs of Robert Lansing.* New York: Bobbs-Merrill Co., 1935.

LARA PARDO, DR. LUIS. *Marcha de dictadores: Wilson contra Huerta: Carranza contra Wilson.* Mexico: A. P. Márquez, 1942.

LAWRENCE, DAVID. *The True Story of Woodrow Wilson.* New York: George H. Doran Company, 1924.

LECHARTIER, G. *Intrigues et Diplomaties à Washington, 1914-1917.* Paris: Plon-Nourrit et Cie., 1919.

LINK, ARTHUR S. *Wilson: The Road to the White House.* Princeton, N.J.: Princeton University Press, 1947.

LODGE, SENATOR HENRY CABOT. *The Senate and the League of Nations.* New York: Charles Scribner's Sons, 1925.

LUQUÍN, EDUARDO. *La política internacional de la revolución Constituciónalista.* Mexico: Biblioteca del Instituto Nacional de Estudios Históricos de la Revolución Mexicana, 1957.

McADOO, WILLIAM G. *Crowded Years.* Boston: Houghton Mifflin Company, 1931.

MACCORKLE, STUART A. *American Policy of Recognition Towards Mexico.* Baltimore: Johns Hopkins University Press, 1933.

MADERO, FRANCISCO I. *Las memorias y las mejores cartas de Francisco I. Madero.* Mexico: Libro Mexicana, 1956.

MANCISIDOR, JOSÉ. "El Huertismo," *Historia Mexicana*, III, 1 (July-September, 1953), 34-51.

MARÍA Y CAMPOS, ARMANDO DE. *Episodios de la Revolución: de la caída de Porfirio Díaz a la Decena Trágica.* Mexico: Libro Mexicana, 1957.

MELÉNDEZ, JOSÉ T. (ED.). *Historia de la Revolución Mexicana.* 2 vols. Mexico: Talleres gráficos de La Nación, 1936.

MENDIOLA, GABRIEL FERRER DE. *Historia de la Revolución Mexicana.* Mexico: Ediciones de *El Nacional,* 1956.

MOORE, JOHN BASSETT. *A Digest of International Law.* 8 vols. Washington: U.S. Government Printing Office, 1906.

MORALES JIMÉNEZ, ALBERTO. *Hombres de la Revolución Mexicana.* Mexico: Biblioteca del Instituto Nacional de Estudios Históricos de la Revolución Mexicana, 1960.

MORENO, DANIEL A. *Los hombres de la Revolución: 40 estudios biográficos.* Mexico: Libro Mex Editores, 1960.

———. *Francisco I. Madero, José M. Pino Suárez, el crimen de la embajada.* Mexico: Libros Mexicana, 1960.

MUNRO, DANA GARDNER. *The United States and the Caribbean Area.* Boston: World Peace Foundation, 1934.

NÚÑEZ DE PARDO, GUILLERMO. *Revolución de México: la Decena Trágica.* Barcelona: F. Granada y compañía, 1913.

OSBORN, GEORGE C. "Woodrow Wilson visits Mobile," *Alabama Historical Quarterly,* XIX (1957), 157–169.

PANIAGUA, EMIGDIO S. *El combate de la Ciudadela narrado por un extranjero.* Mexico: Tipográfica Artística, 1913.

PAPEN, FRANZ VON. *Memoirs.* New York: E. P. Dutton and Company, 1953.

PARKES, HENRY BAMFORD. *A History of Mexico,* 3d ed. London: Eyre and Spottiswoode Company, 1962.

PIKE, FREDERICK B. *Chile and the United States: 1880–1962.* South Bend, Ind.: University of Notre Dame Press, 1963.

PUENTE, RAMÓN. *La dictadura, la Revolución, y sus hombres.* Mexico: Ediciones Bocetas, 1938.

———. *Pascual Orozco y la revuelta de Chihuahua.* Mexico: Eusebio Gómez de la Puente, 1912.

QUIRK, ROBERT E. *The Mexican Revolution: 1914–1915, the Convention of Aguascalientes*. Bloomington, Ind.: Indiana University Press, 1960.

RAMIREZ PLANCARTE, FRANCISCO. *La Ciudad de México durante la revolución constituciónalista*, 2d ed. Mexico: Ediciones Botas, 1941.

RIPPY, JAMES FRED, GUY STEVENS, AND JOSÉ VASCONCELOS. *American Policy Abroad: Mexico*. Chicago: The University of Chicago Press, 1928.

ROBINSON, EDGAR E., AND VICTOR J. WEST. *The Foreign Policy of Woodrow Wilson: 1913–1917*. New York: The Macmillan Company, 1917.

ROMÉRO FLORES, JESÚS. *Del Porfirismo a la revolución constituciónalista*. Vol. I of *Anales históricos de la Revolución Mexicana*. Mexico: Ediciones Encuadernales, 1939.

SILVA HERZOG, JESÚS. *Breve historia de la Revolución Mexicana*. 2 vols. Mexico: Fondo de Cultura Económica, 1962.

SPENDER, JOHN A. *Weetman Pearson: First Viscount Cowdray—1856–1927*. London: Cassell and Company, 1930.

STARR, FREDERICK. *Mexico and the United States*. Chicago: The Bible House, 1914.

TABLADA, JOSÉ JUAN. *Historia de la campaña de la división del norte*. Mexico: Imprenta del Gobierno Federal, 1913.

TANNENBAUM, FRANK. *Mexico: The Struggle for Peace and Bread*. New York: Alfred A. Knopf, 1950.

TARACENA, ALFONSO. *La verdadera Revolución Mexicana*. 6 vols. Mexico: Editorial Jus, 1960.

———. *Madero, víctima del imperialismo Yanqui*. Mexico: Editorial Jus, 1960.

THOMPSON, CHARLES W. *Presidents I've Known and Two Near Presidents*. Indianapolis: Bobbs-Merrill Company, 1929.

TORO, CARLOS. *La caída de Madero por la revolución felicista*. Mexico: Published by the author, 1913.

TORRERA, GENERAL JUAN MANUEL. *La Decena Trágica, apuntes para la historia del ejército Mexicano*. 2 vols. Mexico: Ediciones Joloco, 1939.

TRAMERAGE, PIERRE L'ESPAGNOL DE LA. *The World Struggle for Oil*. Trans. C. Leonard Lesse. New York: Alfred A. Knopf, 1924.

TRAVESÍ, GONZALO G. *La Revolución Mexicana y el imperialismo Yanqui*. Barcelona: Casa Editorial Maucci, 1914.

TREVELYAN, GEORGE MACAULAY. *Grey of Fallodon: The Life and Letters of Sir Edward Grey, afterwards Viscount Grey of Fallodon*. Boston: Houghton Mifflin Company, 1937.

TURLINGTON, EDGAR W. *Mexico and her Foreign Creditors*. New York: Columbia University Press, 1930.

TURNER, JOHN KENNETH. *Hands Off Mexico*. New York: The Rand School of Social Science, 1920.

TWEEDIE, MRS. ALEC. *Mexico as I Saw It*. London: Hurst and Blackett, Limited, 1901.

———. *Mexico from Díaz to the Kaiser*. New York: George H. Doran Company, 1918.

ULLOA ORTIZ, BERTA. "Carranza y el armamento norteamericano," *Historia Mexicana*, XVII, 2 (October–December, 1967), 253–262.

VELÁZQUEZ, JOSÉ VÍCTOR. *Apuntes para la historia de la revolución felicista*. Mexico: Librería de la Viuda de Ch. Bouret, 1913.

VERA ESTAÑOL, JORGE. *La Revolución Mexicana: orígenes y resultados*. Mexico: Editorial Porrua, 1957.

WALWORTH, ARTHUR. *Woodrow Wilson: World Prophet*. New York: Longman's Green and Company, 1958.

WHITEMAN, MARJORIE M. *Digest of International Law*. 11 vols. to date. Washington: U.S. Government Printing Office, 1963–1967.

WILLIAMSON, HAROLD F., et. al. *The American Petroleum Industry*. 2 vols. Evanston, Ill.: Northwestern University Press, 1959–1963.

ZAYAS ENRIQUEZ, RAFAEL DE. *The Case of Mexico and the Policy of President Wilson*. Trans. Andre Tridon. New York: A. & C. Boni, 1914.

Acknowledgments

Inevitably, in a study of this magnitude, there are numerous individuals to whom I owe a debt of gratitude and for whose aid I wish to express my sincere appreciation. Their helpfulness greatly facilitated the research involved.

Since this study had its inception as a doctoral dissertation, I gratefully acknowledge the guidance of Dr. Robert E. Quirk, Indiana University, who immeasurably enhanced the literary presentation of the ideas herein. Dr. Quirk's advice and encouragement was extremely helpful during the initial stages of the project. I also wish to thank all the professors of the Department of History at Indiana University who contributed, in their respective courses, to the development of the skills and theories that manifested themselves in this study. Words cannot express my gratitude for the innumerable ways their advice aided my efforts.

I am deeply grateful to the Henry L. and Grace Doherty Foundation, which granted a fellowship that enabled me to spend a year in Mexico. This not only facilitated research in the Mexican sources, but provided an invaluable experience of living with the Mexican people and an opportunity to absorb the Mexican culture.

I wish to express my appreciation to the following individuals for their assistance in my research: Dr. W. Neil Franklin, Chief of the Diplomatic, Legal and Fiscal Branch, United States National Archives, and his entire staff, especially Mr. Mark G. Eckhoff and Mr. Rudolf Heise; Victor Gondos, Jr., Chief of the Army and Air Corps Branch of the National Archives, and his assistants, particularly Mr. Elmer O. Parker and Mr. John Taylor; Dr. Jorge Ignacio Rubio Mañé and his entire staff at the Archivo General de México; the staffs of the Archivo Histórico Relaciones Exteriores de México, the Archivo

Histórico Defensa Nacional de México, and the personnel of the Public Record Office in London; and the staffs of the manuscript divisions of the United States Library of Congress, the Minnesota Historical Society, Sterling Memorial Library at Yale University, the Latin American Collection at the University of Texas, the Hemeroteca Nacional de México, and many others too numerous to mention. I am also thankful for the cooperation of those individuals who gave generously of their time for interviews.

Finally, I wish to express my appreciation to those of my colleagues in the Department of History at Wisconsin State University—Oshkosh, who read portions of the manuscript and offered helpful suggestions. I am especially grateful to Dr. Justin E. Walsh, whose valuable suggestions and advice throughout the final stage of rewriting have greatly enhanced this study.

Index

ABC powers: nonrecognition of Huerta by, 71; opposition of to American demands on Tampico incident, 149; offer of to mediate the United States–Mexican dispute, 159; agenda for conference proposed by, 160; difficulty of with Carranza, 164–165, 167; proposals regarding Mexican provisional government, 165–166, 171–172; controversy regarding admission of Carrancistas to conference, 167–169; cease-fire proposed by but rejected, 168; considered obliged to evacuate Veracruz, 175; appraisal of the conference by, 176

Angeles, General Felipe: in the attack on Ciudadela, 14; chosen by Madero to command escort on trip to Veracruz, 25; not included in assassination of Madero, 29

Antilla: munitions delivered by to Mexican port, 173–174; Lind pledged no more such incidents, 175

Arms smuggling, 60–64, 173–175

Asquith, Prime Minister Herbert H., 125, 128, 136

Bachimba, battle of, 10–11

Bacon, Senator Augustus O.: opposed recognition of Huerta, 83; critical of Bryan mediation plan, 91; suggested "watchful waiting," 100

Badger, Admiral, ordered to Veracruz, 151–152

Barrios, Angel, rebellion against Madero, 2

Belgium, supports Huerta, 114

Benton, William S., execution of by Villa, 139–140

Blanquet, General Aureliano: occupied Palace, 18; arrest of Madero by, 19; military commander in Mexico City, 25; plans for Madero exile, 25; said to have ordered the assassination of Madero, 29; Huerta's dependence on, 51; named Minister of War, 57; role in Huerta coup, 106; ordered evacuation of Veracruz, 153; left Mexico with Huerta, 178; arrival in New York, 188

Bliss, General Tasker H.: on arms smuggling, 61, 62; on fears of border residents, 157

Bonney, Wilbert, report by on conditions under Madero, 3

Boston *Herald*, quoting H. L. Wilson, 86

Bowman, Thomas, reports Huerta–Carranza negotiations, 33

Boy-Ed, Captain Karl, connection of with Huerta uncertain, 183–184, 185

Bravo, attempted blockade of Tampico, 174

Brooklyn *Daily Eagle*, comment on Torreón battle, 66

Brown, E. N., 72–73

Bryan, William Jennings: policies of, 45; limitations as Secretary of State, 45–47; favored withdrawal

217

Bryan, William Jennings (*cont.*)
of Americans from Mexico, 47–48; urged President Wilson to recognize election victor, 74; disapproval of Franco-British loan to Huerta, 74–75; attempt to forestall passage of alien land law, 75; inadvertent commendation of Ambassador Wilson, 76; reaction to Del Valle reports, 77; suggested use of "special agents" in Mexico, 78; and resignation threatened by H. L. Wilson, 78–79; orders to Del Valle, 79–80; orders to Hale, 80, 82; exchange with President regarding Ambassador Wilson, 81; recall of H. L. Wilson, 85–86; explanation of H. L. Wilson's resignation, 87; refusal to answer reporters' questions regarding Mexico, 88; mediation proposal, 91; selection of Lind as special agent, 92; poor handling of Lind mission, 93, 94–95; personally drafted dispatches to Lind, 94; requested support of other nations for mediation plan, 95; ignorance of Mexican sentiment, 97; plan supported by Latin American nations, 98; arbitration treaties with Latin American nations, 98; misinterpreted Gamboa's second reply to Lind, 99; suggested President Wilson address Congress on Mexico, 99; approved Wilson's address to Congress, 100; refusal to see Zamacona, 103; support for Gamboa in election, 109; misinterpretation of Huerta's noncandidacy, 109; refusal to comment on delivery of note to Mexico, 111; attempt by to invoke Monroe Doctrine, 114–115; urged European governments to withdraw recognition, 115–116, 135; threat of force against Huerta made by, 115–117; directed O'Shaughnessy not to attend opening of Congress, 118; financial pressure used by, 119; agreed to Lind's return, 122; idealistic stand alarmed British, 126; efforts to secure British aid against Huerta,

131–135; charged Cowdray dominated British Mexican policy, 132, 134; view of Carden, 134, 138; rejection of Huerta proposal, 137; objected to British warships at Veracruz, 137; resented visit of British admiral to Huerta, 138; demanded withdrawal of Carden, 138; support of Mayo's actions at Tampico, 145; desired compromise on Tampico affair, 146; advised caution on Tampico demands, 147; requested diversion of arms shipment to Huerta, 153; apologized for detention of *Ypiranga*, 153; reaction to fighting at Veracruz, 154; placed American interests in hands of Brazilian legation, 155; American intentions after Veracruz indicated by, 156; requested British aid in securing Huerta's assent to mediation, 159; and American delegation to Niagara Falls, 162; reply to Huerta's charge of violation of suspension of hostilities, 164; proposed junta to succeed Huerta, 165; change by to single president, 166; Constitutionalists called "victorious party" by, 167; rejection of armistice, 168–169; threat of desertion of Carranza by, 170; insistence on Carrancista provisional president, 171–172; disavowed responsibility for the *Antilla*, 173; instructed delegates to specify nonrecognition of Huerta, 176; pleased by Huerta's resignation, 178; dismissal of Lind, 180; turn from Carranza to Villa by, 180; and return of Huerta to the United States, 182

Bryce, Lord, criticism of Bryan as Secretary of State, 45–46

Buckley, William F.: named counsel for Niagara Falls conference, 161; attempt to secure agreement on neutral president by, 171

Burleson, Albert S., views on Mexico, 48, 73

Burnside, Captain William: criticism of Madero regime, 3; accompanied

Huerta's column against Orozco, 9–10; agreement with Huerta's tactics, 11; report on strength of the Ciudadela, 14–15; view of Madero's death, 30; believed Madero government paying Carranza's state troops, 31; views of pacification efforts, 35; estimate of government forces, 54–55; on rebel successes in the north, 58–59; comment on Lind's proposals that he plan rebel attacks, 122; comment on order to seize customs house in Veracruz, 152; favorable estimate by of peace commissioners, 161

Cabera, Luis, 169–170
Calero, Manuel, 5–6
Camp, Judge J. J., action against Huerta, 186, 188
Campa, Emilio, involvement in Orozco movement, 180
Canada, William: warned against removal of Madero to Veracruz, 26; aided Díaz in election of 1913, 109; report on delivery of arms to Huerta, 151–152; and occupation of Veracruz, 153
Carbajal y Rojas, Francisco: offer of presidency to, 19; accepted by Huerta as nominee for provisional president, 172; named Minister of Foreign Affairs by Huerta, 178; disagreement of with Carranza, 178–179; exile of, 179
Carden, Sir Lionel: arrival in Mexico City, 114; presentation of credentials as British minister to Mexico, 130; background, 130; interpretation of Wilson policy by, 130; association with Lord Cowdray, 130, 132; support of Huerta by, 130–131; urged Huerta to renounce candidacy, 131; Bryan's comments on, 134; negotiations with Huerta, 137; presence of in Mexico objectionable to Americans, 138; recall, 138–139; assigned to Brazil, 139; estimate of Mexican-American relations by, 141;

Huerta urged to accept ABC mediation offer by, 159; comment on Huerta delegates to Niagara Falls conference, 161
Cárdenas, Major Francisco, 28, 29
Carothers, George, comment by on Villa's methods, 65
Carr, Wilbur, 63
Carranza, Jesús, reports brother's rebellion, 33
Carranza, Venustiano, governor of Coahuila: opposed to Huerta, 31; willingness to accept Huerta government, 32; negotiations with Huerta, 32–33; proposed telegraph conference with Minister of Gobernación, 32–33; revolt against Huerta, 33, 34; Plan of Guadalupe adopted by, 35; rebellion called constitutionalism by, 35; revolt against Huerta, 53; supported by smuggled arms, 60; success in the north, 60; visit to governor of Texas, 63; requests recall of United States consul, 63; statement to London *Times*, 65; tacit support of by Wilson administration, 68; Del Valle's description of, 79; rejection of mediation, 91–113; support of urged by Lind, 120; ordnance secured by, 121; refused to join Huerta after Veracruz, 156; refused overtures from Wilson, 157; limited acceptance of ABC mediation by, 159; backing of by Lind, 163; refusal to suspend hostilities, 164–165; refusal to accept provisional government, 168–169; delegates to conference named by, 169; limitations on delegates, 169–170; advance rejection of results of mediation by, 170; refusal to meet Huerta delegates, 176; rejection of Carbajal y Rojas as provisional president, 178; request for guarantees refused by, 179; split with Villa, 179; retreat of to Veracruz, 179; United States recognition of, 191
Castro, Cipriano, visits United States, 30

Catholic Party: alliance with Huerta, 51–52; opposed to early elections, 56; nomination of Gamboa for presidency by, 104; liberals feared president from, 104; liberals' rejection of party member as Minister of Public Instruction, 104–105; membership in new Chamber, 110

Cepeda, Enrique: connection of with Huerta in the Mondragón revolt, 14; and the Huerta coup, 20; took news of coup to American Embassy, 20

Chamizal tract, United States demands cession as price of recognition, 36, 70

Chapultepec: Madero's departure from, 13; Huerta comments on not occupying, 52

Chihuahua (city): capture of by Orozco, 9; recapture from rebels by Huerta government, 66; captured by rebels again, 66

Chihuahua (state), Huertista Congress deprives of statehood, 157

Ciudadela: captured by Mondragón-Díaz forces, 12–13; described, 13; artillery battle over, 14

Ciudad Juárez: captured by Orozco, 9; captured by rebels, 58–66; Villa executions at, 67

Ciudad Porfirio Díaz: recaptured by government, 65; captured by rebels again, 66

Clifton House, site of Niagara Falls conference, 165

Cobb, Zaccary, 187

Cólogan, Bernardo J.: pressed Madero to resign, 17; statement regarding role as author of H. L. Wilson speech, 87

Colquitt, Governor O. B.: sympathy with the Mexican rebels, 63; attitude on interned troops, 67

Conejos, battle of, 10

Conger, Sidney, 103

Constitutionalists, Carranza names movement, 35

Copp, Ensign Charles C., 143

Cowdray, First Viscount (Weetman Pearson): Mexican oil concessions, 126; connection of with Asquith government, 126; association of with Sir Lionel Carden, 130; charged by Bryan with dictating British Mexican policy, 132–134; withdrawal of support from Huerta, 136–137

Cradock, Rear Admiral Sir Christopher: controversy regarding precedence of Americans over, 137, 138; visit to Huerta by, 138

Creel, Enrique, Orozco envoy to Huerta, 180

Cuba, cruiser offered to convey Madero to exile, 24

Cuernavaca: Huerta's base of operations in Morelos, 8; Madero trip to for troops, 14

Da Gama, Dr. Dominico: named mediator by Brazil, 160; questioned installation of a Carrancista as provisional president, 166; claimed war averted by Niagara Falls conference, 176

Daniels, Josephus: views regarding Mexico, 48, 73, 74; ordered preparations for military intervention in Mexico, 74; attitude of on Tampico affair, 146, 150; orders given by to intercept delivery of arms to Huerta, 151–152; ordered Mayo to pull ships out of Tampico and send them to Veracruz, 151–152; agitation at bloodshed in Veracruz landing, 154

D'Antin, Louis, 103

Dearing, Fred Morris: comment on ambassador's reports, 5; recommended recognition of Huerta, 69–72; involvement in Bryan's inadvertent commendation of Ambassador Wilson, 76; support of H. L. Wilson by, 78

Decena Trágica. See Ten Days Revolt

De la Barra, Francisco: appointment of Huerta as commander in Morelos, 8;

orders to Huerta in the Zapatista raids, 8–9; convinced Ambassador Wilson to accept official explanation of Madero death, 30; rejected talks with United States prior to recognition, 71; and Del Valle, 80

De la Lama, Adolfo: traveled to Europe to seek loans, 119; importance of at Niagara Falls conference, 162

Delgado, José C., 181

Del Valle, Reginald: mission as special agent, 79–80; unfavorable report on Carrancistas, 79; relations with press, 80; recall, 80; low rating of Hale by, 84–85

De Oliveria, Cardozo, placed in charge of United States interests after severance of diplomatic relations, 155

Diario Oficial: criticism of *El País* by, 111; first report of Tampico incident in Mexico, 154

Díaz, Félix, 24, 84, 85; rebellion against Madero, 2; release from prison by Mondragón, 12; negotiations with Huerta, 14; conspiracy with Huerta against Madero, 14; meeting with Huerta after the coup, 20–21; Pact of the Embassy, 21; said to have ordered the assassination of Madero, 29; election date dispute, 56; offered post of Minister of Gobernación by Huerta, 56; cancellation of Pact of the Embassy, 57; named ambassador to Japan, 57; denial of charges against Ambassador Wilson, 77; comment on by Hale, 82; recall to Mexico, 104, 108; as candidate for President, 109; carried state of Oaxaca, 110; granted asylum by the United States, 111; coup planned by, 119; joined Huerta in El Paso, 118

Díaz, Porfirio, xxi, 3; Huerta and the flight of, 8

Dolphin, 142–143, 151–152

Domínguez, Senator Belisario: advocacy of Huerta's removal by, 105; assassination of, 105

"Dooley, Mr.," quotations from, 59, 64, 66

Douglas Hardware Company, sale of ammunition to Mexican rebels by, 61

Dresden: German cruiser evacuated Americans from Tampico, 155; carried Huerta to exile, 178–179

Durango, battle of, 58–59

Earle, Lieutenant Commander Ralph T.: attempt by to secure oil at Tampico, 142; protest by to Morelos Zaragoza, 143

Ecuador, opposition to Bryan's Mexican plans, 98

Edwards, Clement, 2, 2 n.

Election of October, 1913: dispute over scheduling, 56–57, 104; apathy, intimidation, control of by Huerta, 110; protested by press, 111

Elguero, Luís, Huerta delegate to Niagara Falls conference, 161

Ellsworth, Luther: reports on Carranza rebellion, 33; reports on arms smuggling, 63–64; Carranza requests recall, 63–64

El Paso, Texas, Huerta arrest and hearing in, 187–191

Emerson, Captain Edward, biographical sketch of Huerta, 8 n.

Emery, Sloan W., 103

Esteva Ruiz, Roberto: and the Tampico incident, 145–146; refusal by of Mayo's demands, 147; lack of contact with delegates to Niagara Falls, 162

Fall, Senator Albert, 83

Fletcher, Rear Admiral Frank: precedence over British admiral secured by, 138; uninformed of Tampico incident, 144; found no cause for complaint in arrest of sailor at Veracruz, 148; occupation of Veracruz by, 152–153

Fort Bliss, Texas, Huerta detained at, 190

France, attitude toward Wilson proposal, 97, 114

Funston, General Frederick, 189

Gamboa, Frederico: reception of Lind, 96–97; reply to Lind demands, 97; offer to go to Washington rejected, 98; second reply to Lind, 99; candidacy of for presidency, 104, 109; triumphed in Jalisco, 110

García Granados, Alberto: Carranza requests conference with, 32–33; resignation as Minister of Gobernación, 56

García Naranjo, Nemesio: advice to Huerta against return to Mexico, 182; and Huerta's finances, 184

García Pena, General Angel, 12

Garrison, Lindley M.: praise of accuracy of Huerta map, 8; report from on frontier smuggling, 62; orders release of interned Mexicans, 67; favored recognition of Huerta, 73; critical of Bryan mediation plan, 91; advocated armed intervention, 112; and arrest of Huerta, 187

Garza Aldape, Manuel: named to Huerta's cabinet, 57; and acceptance of Lind mission, 93–94; named Minister of Gobernación, 104; role in dissolution of Congress, 104–106; summoned to appear before Congress, 105, 106; break with Huerta, 117; proposal for United States–Mexican agreement, 117

Germany: view of Huerta coup, 114; economic interest in Mexico, 116–117; interpretation of Wilson policy, 128; ships of at Veracruz, 155; aid of to Huerta, 178; reasons for support of Huerta's plot by, 182–185; and the supply of munitions to Huerta, 184; Zimmermann telegram, 185

Gómez, José F. ("Che"), rebellion of against Madero, 2

González Salas, General José: defeated by Orozco, 2, 9; resignation from Madero cabinet, 9; suicide, 9

Grayson, Admiral Cary Travers, comments on Wilson's reaction to Mexican problems, 149, 154

Great Britain: recognition of Huerta government by, 37, 70–71, 87; opposition to Lind mission, 97–98; view of Bryan's refusal to receive Zamacona, 103; approval of Huerta coup by, 106–107; view of Huerta election control, 109; support of Huerta criticized by President Wilson, 115; approval of concessions offered by Portillo y Rojas, 119; view of Lind, 123; protection of investments, 125; need by Royal Navy for Mexican oil, 125–126, 136; effort by to promote *rapprochement* between United States and Mexico, 126; difficulties in negotiating with United States, 127, 128; aid to Lind mission, 129, 130; forced by United States to withdraw support for Huerta, 136; warships of in Veracruz resented by United States, 138; transfer of Carden to Brazil, 139; proved powerless to oppose Wilson's policy, 141; Americans taken from Tampico by ships of, 155; support in press for occupation of Veracruz, 156; support of mediation offer, 159; change of Mexican policy by, 179

Grey, Sir Edward, 17, 116, 126; sought stability in Mexico, 37; instructions on Wilson plan, 97; comment on United States criticism of Carden, 132; explanation by of British attitude toward Huerta, 132, 133; reaction to Page's explanation of Wilson's policy, 133; opposition to *démarche* by European powers, 133–134; interpretation of American attitudes, 133–134, 137, 139; withdrawal of support of Huerta, 134, 136

Guatemala, attributes recognition of Huerta to actions of H. L. Wilson, 78

Guaymas, battle of, 58

Hackley, George, 102–103

Haff, Delbert J., plan proposed by for recognition of Huerta, 73

Haiti and Santo Domingo, revolutions in, 124

Hale, William Bayard: mission to Mexico, 80–82; indictment of H. L. Wilson, 81–82; acceptance of report by Wilson and Bryan, 82–83; continued attacks on Huerta regime by, 84; opinion of Del Valle, 85; Huerta government's reaction to, 85; indicated United States approval of Díaz, 85; suggested mediation plan, 91; report on Huerta's activities, 91; meeting with Lind in Veracruz, 94; support of Lind proposal for use of force, 102; sent back from Mexico by Lind, 102; recommended negotiations with rebels, 112; sent to negotiate with Carrancistas, 112–113; views of Carrancistas, 113

Hamm, Theodore, 53, 59

Hanna, Philip, 33; imprisonment and release by Mexicans after Veracruz invasion, 154–155

Hinojosa, Colonel Ramon H.: detained Americans at Tampico dock, 143; arrested for role in Tampico affair, 146

Hohler, Thomas B., and United States–Mexican salute, 150

Holland, Philip: reports from on Madero regime, 5, 6; and the Carranza revolt against Huerta, 32, 33, 34, 53

Hopkins, Sherbourne G.: Carranza agent, 63–64; received assurance of noninterference with arms shipments from Lind, 175

Hostetter, Louis, report by on Huerta's break with Maytorena, 33

House, Colonel Edward M., 135, 149, 178–179; comment on dealing with President Wilson, 45; comment on President's relations with his Cabinet, 48–49; favored recognition of Huerta, 72–73; contact with E. N. Brown, 73; discussion of armed intervention in Mexico with W. Wilson, 74; approval by of Wilson's Mobile speech, 115; discussion of ending

arms embargo with W. Wilson, 121; comment on Tyrrell visit, 135; attitude of on Tampico affair, 146; alarmed by Wilson's reaction to Tampico incident, 149; congratulated Wilson on Huerta's flight, 178

Huerta, Victoriano: historical significance of, xi; effect of American policies on, xii; defeat of Orozco rebellion, 2, 9–12; summary of character, 6–7; addiction to alcohol, 7; early military career, 7–8; command of Porfirio Díaz exile escort, 8; campaign in Morelos, 8–9; campaign in north against Orozco, 9–11; promotion to General of Division, 11; dispute with Madero, 11; named commander of Mexico City by Madero, 13; strategy against Díaz-Mondragón forces, 14; difficulties in attack on the Ciudadela, 15; movement against Madero, 18–19; received Senate appeal to oust Madero, 19; offer to install Supreme Court President in national presidency, 19; success of coup, 20; meeting with Díaz, 20–21; and Pact of the Embassy, 21; legal basis of government, 21–22; confirmation as President, 22–23; attitude toward menace of Madero, 24–25, 27; attitude toward American public opinion, 28; version of Madero assassination, 29; accused of ordering the assassination by Cárdenas, 29; feelings on American reaction to Madero assassination, 30; support of state governors secured, 31; opposition of Carranza to, 31; refusal of Carranza's demands, 34, 35; pacification efforts, 35–36; efforts to secure recognition, 36, 37, 70–71; recognition of by the United States delayed, 36–37; recognition by Great Britain, 37; President Wilson's concept of, 43–44; goals and self-confidence of, 51; alliance with Catholic party, 52; elimination of rivals, 52; simplicity of life while in office, 52–53; amnesty

Huerta, Victoriano (*cont.*)
declared, 53; early rebellions against, 53; removal of state governors by, 54; reconstruction of army, 54–55; plea to Congress for pacification, 55–56; sought support of upper classes in speech to Jockey Club, 56; scheduled election, 56; purged Díaz men from his cabinet, 56; forced exile of Mondragón, 57; forced resignation of other officials, 57; Díaz named ambassador to Japan, 57; entire administration militarized by, 66; European recognition of, 71; denial of Rojas charges against H. L. Wilson, 77; accusation by Hale of H. L. Wilson's support of Huerta's coup, 82; thanks extended to H. L. Wilson by, 87; cordiality to O'Shaughnessy, 88; dismissal of Minister of Hacienda, 91; rejection of mediation plans of Bryan and Wilson, 91; conditions set for acceptance of Lind, 94; prestige raised by Lind mission, 95–96, 97, 99, 101; dislike of Lind, 103; appointment of Zamacona as special agent, 103; reluctance to allow Díaz to resume candidacy, 104; rebuffs attempt to postpone elections, 104; opposed by Chamber of Deputies, 104, 105; resignation demanded after death of Dominguez, 105; Chamber dissolved by, 106; assumption of dictatorial power by, 106; electoral preparations, 108; officially not a candidate in election of 1913, 109; secured landslide in election, 110; new Congress composed of Huertistas, 110; given extraordinary powers by Chamber of 1913, 110; press censorship by, 111, 148; new Wilson demand for resignation, 111; to retain office in spite of election, 112; President Wilson's desire for resignation, 115; pressure against by Bryan, 115–116; financial maneuvers by, 118–119; ordnance secured by, 121; cultivation of British support by, 127, 131; urged to renounce candidacy by British, 129–131; renunciation of candidacy by, 131; general European support of, 133; withdrawal of British support, 136–137; proposal for retirement submitted by, 137; and the Tampico incident, 146, 147, 148, 149; delivery of arms to, 151, 153–154; effect on of American occupation of Veracruz, 154, 155; diplomatic relations with United States severed by, 155; amnesty for revolutionaries decreed by, 156; punitive measures adopted by, 156–157; acceptance of ABC mediation by, 159; delegates to Niagara Falls conference named by, 161; instructions to delegations, 161–162; charges American violation of cease-fire agreement, 164; willingness to resign, 165–166, 167; insistence on candidacy of Carbajal y Rojas, 172; protested shipment of arms to Carrancistas, 173; blockade declared by, 174; effect of Niagara Falls conference on, 176–177; resignation of, 178; departure from Mexico, 178–179; settlement of in Barcelona, 179; disturbed by anarchy in Mexico, 180; plan of revolt, 180, 182; return to New York, 181; press statements by in New York, 181; residence in New York secured by, 182; involvement of Germans in revolt plans, 182–185; question of finances of, 184, 185; evidences of revolt planned by, 186; trip to Mexican border by, 187; arrested in El Paso, 187, 189; court hearing postponed, 189, 190; sent to Fort Bliss, 190; reasons for choice of Texas as a base, 191; effect of Orozco's death on, 191; fatal illness and death, 191

Internment of troops, 67–68

Italy: attitude toward Wilson's policy, 114; delayed sending minister to Mexico, 114

Iturbide Bridge, 142–143

Knox, Secretary of State Philander: criticism of Ambassador Wilson, 5; approved ambassador's demand for protection of foreigners, 15; and recognition of Díaz, 15; opposed forced resignation of Madero, 17; rejects ambassador's plan for military action, 18; conditions for recognition of Huerta stated by, 36
Kruttschnitt, Julius, 74

Lamar, Joseph E.: named by Wilson to Niagara Falls conference, 162; report to Bryan on conference, 165; suggestion by for admission of Carrancistas to conference, 167–168; urged break with Carranza, 170; demand by for use of port of Tampico, 173; convinced Wilson to authorize signing of protocol, 176
Lansing, Robert: comment on Woodrow Wilson, 40; directed by Wilson to find precedent supporting the United States' stand in whaleboat incident, 145; precedent to Tampico case noted by, 148; advised against declaring war on Mexico, 151; statement by on purpose of Niagara Falls conference, 161–162; German aid to Huerta suspected by, 185–186
Lascuráin, Pedro S.: urged by Ambassador Wilson to secure resignation of Madero, 16–17; reception of Madero–Pino Suárez resignations, 22; brief presidency, 22–23; gave assurance of Madero's safety, 26; proposed by Niagara Falls conference for provisional president, 165, 171; named by Huerta as Minister of Foreign Affairs, 172; unacceptable to United States delegation, 172
Latin America: fear of United States intervention led to support of Huerta by, 117; opposition to occupation of Veracruz, 156; approval of mediation by ABC powers, 160; misunder-

standing of result of Niagara Falls conference by, 176
Lea, Tom, attorney for Huerta and Orozco, 188
Lehman, Frederick W.: named by Wilson to the Niagara Falls conference, 162; report by to Bryan on the conference, 165; suggestion by for admission of Carrancistas to conference, 167–168; break with Carranza urged by, 170; use of Tampico for delivery of arms demanded by, 173; convinced Wilson to authorize signing of protocol, 176
Lind, John: background, 92; proposed United States purchase of Mexico City cathedral, 92; arrival in Mexico, 93, 94; previous offer of Swedish post, 94; met by Hale at Veracruz, 94; favored ultimatum to Huerta, 96; meeting with Gamboa, 96; failure of other nations to support proposals, 97–98; opinion of Gamboa offer, 98; plan resubmitted and success claimed, 99; loan offer made by, 99; extension of mission, 101; suggested use of force, 102; residence in Veracruz, 102; sent Hale back to United States, 102; pro-Carranza position of, 102–103; disliked by American colony, 103; supported Díaz for President in 1913, 109; prediction that Huerta would announce his candidacy, 109; demanded that Huerta dismiss new Congress, 111; ordered to receive Huerta answer to ultimatum, 111–112; continued pressure against Huerta by, 117; negotiations with Portillo y Rojas, 119; urged support of Carranza and Villa, 120; urged lifting of arms embargo, 120–121; conference with Wilson, 121; return to United States, 121; proposed direct military aid to rebels, 122, 124; proposed seizure of Mexico City, 122; recall of, 122–123; British view of, 123; appraisal of work of, 123–124; mission aided by

Lind, John (*cont.*)
Stronge, 129; view of British interests in Mexico, 130; view of controversy regarding precedence of British admiral, 138; reports of British efforts to frustrate United States policy, 138; direct action advised by in Tampico case, 147; characterization of Mexican delegates to Niagara Falls conference, 161, 163–164; support of Carranza by, 163; pivotal role in Niagara Falls conference, 163; influence of on Wilson, 170–171; gave assurance of noninterference with arms shipments via Havana, 175; dismissal by Bryan because of pro-Carranza outlook, 180

Lobos Island, Mexican complaint of United States seizure of, 164

Lodge, Senator Henry Cabot: called for intervention against Huerta, 83; support of Huerta by, 131; comment on Wilson's reaction to fighting at Veracruz, 154

London *Chronicle*, comment by on Tampico affair, 149

London *Evening Post*, comment by on Tampico incident, 149

London *Times:* comment by on Wilson's Mexican policy, 44; interview with Carranza reported, 65–66; criticism of Villa, 67; comment on Gamboa's reply to Lind, 98; criticism of Wilson's address to Congress, 100–101; approval of Huerta coup, 107; criticism of Wilson's program by, 124; reaction of to Benton murder, 140; comment on Wilson and the Tampico incident, 148, 149, 150

Long, Boaz W.: equivocal stand on recognition of Huerta, 72; comment on Hale mission, 80

Maass, General Gustavo, 153
McAdoo, William G., 112, 145, 178
McReynolds, James C.: comment on controlling arms smuggling, 62; proposal of in election crisis of 1913, 112

Madero, Alfonso, support of Carranza and attack on H. L. Wilson by, 86

Madero, Ernesto: statement on H. L. Wilson, 77; connection of with Robert Murray, 81

Madero, Francisco I.: sweeping promises made, 2; criticism of methods of, 2; early rebellions against, 2; mounting pressure against, 5; accord with Zapata, 8–9; appointment of Huerta to subdue Orozco rebellion, 9; promotion of Huerta after defeat of Orozquistas, 11; and the Mondragón insurrection, 12–14; appointed Huerta military commander of the plaza, 13; trip to Cuernavaca for troops, 14; protested ambassador's actions to Taft, 17; retirement of demanded, 17; arrest by Blanquet, 19; resignation of, 22–23; imprisonment, 24; family requested ambassador's intercession in behalf of, 25, 27–28; plan for exile, 25–28; fate discussed by cabinet, 27; assassination of, 28–29; President Wilson's attitude toward, 42–43; Hale's view of fall and assassination of, 82

Madero, Gustavo: strong man of Madero administration, 2; action against Mondragón-Díaz uprising, 12; seizure of by Huerta, 19; assassination of, 24

Madero, Mercedes González de: appealed to Ambassador Wilson to protect Francisco Madero, 27; alleged appeal for personal intercession of President Taft, 28

Madero, Sara Pérez de: appealed to Ambassador Wilson to protect Francisco Madero, 27; endorses Rojas's charges against H. L. Wilson, 77

Márquez Sterling, Manuel, 18–19; attempts to save Madero, 24–25, 28; spent night with prisoners, 27

Marshall, Vice President Thomas, 95

Matamoros, battle of, 58–59

Mayo, Rear Admiral Henry T.: Commander of the American squadron at Tampico, 142; protested Tampico incident, 143–144; demands made by, 144; approval of by Wilson, 145; lack of instructions from Bryan on acceptance of apology, 146–147; preparations for intervention made by, 151; ordered to pull ships out of Tampico and send them to Veracruz, 151; distressed by order, 152; hesitation, 152; effect of delay on situation at Veracruz, 152; effect of evacuation on Americans at Tampico, 152, 155

Maytorena, Governor José, negotiations of with Huerta, 33

Mazatlán, federals victorious at, 66

Mercurio, El, criticism of American occupation of Veracruz, 156

Mexican-American arbitration agreement, allowed to lapse, 71

Mexican Herald, comments on the Huerta coup, 20, 23

Mexico: Ambassador Wilson sails back to the United States aboard, 86; ammunition delivery to Huerta, 151

Miller, Clarence: accompanied naval officer to protest whaleboat incident, 143; authority of superseded by Mayo at Tampico, 145; opposed to withdrawal of United States ships from Tampico, 152

Mobile address, 115, 117

Moffett, Commander William A., and the Tampico incident, 144

Moheno, Querido: announced nullification of election, 112; appeal for end of financial pressure, 118

Monclova, captured by government, 58

Mondragón, General Manuel: rebellion against Madero, 12; capture of Ciudadela, 12–13; said to have ordered assassination of Madero, 29; Minister of War under Huerta, 56; forced into exile, 57; arrival in New York, 188

Monterrey: rebel attack repulsed, 66;

demonstration against United States consul general after United States landing at Veracruz, 154

Monterrey, arms shipment to Huerta diverted by United States, 153

Moore, John Bassett: urged recognition of Huerta government, 72, 100, 131; critical of Woodrow Wilson's policy, 78; opposed Wilson's note to European powers, 114–115

Morelos: Huerta commander in, 8; Huerta-Madero dispute over activities in, 8–9; Pascual Orozco, Sr., trip to negotiate with Zapata, 53; *reconcentrado* policy employed against Zapatistas, 59; federal commander claims victory in state, 65; Huertista Congress deprives of statehood, 156

Morelos Zarangoza, General Ignacio: release of Americans by at Tampico, 143; report of incident made by, 144–145

Morgan, Colonel George, 187

Murray, Lord, of Elibank, 126, 136

Murray, Robert H.: attack on Henry Lane Wilson, 76; connection of with Hale, 80–81; association with Maderos, 81

Muller, Dr. Lauro, 75

Nación, La, closed by government for protesting election control, 111

Naco, Arizona, arms smuggling in, 60–62

Naco, Mexico, captured by rebels, 58

Naón, Dr. Romulo S., 175; named mediator by Argentina, 160, 168; reception of Carranza's messenger, 168; attempt by to break conference deadlock, 172; offended by Wilson's reticence regarding protocol, 176

New Hampshire: Lind's passage on, 94; fired salute to Mexico, 94

Newman, New Mexico, 187

New York *Times:* comment on recognition, 37–38; comment on Bryan, 47; favorable comment on Huerta, 67; praise of H. L. Wilson, 76, 86, 87;

New York *Times* (*cont.*)
support of recognition of Huerta, 98; comment on arms shipment to Carranza and Wilson attitude, 174; reported Huerta's statements, 181–182; comment on Huerta's statements, 181–182; Voska's exposé of Huerta's contacts with Germans, 183

New York *World:* comment on assassination of Madero, 29–30; approved recognition of Huerta, 38; attacks Henry Lane Wilson, 76, 77, 87; praise for Huerta's concessions by, 167

Niagara Falls, Canada, site of ABC mediation conference, 160

Niagara Falls conference: hostilities of Carranza threatened conference, 160; delegates to named by Huerta, 161; by Wilson, 162; proposal by for resignation of Huerta, 165; changed plan offered by mediators, 166; invitation from to Carranza to attend, 169; compromise agreement proposed by, 171; negotiations terminated, 175–176; protocols signed, 175, 176; appraisals of results, 176–177

Nicolson, Sir Arthur: approval of Huerta coup, 107; criticism of American policy, 139, 156

Nogales, Arizona, arms smuggling in, 60

Nogales, Mexico: captured by rebels, 53; site of Hale's talks with Carancistas, 112

Obregón, General Álvaro: effect of Veracruz on, 156; defeat of Villa, 180

Ojinaga: captured by rebels, 66; Villa seizure and executions at, 67

Olmstead, Loring, 102–103

Orozco, General Pascual, Jr.: insurrection against Madero, 2; early success of, 9–10; defeat of by Huerta, 10–11; joined Huerta regime, 53; plan for revolt, 180; possible German aid to,

185; meeting of with Huerta, 187; arrest, 187; escape of, 189; death of, 191

O'Shaughnessy, Edith: comment on Lascuráin's term, 22–23; treatment by Huerta, 88

O'Shaughnessy, Nelson J., 117, 118, 124, 140; State Department comment on qualifications, 78; became chargé d'affaires, 88; friendship with Huerta, 88; and the Lind mission, 92–94, 96; opposition of European missions to Lind plan, 98; comment on Huerta dispute with Congress, 104; ordered by Wilson to demand Huerta's resignation, 111; view of Garza Aldape's proposal and resignation, 117; did not attend opening of Congress, 118; reported resistance by Carden to American policy, 138; fear of consequences of Carrancista triumph, 140; and the Tampico incident, 145–146, 147, 148, 149–150; negotiations regarding return of Mexican salute to flag, 149–150; left United States affairs in British care after Veracruz landing, 155; handed passports by Huerta, 155; escorted to Veracruz, 155

Pact of the Embassy (Pact of the Ciudadela): negotiation, 20–21; provisions, 21; canceled, 57; misunderstood by President Wilson, 84; explained by H. L. Wilson, 86

Page, Walter Hines: comment on Bryan, 47; wanted Huerta forced out, 116; support by of Wilson's Mexican policy, 127, 128, 132–133; opposition of to Carden, 132; criticism of British attitude by, 133; comment by on Tyrrell mission, 135; use of Panama tolls question to pressure British, 136; charges against Carden, 138; reaction of to Benton murder, 140

Paget, Sir Ralph: comment on United States response to Huerta's renunciation of candidacy, 131; comments on

Wilson policy, 131, 156; statement by on British attitude to the Tampico incident, 148–149; comment on United States willingness to use Carden, 159

País, El, charge of government control of election, 111

Panama Canal tolls question, used by Wilson to influence British policy in Mexico, 135–136

Parral, captured by rebels, 58

Pass Christian, Mississippi, site of Wilson-Lind conference, 121

Pearson, Weetman. *See* Cowdray, First Viscount

Phelps Dodge Company, sale of ammunition to Mexican rebels by, 61

Pimienta, Lieutenant Rafael, assassination of Madero and Pino Suárez, 28–29

Piña, Joaquín, comments on Huerta's character, 7

Pino Suárez, José María: selection for vice presidency, 2; resignation of, 22; imprisonment with Madero, 25; assassination of, 28–29; comment on assassination of, 82

Pittsburgh, entertained Carrancistas, 64

Plan of Guadalupe: issued, 35, 53; cited by Carranza to bar agreement on provisional president, 170, 176–177

Portillo y Rojas, José López, concessions offered by, 119; proposal made by to end Tampico deadlock, 150; denied that whaleboat flew United States flag at Tampico, 154

Providence *Journal,* release by of the Voska exposés, 183, 185

Puerto México: *Ypiranga* landed arms at, 154; rumors of United States seizure of, 154; Huerta departed for exile from, 178

Rabasa, Emilio: Huerta attempted to name as ambassador to the United States, 37, 70; named as head of delegation to Niagara Falls conference by Huerta, 161; offer by for withdrawal of Huerta, 166, 167

Ratner, Abraham, 181, 182

Rathom, John, 185

Recognition of governments, xi, xii, 43; New York *World* comment on, 38; use of nonrecognition in Mexico, 43–44, 70–71, 73–74, 135, 151, 162, 170–171, 176; use of recognition in Peru and China, 44; European recognition of Huerta, 71; State Department counselor cites precedents regarding, 72, 114–115

Reconcentrado policy, employed by government in Morelos, 59

Rellano: site of Gonzáles Salas' defeat by Orozco, 9; Huerta defeated Orozco in second battle of, 10

Reyes, General Bernardo: rebellion against Madero, 2; release from prison by Mondragón, 12; death of, 12

Reyes, Rudolfo, cancellation of Pact of Embassy, 57

Rintelen von Kleist, Captain Franz, contacts with Huerta in Spain and New York, 183, 184

Rivera, General, 19

Riveroll, Colonel Jimenez, attempt to seize Francisco Madero, 19–20

Rodríguez, Agustin, named by Huerta as delegate to Niagara Falls conference, 161

Rojas, Luís Manuel, attack on H. L. Wilson by, 76–77

Roosevelt, Franklin D., demand by for use of port of Tampico, 173

Sacramento, prevented blockade of Tampico, 174

Salazar, General José Inés, involvement of in the Orozco movement, 180

Saltillo: United States consul there reports Carranza's decision to conform to Huerta government, 32; delay in telegrams to, 34; captured by federal troops, 34, 53; rebel attack repulsed, 58; arrest of United States

Saltillo (*cont.*)
consul there after seizure of Veracruz, 155
Salutes: by *New Hampshire* when conveying Lind to Veracruz, 94; O'Shaughnessy agrees to simultaneous return of, 149–150; protocol proposed guaranteeing return of, 150; *Zaragoza* refused by United States forts at New Orleans, 150; regulations regarding salutes to unrecognized governments, 150
San Francisco *Examiner*, comments on Tampico affair, 146, 151
Sawtelle, William H., 78
Scott, Ernest, 134
Shearwater, furnished coal by Huerta government, 127
Silliman, John: comments on Carranza's revolt, 35, 53; arrested and deported after taking of Veracruz, 155
Slade, J. J., Jr., 103
Smith, Senator William A., 95
Spain, suggestion of European support of Huerta, 133
Speyer, James, 72
Spring-Rice, Sir Cecil, 156; criticism of Bryan by, 46, 47, 126–127; effort to approach Wilson by, 126; attempt by to understand Wilson's policy, 128; informed by Bryan of W. Wilson's intransigence, 131; comment by on Tampico case, 147
Standard Oil Company, effect of on American policy in Mexico, 132
Stronge, Sir Francis: approval of H. L. Wilson's opposition to Madero, 17; opinion on death of Madero, 30; favored recognition of Huerta, 37; comment on by Hale, 82; corroborates Cólogan's role in H. L. Wilson's speech, 87; approval by of Huerta, 127; criticism of Wilson's Mexican policy, 128–129; effort by to aid Lind, 129; request by to Huerta to renounce presidency, 129–130
Súarez Mújica, Eduardo, Chilean named mediator, 160

Sunshine, landing of arms by at Tampico, 173

Tacoma, prevented blockade of Tampico, 174
Taft, President William Howard, xix, 5; and the Ten Days Revolt, 15, 17–18; reaction to the Huerta coup, 20; alleged request for personal intercession of, 28; end of administration prevented recognition of Huerta, 36–37, 38; internment policy, 67
Tamariz, Eduardo: named Minister of Public Instruction by Huerta, 105; opposed by liberals, 105; remained in Chamber, 105; named Speaker of new Chamber, 110
Tampico: rebel attack repulsed, 66; incident at, 142–145; United States blamed for second Tampico incident, 154; anti-American demonstrations at after seizure of Veracruz, 155; evacuation of Americans from, 155; arms entering and American rejection of blockade of, 173–175
Ten Days Revolt: described, 10–19; Ambassador Wilson's support for, 76; Hale investigation of Ambassador Wilson's conduct during, 80–81; reviewed by Ambassador Wilson, 86; British agreement with Ambassador Wilson's position during, 127
Thompson, Charles W., comment by on Wilson, 49
Tlalpan Military School, cadets from in the Mondragón insurrection, 12
Torreón: Huerta's base of operations, 9; rebel attack repulsed, 59; captured by rebels, 65; comments on atrocities at, 65–66; recaptured by federal forces, 66; retaken by rebels, 66–67
Treviño, General Jacinto B., 54
Tyron, Max: offer of oil supply from, 142; involvement in Tampico incident, 143
Tyrrell, Sir William: sent by Grey to Washington, 134; informs Wilson of

British withdrawal of support for Huerta, 134; conclusions on Wilson–Bryan rigidity, 134–135; clearer view obtained by, 135

United States government: attitude on protection of American investors, xii; effect of on Huerta regime, xii; policy of dominance of the Caribbean, 44; atrocities reported to, 58–59; smuggling across border, 60–68; internment of troops, 67–68; question of adherence to Pact of the Embassy, 84; lifting of arms embargo, 121; turn to Carranza by, 124; attempted to convince mediators to admit Carrancista delegates to Niagara conference, 167; supply of munitions to Constitutionalists by, 173–175; use of naval force for landing of arms, 174–175; Justice Department and Huerta-German threat, 184; concern of with threat of Huerta revolt, 186; difficulty in finding charge against Huerta by, 188, 190; Justice Department order to put Huerta in Fort Bliss, 190; recognition of Carranza, 191

Urrutia, Dr. Aureliano: named to Huerta's cabinet, 57; replaced by Garza Aldape, 104

Velasco, General José Refugio, upsets plans to exile Madero, 26

Veracruz: Félix Díaz attempted revolt at, 2; plan to transfer Madero to, 25; Lind's arrival at, 94; Lind's residence in, 101–102; Portillo y Rojas' negotiations with Lind in, 119; Bryan objection to British warships at, 137; arms deliveries to, 151; invasion of, 151–153; Mexican patriotism aroused by, 154; foreign reaction to invasion, 155–156; reaction to in the United States, 157; failure of to oust Huerta, 158; Huerta's protest at landing of American arms at, 164; evacuation of urged by Mexico, 175; Latin American belief

that mediation led to evacuation of by United States, 176

Vera Estañol, Jorge: attempted to refuse cabinet appointment, 21; resignation from cabinet forced, 57

Villa, General Francisco: "Mr. Dooley" comment on, 59; atrocities in Torreón, 65; executions by, 67; approach by Díaz for support, 119; support of urged by Lind, 120; execution of British citizen by, 139; British criticism of, 140; support of United States and break with Carranza, 157, 179; defeat by Obregón, 180; supported by Bryan, 180

Villar, General Lauro: defense of Madero during Ten Days Revolt, 12–13; wounded, 13

Von Bernstorff, Count Johann, 153, 185, 186

Von Hintz, Admiral Paul, urged safety for Madero, 27

Von Papen, Captain Franz, 183–185

Voska, Emil, reports by of Huerta's contacts with German agents, 183–184

Warren, Charles, involvement in legal detention of Huerta, 186, 189–190

Washington *Post*, 160; comment on death of Madero, 30; comment on Villa, 67; approval of Ambassador Wilson, 87; comment on hopelessness of mediation plan, 91; comment on Lind mission, 98; caution about mediation, 160; comment on deadlock in Niagara Falls conference by, 166–167; comment by on *Antilla* affair, 174

Watchful waiting: phrase suggested by Senator Bacon, 100; discussed, 100; terminated, 121

Wilson, Henry Lane: hostility of to Madero, 3, 4; dean of the diplomatic corps, 4; objectives of, 4; relations with Secretary Knox, 5; ignored Díaz request for recognition of belligerency, 15; decision to protect foreign interests, 16; refusal to

Wilson, Henry Lane (*cont.*)
abandon the embassy, 16; conference with friendly envoys, 16; attempt to secure the resignation of Madero, 17–18; requested United States military forces, 18; and the Huerta coup, 18, 20; participation in Pact of the Embassy, 20–21; announcement of completion of the Revolution, 23; indifference to Madero's fate, 24–25, 30; secret anti-Madero actions, 26; showed consular reports to Díaz, 26; and protection of Madero, 27, 28; version given by of assassination of Madero, 29; efforts to establish Huerta rule, 32, 34; urged recognition of Huerta regime, 36, 37, 69, 70, 71; break with President Wilson, 75–77, 83; supported by American colony in Mexico, 76; opposed by American newspapers, 76; support for by embassy staff, 77; reluctant retention in office, 78; Hale's investigation of his conduct during Ten Days Revolt, 80, 83; Hale's description of, 81; criticism of Hale, 85; recalled for consultation by Bryan, 85–86; press statements on return to United States, 86; reactions of press, 86; report on Mexican situation by, 86; meeting with President Wilson, 86–87; appearance before Senate Committee on Foreign Affairs, 87; resignation requested by Bryan, 87; comment on mediation plan, 91

Wilson, President Woodrow: attitude toward intervention in Mexico, xi–xii; failure of policy, xiii; benefits from Mexican policy, xiii; effect of on Huerta, xiii; Mexican policy compared with later war policy of, xiv; early career of, 39; basic beliefs of, 39–40; limitations of in foreign affairs, 41; ignorance of diplomacy, 41; ignorance of Latin America, 42; approval of Madero, 42–43; use of recognition issue by, 43; policy of in Peru and China incon-sistent, 44; refusal to accept criticism or advice, 45; tendency to act as own Secretary of State, 47; agreement with Bryan on policy toward Mexico, 47; failure to consult cabinet on Mexico, 48; absorption with domestic matters, 49–50, 75; enforcement of neutrality laws, 61–64; internment policy, 68; Latin America policy statement by, 69; allowed lapse of Mexican-American arbitration agreement, 71; cabinet support of Huerta, 73; almost accepted plan for recognition of Huerta, 73–74; insistence on maintaining naval squadron in Mexican waters, 74; consideration of armed intervention in Mexico, 74, 98, 112; and the alien land law, 75; conflict with Henry Lane Wilson, 75–77; use of special agents by, 78–79; acceptance of Hale's report, 81, 82–83; misunderstanding of Pact of the Embassy by, 83–84; meeting with H. L. Wilson, 86–87; cancellation of the ambassador's appearance before House committee, 87; decision to pressure Huerta out, 89; mediation plan for an acceptable government, 90–91; Lind's mission to Mexico sent by, 92; inept launching of Lind mission, 93; brief halt and renewal of Lind mission, 95, 96; surprised by rejection of Lind proposals, 97; misinterpretation of Gamboa's second reply to Lind, 99–100; address to Congress, 99–100; decision to impose arms embargo, 99; instructed Lind to remain in Veracruz, 101; praised nomination of Gamboa for presidency, 104; support of for Gamboa's presidential candidacy, 104, 109; protest of Huerta coup by, 106; new ultimatum sent to Huerta, 111; new mediation plan sent via Hale, 112, 113; plan rejected by Carranza, 113; note to European powers urging withdrawal of recognition prepared but not sent, 114–

115; Mobile address, 115, 117; refusal to back any particular individual to succeed Huerta, 116; employment of financial pressure against Huerta, 118; concessions offered by Portillo y Rojas rejected by, 119–120; lifting of arms embargo, 121; effect of lifting of embargo by, 121, 122; comment on Lind's role, 123; increased determination against Huerta, 124; rigid stand on Mexican question, 126–127, 131; opposed by European diplomats, 128, 129; view of British policy, 134–135; use of canal toll question to influence Britain's Mexican policy, 135–136; rejection of Huerta's plan of retirement, 137; resented visit of British admiral to Huerta, 138; disregard of rebel atrocities, 140; first news of Tampico incident received by, 145; directed Lansing to find precedent to support his policy, 145; directed O'Shaughnessy to protest Tampico incident, 145, 147; adamant on firing of salute, 147; conferred with Lind about action at Tampico, 147; discussed Tampico incident with cabinet, 147; ordered Atlantic Fleet to Mexico, 148; charges made against Mexico, 148; ultimatum to Huerta, 150; rejected compromise on flag salute, 150; resolution of Congress authorizing invasion requested by, 152; seizure of customs house at Veracruz ordered by, 152; mistaken views of Mexican resistance to American landing, 154; arms embargo restored, 157; acceptance of ABC mediation offer, 159; agenda for Niagara Falls conference proposed by, 160; desire for Carranza to take part in mediation negotiations, 161, 168–169; selection of delegates to Niagara Falls conference, 162; attempt by to avoid indirect recognition of Huerta, 162; personal control of negotiations at Niagara Falls, 162; influence of Lind on, 163–164; insistence on Carrancista provisional president, 167; rejection of armistice, 168; views on provisional government, 170–172; release of smugglers ordered by, 175; objection to protocol phraseology, 176; jubilation over Huerta's fall, 179; turn by from Carranza to Villa, 180; alarm at return of Huerta, 182; interest in Huerta's detention, 188, 190

Ypiranga: scheduled ammunition delivery to Huerta, 151–152; detained by United States warship, 153–154; United States apology for detention, 153; delivery of arms to Puerto México, 154; cited in *Antilla* affair, 174

Zacatecas, battle of, 58, 66
Zamacona, Manuel, sent by Huerta to Washington, 103
Zapata, Emiliano: rebelled against Madero, 2; attempted accord with De la Barra government, 8; defeat of by Huerta, 8–9; negotiations with Huerta regime, 53; government use of *reconcentrado* policy against, 59; headquarters captured by government, 65
Zaragoza: Lind desired to capture for Carrancistas, 122; United States forts at New Orleans failed to return salute, 150; attempted blockade of Tampico, 174
Zubaran Capmany, Rafael: named by Carranza to attend Niagara Falls conference, 169–170; conference with Lamar and Lehman, 170